THE GILETS JAUNES AND THE NEW SOCIAL CONTRACT

Charles Devellennes

First published in Great Britain in 2022 by

Bristol University Press
University of Bristol
1-9 Old Park Hill
Bristol
BS2 8BB
UK
t: +44 (0)117 954 5940
e: bup-info@bristol.ac.uk

Details of international sales and distribution partners are available at bristoluniversitypress.co.uk

© Bristol University Press 2022

British Library Cataloguing in Publication Data
A catalogue record for this book is available from the British Library

ISBN 978-1-5292-1221-1 paperback
ISBN 978-1-5292-1220-4 hardcover
ISBN 978-1-5292-1222-8 ePub
ISBN 978-1-5292-1223-5 ePdf

The right of Charles Devellennes to be identified as author of this work has been asserted by him in accordance with the Copyright, Designs and Patents Act 1988.

All rights reserved: no part of this publication may be reproduced, stored in a retrieval system, or transmitted in any form or by any means, electronic, mechanical, photocopying, recording, or otherwise without the prior permission of Bristol University Press.

Every reasonable effort has been made to obtain permission to reproduce copyrighted material. If, however, anyone knows of an oversight, please contact the publisher.

The statements and opinions contained within this publication are solely those of the author and not of the University of Bristol or Bristol University Press. The University of Bristol and Bristol University Press disclaim responsibility for any injury to persons or property resulting from any material published in this publication.

Bristol University Press works to counter discrimination on grounds of gender, race, disability, age and sexuality.

Cover design: Liam Roberts
Front cover image: Shutterstock/Marcos Silva

Contents

Acknowledgements   iv

Introduction   1

1   Critical Times for the Social Contract   19

2   Violence   41

3   Liberty   57

4   Democracy   75

5   Economic Justice   91

6   A Renewal of the Social Contract   113

Conclusion   133

Appendix: The 42 demands of the gilets jaunes, posted online on 28 November 2018   151

Notes   155
References   157
Index   169

Acknowledgements

Writing a book on a topic that is evolving before one's eyes can be a challenge, and the present volume would not have been possible without all those who shared their experiences on the ground, through traditional news outlets, social media and in person. Although I was able to make several visits to France during this project, much of the information I gathered on the movement was through others' accounts shared online, and I am forever in their debt for making me understand what was happening around them. I am grateful to all those who, over the past year, have contributed to project as it now stands. In particular, Philip Cunliffe and David McLellan provided early comments that helped shape the rest of the book, and their input at such an early stage truly formed my thinking. I have enormously benefited from the input of friends and family, who provided me with comments on drafts and in-depth discussions about my research, among them Robert Wilson, Ben Turner, Benoît Dillet, Alexandre Christoyannopoulos, Lucas Van Milders, Henry and Hugo Deslongchamps, Yves and Fabienne Devellennes, Tadeuzs Markiewicz and Ana Maria Lobos. The wonderful staff at Bristol University Press have been patient and supportive throughout the writing, and special thanks go to Stephen Wenham for his many suggestions to improve on the manuscript. The three anonymous reviewers who helped consolidate the arguments of the book through their constructive criticism have also allowed me to improve the points I was making. Last but not least, my wife Yana Bezirganova's unending support of the book helped overcome many hurdles during the writing – I could not have done it without her.

Introduction

The *gilets jaunes*, a group of French protesters named after their iconic yellow vests donned during demonstrations, have formed a new type of social movement. Although historical parallels have been drawn by commentators – ranging from the peasant revolts of pre-revolutionary France (the *jacqueries*), the French Revolution, the Paris Commune of 1871, the workers' movements of 1936 or 1947–48, to the *évènements* [events] of 1968 – no comparison entirely corresponds to the movement and its consequences. It is a *sui generis* movement rather than a repetition of a previous upheaval. The gilets jaunes are not quite a revolution as they do not seek to take over the functioning of the state, not quite akin to the student revolt of 1968 relived half a century later, not a workers' movement organized through trades unions and workers' representation, and not an attempt to establish a communist utopia. If anything, the movement has claimed to be apolitical and breaks away from the better-organized and more engaged movements of the past. It has no links with existing political parties and has resisted attempts by politicians to join or co-opt the movement. The 'apolitical' claim of many in the movement is more a reaction to politicians' attempts to jump on the bandwagon than a statement about the movement's aspirations, which are inherently engaged and demanding. I will show that the movement is non-partisan rather than apolitical – it makes many political claims, although it is true that it has not been attached to any political party and that it does not fit neatly on the left/right political spectrum. A *popular* movement at its heart (it encompassed all layers of French society at some level, including in overseas territories), it has challenged the foundations of political order in a country that prides itself on its revolutionary past, on its resistance to authoritarian political authority, and on its proclamation of human rights. Scenes of violence, by protesters and police, have rocked the liberal consensus that the post-Cold War state has reached its final form and that the end of history has arrived, as Francis Fukuyama (1992) once claimed – with only twists and tweaks needed to reform political organization. It also challenges the claim that future conflicts will be between clashing civilizations, as Huntington (1996) had argued, as the movement is clearly a French phenomenon with few links outside of the hexagon.[1] It does have broader consequences for how we think about politics more generally, however. It shows that history has not ended, that social struggle still persists, and that it will take novel forms in the twenty-first century. The analysis of such a movement will help us reflect on its significance beyond the French context. The conditions that enabled the gilets jaunes to rise up on France are present elsewhere, and one would do well to ponder how a response to the movement can help reframe political legitimacy, and revive politics for the twenty-first century.

The gilets jaunes have been variously interpreted since they began their occupation of French roundabouts on 18 November 2018. At first received with enthusiasm on the right of the French political establishment, and caution on the left, the reception to their demands and acts of rebellion have polarized opinion in the larger population. If there was widespread sympathy for the movement from the French public, both on the left and on the right of the political spectrum, in the first three weeks of the movement, the fourth weekend saw scenes of violence erupt on the Champs Élysées, notably around and within the Arc de Triomphe, which towers over the first roundabout built in France. From this day, 1 December 2018, the headlines of newspapers and stories of the news media became almost exclusively focused on the violence of the protests, turning every clash between protesters and police as a threat to social order and the beginning of a more general political, cultural and civilizational meltdown. Whereas mainstream media followed this editorial line for months on end, alternative media focused on the flipside of the story. Images of state violence became ever-present on Twitter and independent media outlets, making it clear that it was the use of disproportionate force by police units that was at the centre of the events. Although violence has been part of the story, I will show that the use of violence is not the only tale to be told about the role of the protesters in the contemporary French context. Their contribution to the political landscape of France is quite different. They have provided a fundamental challenge to the social contract in France, the implicit pact between the governed and their political leaders. Many of the unwritten rules of conflict management, which typically regulate trades unions' activities and their interaction with law enforcement, were completely sidestepped by protesters, leading to ever-increasing tensions between law enforcement forces and protesters on the streets. The movement has seen the numbers of participants diminish over time, but the underlying tension between the haves and the have-nots, the winners of globalization and those at risk of *déclassement* [social downgrading], are enduring and persistent. Before we go on to discuss my own specific understanding of the movement and its significance, let us look at the various causes and analyses of what they mean that have been brought to the fore so far, mainly by French news media and academic commentary.

The origin of the gilets jaunes

The movement that erupted in France in November 2018, and that has become known as the gilets jaunes movement from the high visibility jackets worn by many of its supporters during protests, has many causes. The most immediate trigger for the movement was without doubt the new tax on fuel introduced by Emmanuel Macron's government, which would have imposed particular hardship on the least well-off in French society. Whereas the poorer members of French society typically live in the inner cities or in the infamous *banlieues*, those sleeper suburbs where cheap social housing is available, the gilets jaunes themselves have largely come from the social class just above this. Out of this segment of the working class, it is those who live outside the cities in what geographer Christophe Guilluy (2016) has called 'peri-urban France' who have been the worst affected by the new tax. Those living in these semi-remote areas, on the outskirts of big cities but further out than the banlieues, often rely heavily on their own car as a mode of transportation, given the few alternatives available to them in terms of public transport. They use their vehicle to go to work, take their children to school, and do their shopping, making life without motorized transport impossible because of their geographical location. Even a marginal increase in the price of fuel often means the need to cut out other essential expenses, such as food or clothing, in order to make ends meet. Given the fixed nature of other costs, such as rent, mortgage payments, insurance or university tuition for the children, the rise in the price of fuel was more than a mere small increase that could be taken out of the family's holiday budget. For many it was the straw that broke the camel's back, following a decade of austerity, a steady decline in public services and unequal access to those services due to geographic inequalities, and lack of opportunities in employment. The organization of a movement against the tax was more than a mere reactionary protest against an all-intrusive state. It was, for many, a desperate plea to be seen and be heard, to be recognized as human beings with legitimate interests and needs, and for more than a few of the participants it was an economic necessity. The choice of the roundabout for their site of protest was made precisely because they all drive round it on a daily basis to go from their home to the centres of economic activity. Often coming from middle-class or skilled-labour families, these protesters, many in their mid-twenties, thirties or forties, have suffered a *déclassement*, in the words of Pierre Vermeren (2019) – a downward change in class from their parents' generation, a social downgrading between generations.

There are important economic reasons for such a *déclassement*. A large public deficit for the French state since the 1970s, the economic crisis of 2008, trade imbalances and the growth of rentier capitalism are all to blame, according to Vermeren. Where gross domestic product (GDP) per capita adjusted for purchasing power parity in France was at $45,200 in 2008, it had fallen to $38,400 a decade later, in 2017. The economic situation is aggravated by the unequal effect this has had on poorer regions and on those living away from urban centres, where cheap and reliable public transport is unavailable and cannot mitigate for part of this fall in revenue available for daily activities (Vermeren, 2019: 115). Those living in the *diagonale du vide* [the empty diagonal], crossing France from the north-east to the south-west, have known difficulties inherent to remote locations where public services are few and far between, and on the decline. Unlike those who have flocked to the cities and urban metropolises of France, those who have stayed behind in such historic regions as Lorraine, the Massif Central or the Gers have suffered greatly from economic decline and population drain. But the economic plight has now spread even beyond this empty France, and is seen in regions beyond the diagonal. According to Vermeren, the fall in the standards of living of many workers in France is at the centre of the protests against a further burden being imposed on them in the form of increased taxation. Compared with their parents' generation, these French workers have seen a steady decline in their economic well-being, alongside a retreat of the state from public services and welfare provision. Living less affluent lives than their elders, brought to the brink of poverty by a persistent and enduring economic crisis leading to negative or near-zero growth, the combination of negative economic indicators has taken its toll on those at the bottom of the pay-scale. Yet it was not only the economically desperate who answered the call for action. Even those who have not quite been pushed to the bottom often joined the gilets jaunes on the roundabouts. They, too, though not in dire need of tax breaks, have felt the toll of economic recession for those living outside the globalized cities such as Paris, Bordeaux, or Lyon which keep on providing important new economic opportunities for growth. This feeling has reflected itself as a disillusionment of progress, according to Raymond Aron's terminology, where the promises of modernity have ceased to deliver for ordinary people (Chauvel, 2019: 86). Where we once dreamed of a future with flying cars and robots performing the menial tasks necessary for economic activity and growth, bright metropolises and space exploration, we can now imagine only a world of increased pauperization and rising inequalities. Even our fictions have reflected this tendency. In the popular TV series *The Expanse*, the future of humanity is divided between 'earthers', 'martians' and 'belters', all struggling to exploit one another in a world where humanity has become a multi-planetary species. Even on Earth, in this fictional series based on the work of Daniel Abraham and Ty Franck, writing under the pseudonym James Corey (Corey, 2011), the vast majority of the population live on a form of basic income barely sufficient to survive while the elites carve up the revenues from the rich minerals of the asteroid belt for themselves. Our imagined future is reflected by our existing present: one of inequalities, social struggle, and lack of perspectives for our future, where those living on the periphery of the system lack opportunities for human flourishing and self-improvement. Not unlike the belters of this fictional dystopia, the gilets jaunes have reacted with anger and political violence to the perceived inequalities of a society that carves out the best share for its most affluent members. In France in 2018, the new tax on fuel was perceived as a fundamental attack on the least advantaged members of society for what it did: introducing a tax that disproportionately affects the working poor, while simultaneously introducing tax breaks for the wealthiest.

The economic crisis is thus directly linked to fiscal policy, and the decision by the government in 2018 to introduce a new tax on fuel, as well as decisions about public expenditure on services and transport alternatives. As Thomas Piketty notes, it is the issue of fiscal justice, rather than a widespread rejection of taxation, that has come to the fore in the gilets jaunes protests. In particular, the suppression of the *impôt de solidarité sur la fortune* (ISF), a solidarity tax on wealth scrapped by Emmanuel Macron immediately after rising to power, has shown where the priorities of the new centrist party lie. The tax, first introduced in 1990 during Mitterrand's presidency, fell on those whose assets put them roughly in the top 1–2 per cent of society. A progressive tax on wealth introduced by the socialist president, it collected between 0.5 per cent and 1.5 per cent of the worth of the assets, mostly real estate, that are covered under the tax. Over a third of all taxpayers subject to the ISF lived in the greater-Paris region, with most of the rest living in the other major urban centres or on the Côte d'Azur, France's wealthy Mediterranean coastline. This tax on the wealthiest citizens, systematically reduced under conservative governments and increased again by François Hollande in 2013, was a symbol of progressive taxation in France which was raising €4 billion annually for the French treasury when it was cancelled in 2017. Emmanuel Macron blamed fiscal evasion for his decision, despite the fact that the overwhelming majority of those paying the tax showed no sign of flight from the country. The worst year for these rich exiles was 2013, when 713 of them (out of 312,406 who paid the tax) opted to leave France (Pluyette, 2016) – an attrition rate of 0.2 per cent among the most internationally mobile group in society. In other words, it is doubtful that these several hundred individuals all left because of the tax, and the threat of fiscal exile remains an epiphenomenon rather than an endemic feature of French fiscal life. On the contrary, the tax had been extremely successful and had more than quadrupled in receipts since 1990, outpacing GDP growth by over 100 per cent. In fact, Piketty (2019a) argues, the tax could have easily been strengthened against those who hide their wealth to evade paying it. He speculates that by improving it with minimal administrative efforts the state could have raised €6 billion a year, instead of the €1 billion-a-year raised from the Impôt de la Fortune Immobilière (IFI), a tax on real estate that replaced the ISF in 2018. That's a potential loss of revenue of €30 billion over the entire term of Macron's presidency, to the benefit of the richest in French society. The €8 billion of additional revenue that the tax on fuel was supposed to generate frames the equation as a question of social justice, for it was introduced immediately after this tax gift to the highest percentile of French real estate owners. In addition, the tax on fuel was justified in terms of combatting climate change, with all observers noting this farcical attempt at public relations: a mere 10 per cent of the revenue was to be invested in financing green projects (Piketty, 2019a: 80–3).

Beyond the fiscal question lies the retreat of the French state more generally. Structurally weakened by the inability of successive governments to balance budgets, even in times of growth, the French state lies at the limit of what lending markets are willing to tolerate before they start imposing higher interest rates. Moody's, Standard and Poor, and Fitch all rate French debt as AA or Aa2, the third-best rating category below the reliability of Germany, the United States, Finland or the Isle of Man (for example), showing that the markets do not take kindly to higher-than-planned borrowing over time. Whereas France had a debt-to-GDP ratio of around 60 per cent in the mid-1970s, the current levels, which hover around 100 per cent and are set to rise further in 2020, offer poor prospects for international investors. Combined with France's recurrent pension deficit crisis and the cost of the welfare state in times of economic crisis, it is all the more surprising that tax breaks are offered to those who earn the most, and tax burdens are imposed on those who cannot afford some of the bare necessities. As both David Graeber (2019) and Thomas Piketty (2019a) note, this attitude towards debt is not a natural consequence of the economic system, and plenty of policy alternatives exist and can be invented to remedy the situation. It is a lack of political will, from all three parties that have ruled France since François Mitterrand's liberal turn of 1983, that is at the roots of this economic insecurity. The economic situation is dire, but it is not hopeless. Historically, much higher levels of debt have been dealt with in numerous ways, including gradual repayments through balanced budgets, economic growth, devaluation, default, increased taxation or one-off extraordinary levies. As we will see in the Conclusion, the imaginary of economic justice need not be limited to these measures, and an intergenerational justice may demand new ways to think about debt and its repayment. The gilets jaunes themselves have made suggestions and proposals to that effect, as they perceive that the demand for restructure is pressing indeed.

Some of the demands made by the gilets jaunes seemed to have hit home during the outbreak of the COVID-19 coronavirus pandemic. Following the spread of the virus in France, the French government decided on a strict lockdown of the French population from 17 March 2020, which is still in effect at the time of writing in May 2020. The lockdown effectively marked an end to the weekly protests by the gilets jaunes, after 70 consecutive Saturdays of demonstrations. Attempting to alleviate the economic disruption of the lockdown introduced to fight the pandemic, the French government announced a series of economic measures. These included the protection of wages for those unable to work, financial aid to businesses, the deferral of taxes and social charges, and low-interest loans guaranteed by the state – on top of existing measures to provide unemployment insurance and family benefits. The precise cost of these measures is yet to be determined, but it is likely to be substantial, with a figure of an increase in state spending worth around 15 per cent of GDP put forward by some commentators (Vignaud, 2020), bringing the French national debt to new highs not reached since the 1930s. What this shows is that the state is capable of increasing its involvement in economic life, which was one of the demands of the gilets jaunes during their year-and-a-half of uninterrupted protests. What remains to be seen, however, is whether this will break the pattern of liberal-libertarian ideology surrounding the presidency of Macron, which will be discussed in Chapter 5. Without a rethinking of the democratic structures behind decision-making, the outcome of increased state involvement in economic life is unlikely to lead to outcomes that will please those who took part in the gilets jaunes protests from 2018 to 2020. If anything, the pandemic has shown that inequalities are deeply engrained, with many of those who had taken part in the protests classified as essential workers during the confinement, allowing the backbone of the economy to keep on functioning while others stayed at home, and they have therefore been those most at risk of catching the disease (Fourquet and Morin, 2020).

Who are the gilets jaunes?

The sociology of the gilets jaunes has also widely been commented on. Comprising women and men from all walks of life, they do share some features that can help us understand where the vast majority of protesters come from. Often described as the 'white poor' – as opposed to the poor working classes from the inner cities or banlieues, who largely come from immigrant families with various non-white origins – they are the French equivalent of the American 'white trash' or the British 'chav'. Portrayed as the losers of their generation, they are certainly those who have lost most from the economic crises and fiscal changes described above. But they are not the poorest in French society. While a majority are still renting their accommodation, many of them do own their own house and have a car, but also have the debt that comes with these two personal assets. Relying on mortgages and credit, and having to pay monthly repayments to reimburse the cost of their vehicle, these workers have often very low disposable incomes and very few savings – particularly after more than a decade of austerity. They have been driven out of cities not so much out of personal choice, but because the bungalows of peri-urban France are the only places left they can afford given the rise in house prices in the city centres. Pierre Rosanvallon (2019: 174) describes them as coming from a society of the little people (*une société des petits*), as opposed to the society of the excluded who are on welfare or who have found themselves unemployed. They are either from the working class or from the lower-middle class, are sometimes small entrepreneurs, with a few employees they manage directly, who are classed as artisans or shopkeepers. Rosanvallon estimates that five million French people fit into this category, which is described by Isabelle Coutant (2019: 147) as the '*petits-moyens*'. The *petits-moyens*, which translates both as 'small means' and as the 'small-middle', illustrate this double sociological category. It can perhaps best be translated as the *small-mean class* – with reference to both the arithmetic mean and the small means that form their economic reality. They are those who have limited means to get by if something goes wrong in their life – a sick child, a car accident, a parent who becomes a dependant – and whose small economic means make them particularly vulnerable to changes in the cost of living. And they are those who are not quite at the bottom of the social hierarchy, but are either at the top of the lowest social stratum or at the bottom of the middle. Either upper-working class or lower-middle class, the hybridity of the participants demands a rethinking of our social categories. The *small-mean class* is a sociological category that best explains the bulk of the participants in the gilets jaunes movement.

Home-owners with no savings, they are often just a month or two away from having their home repossessed by the bank or their car sold at auction, and have to depend on charity and foodbanks when times get tough. Whereas in times of economic boom they typically have opportunities for advancement and mobility, in times of shrinking economic activity they are often the first to be hit by tightening budgets for state services they depend on, and rising inflation coupled with wage stagnation. As Olivier Ertzscheid (2019: 137) shows, however, they are not particularly close to the far right and typically are apathetic towards political parties. Analysing their Facebook posts in gilets jaunes organizing pages, Ertzscheid found very little use of racism, an almost complete absence of far-right vocabulary, and often profound concern for ecological issues. Neither left nor right (nor centre), they are simply concerned with the end of the month and paying their bills. For many, being involved in the gilets jaunes movement either online or in person was their first foray into political life. Their calls for economic justice, fiscal fairness and affordable living have echoed deep in French society, as it is evident that their demands were shared by a wide proportion of the French public, at least initially.

Politically they have not been aligned with any single party. Although they clearly gravitate more towards protest parties on the extremes, even this link between the gilets jaunes and the extreme right or left is not as clear as is often claimed in the news media, as we will see. They may have started as an anti-tax movement, traditionally more the remit of the right, but the movement quickly moved to demands for economic justice and direct participation in politics. Lacking a leader, a strong woman or man at the head of the movement, and resisting attempts by Marine Le Pen, leader of the Rassemblement National, Nicolas Dupont-Aignant, leader of Debout la France, Laurent Wauquiez from Les Républicains and Jean-Luc Mélenchon from La France Insoumise, they have stayed clear of party lines and affiliations (Bristow, 2019). Their calls for increased democracy and their refusal of representation are clearly political, however, despite the claims of some protesters. Refusing to 'do politics', they have engaged in one of the most fundamental political activities of all times: rethinking the social contract and what unites us all. There is widespread consensus among commentators that the gilets jaunes have been a reaction to a breaking of the social contract in France. For Samuel Hayat (2019a: 24) and David Guilbaud (2019: 121), it is Macron that has broken the implicit pact of French society with its leaders; for Rosanvallon (2019: 180), it is the 'right to govern' that is being questioned by these protests; for Dominique Rousseau (2019: 71), it is the question of legitimacy that is at stake; and for Olivier Christin (2019), it is the very principle of modern politics – the contract – that is at stake. In France at least, this analogy is not questioned, although of course the details of the link between the gilets jaunes and the social contract are left open for debate. What I propose to do in this book is to go one step further than these commentators. They are, of course, correct in assessing a breakdown of the social contract, and the crisis of representation is both persistent and enduring in French society. But I want to propose that the movement of the gilets jaunes itself has also been an opportunity to rethink the social contract anew. Through their actions, propositions and even through their use of violence, the gilets jaunes have put together a challenge to the existing social contract tradition and have proposed the beginning of a renewal of the tradition. This book will expand on this theme, theoretically and politically, to propose a sketch of the new social contract that can emerge today and for the future.

Neither left nor right

The most enduring crisis of political representation that France has faced since the Revolution that toppled the *Ancien Régime* in 1789 has been raging in France since the year of my birth, 1983. François Mitterrand, the first socialist president of the Fifth Republic, decided to follow the liberal advisers from within his party and accept austerity measures, and to move away from traditional socialist policies of the first two years of his presidential mandate. This important year for French politics crystallized the liberal consensus, whether on the left or the right of political spectrum, that governments have to withdraw from economic life and abandon the welfare state, or at least halt its growth and limit its remit. Not unlike the later claim by Fukuyama (1992) that we had reached the end of history, the political turn to the right by Mitterrand was a signal of a wider social phenomenon, where differences between political parties became ones of degree rather than ones of kind. Between 1981 and 2017, France saw a rotation between left and right, including cohabitation governments (where the President was on one side of the spectrum, and the Prime Minister and government on the other), that made differentiating between the politics of the left and right an increasingly difficult exercise. The most immediate consequence of this centring of French politics has been the electorate's increased removal from political activism and participation, and the settling of a more apathetic mood to the swing between left and right. The crisis of representation was made evident by low voter turnout in elections, and the rise of so-called populist parties, not least of which the Front National under the leadership of Jean-Marie and then Marine Le Pen. When left and right seemed to agree on the main lines of the political economy, only the far right seemed to propose an alternative, culminating in 34 per cent of French voters (over ten million people) casting their ballot for Marine Le Pen on 7 May 2017. Emmanuel Macron, who assumed the French presidency following his victory on that day, had run on a platform of being neither left nor right, combining his experiences as a banker and as a minister under a socialist government to show that he could play both sides of the traditional political spectrum.

Thomas Piketty (2019b: ch 14) has speculated that the left/right divide, which started in France during the Revolution, is perhaps at its end today. Instead of this traditional dichotomy, he proposes to read the new political landscape as either a 'four quarters' race, or a 'three thirds' one. France in 2017, he explains, saw four candidates achieve very close scores in the first round of the Presidential election, despite clear incentives in the political system for a two-horse race. The four horses of the apocalypse of traditional representation are divided along two axes. In the first place, they differ between each other based on their internationalist or nativist tendencies, and in the second instance they are opposed to one another in terms of their positioning regarding equality or inequality. The four tendencies are thus the internationalist-egalitarians (led by Mélenchon), the internationalist-inegalitarians (led by Macron), the nativist-egalitarians (led by Le Pen) and the nativist-inegalitarians (led by François Fillon). We could summarize these by reference to four ideologies: socialist, liberal, nationalist, and conservative. Piketty further speculates that the liberals and conservatives could find common ground (in their acceptance of inequality), with the more egalitarian among the conservative camp shifting towards the nationalist side. What was traditionally a two-horse race between left and right thus turns into a three-horse race between socialists, liberals and nationalists; or a four-horse race with the conservatives added into the mix. The 'fifth quarter', as Piketty himself speculates, are those who have largely abstained from participation in the 2017 election, or those who voted in protest rather than for ideological reasons. The 'fifth quarter' are the gilets jaunes, among others. Neither socialist nor liberal, neither nationalist nor conservative, they are the ones who have been left out of the new emerging political spectrum. Although Piketty clearly places the gilets jaunes on the 'nativist' side of the ideological spectrum, it is not clear that they are easily drawn by the nationalist rhetoric. The gilets jaunes offer an opportunity for the defenders of equality to rethink their policies and re-appropriate the struggles of the working poor, from whom the gilets jaunes are largely drawn. A new model of representation is emerging, and the inclusion of all within it, including those who have lost out from globalization and the liberal consensus of the past, is an important challenge of the struggles of 2018–2020.

As Piketty admits, his classification is rather crude and open to critique. The sincerity of the nationalist discourse with regards to equality, in particular, is more than dubious. Where the Rassemblement National has held positions in power in local politics, notably by winning a few mayoral elections, such as in Béziers, Fréjus, Beaucaire or Hénin-Beaumont, they have tended to apply strict austerity measures resulting in the closure of local social services and the selling off of municipal assets, thus widening inequalities in their towns (Delaporte, 2019; Causit, 2020). Although Marine Le Pen clearly attempted to position herself as a defender of the French working class, and has to an extent succeeded in doing so, the gilets jaunes show there is considerable space for a more egalitarian critique of the nationalist ideology. By opposing the suppression of taxes for the wealthiest, demanding direct participation in politics through referenda, and asking for a rise in purchasing power for the working poor, the gilets jaunes have clearly positioned themselves as a challenge to both socialists and nationalists, who have up until now favoured many of these positions.

As the 'fifth quarter' of the new ideological spectrum, the gilets jaunes pose a fundamental challenge for any constitutional and institutional settlement of the political crisis in the future French state. The small entrepreneurs, peripheral workers and precarious staff that took to the roundabouts of France in 2018–20 asked for more direct control of the political machine that is undergoing profound changes in France. Whereas the other four quarters of the political spectrum function in more traditional terms – all accept the principle of political representation and are organized as political parties – and thereby do not challenge the terms of the social contract *per se*, the gilets jaunes have challenged the general consensus. In other words, while the recalibrating of political representation does not represent a challenge to the social contract *per se*, the movement of the gilets jaunes has provided such a challenge. To answer their claims, one needs to think outside the box, and traditional responses to political struggles are no longer sufficient. Their challenge is not primarily aimed at particular policy initiatives, and is not even strictly ideological in either the traditional sense or the new sense that Piketty proposes, but is rather about the role that the wider citizenry can play directly in the political process. This challenge is one that puts more direct pressure on the political establishment. This is why historical analogies, particular to the jacqueries, the Revolution of 1789, the Commune of 1870–71, or the events of May 1968, have had a powerful appeal for those trying to understand the movement. Let's take these in turn to show that, although historical analogies help us understand the gilets jaunes in the French context, none of them explains the movement as a whole.

The gilets jaunes in France's history of social movements

Four historical uprisings in French history have been used as analogies for the crisis of the gilets jaunes: the jacqueries of *ancien régime* France; the French Revolution; the workers' movement, starting with the Commune of 1870 and continuing with industrial action in 1936 and 1948–49; and finally the May 1968 events. While comparison with the past is inevitable and ultimately useful to situate the current predicament, I will show that too many dissimilarities exist between these historical events, and that the gilets jaunes movement has to be understood on its own terms. Throughout the book, I will come back to these important historical events as points of comparison with the events of 2018–20. Where similarities exist with the past, they help to illuminate the situation of the present. But the important differences between the past and the current movement also help us to sharpen our understanding of what the gilets jaunes mean today. By identifying four main differences with four historical struggles in French history, I hope to make a more general contribution to a theory of the gilets jaunes movement, and its significance for France and the world.

The jacqueries, the peasant movements of rebellion that started in the fourteenth century, but whose name is associated with a series of revolts against the state throughout the late Middle Ages and the early Modern period, bear some resemblance to the gilets jaunes movement. Occurring at the birth of the French state, and during its period of growth and consolidation, they were primarily revolts against the nascent fiscal regime that was to become the embryo of the modern state as we know it today. Moving away from its feudal roots, the French state slowly acquired the power to tax its subjects directly, rather than relying on local nobles to collect taxes for the Crown. It is Noiriel's analysis that 'it is the birth of royal taxation that crafted the French people as a community of individuals subjected to the state' (Noiriel, 2018: 40). The jacqueries were a form of resistance to this rising administrative and political entity, but the French people remained largely bound by the feudal order still in a period of transition until the French Revolution. Following the imposition of the *gabelle*, a tax on salt levied during the Hundred Years' War, a series of popular movements emerged throughout the Kingdom – in Flanders, Île-de-France, Normandy, Auvergne and Languedoc between 1378 and 1382. In Paris, thousands of armed rioters murdered tax collectors and rich citizens, as well as Jews, in the revolt of the *Maillotins* while the King was away putting down a revolt in Flanders. Hundreds died in the riots, and the leaders were executed when the royal armies regained control of the city. The peasant revolts continued sporadically until the early eighteenth century, particularly during times of increased international conflict and new taxes. During the reign of Louis XIV, countless revolts against the new fiscal regime occurred, all easily put down by the Sun King's armies with brutal efficiency. What all these jacqueries have in common is the local nature of their organization. Still based on the interpersonal relations of the *Ancien Régime*, they were small in their scale, if dramatic in their effects. Unlike the jacqueries, the gilets jaunes are a national movement that has benefited from advances in communications technology – particularly Facebook and the use of other social media platforms. They began from the outset as a nationwide movement, and if particular groups crystallized around their region, *département* or individual roundabout, they managed to organize actions beyond their localities, notably by converging on metropolises and the capital city. The first feature that differentiates the gilets jaunes from other movements is thus their *national* character. They are not a local movement, and if they are not actually an urban movement (thereby resembling some of the jacqueries which started in the countryside), they are a peri-urban national movement that depends on modes of transportation and communication which make their organization uniquely different from medieval peasant revolts.

The national event *par excellence* in the history of France is, of course, the Revolution. Commentators on the gilets jaunes movement have pondered about its revolutionary potential, and the likelihood of the movement's success has often been measured against those of the French Revolution. Sophie Wahnich (2019: 29–43) has drawn parallels between the two historical events, placing the centrality of the revolutionary song, particularly the *Marseillaise*, at the centre of similarities. For the movement to be successful, it would need to initiate a new type of regime fundamentally different from that of the past, some claim. But even this is to read the Revolution in an all-too-teleological manner. Although certainly radical and much more violent than the events of 2018–20, the French Revolution did not abolish the monarchy immediately, and attempted to work with the structures of the past until it was clear that such a desire would not come true. More importantly, the Revolution aimed at seizing power, and taking over the organs of the state. This is, almost by definition, what a revolution is: an attempt to take power into one's own hands. There is no evidence that the gilets jaunes were attempting a revolution in that sense. Of course, there is an element of empowerment that comes from their demands and actions, as we will discuss later in the book. But there was never an attempt to seize control of the state. Unlike the French Revolution, there was no tennis court oath, no establishment of an alternative locus of power such as the national assembly gathering in Versailles, and no attempt to overthrow the power of the state. Even the slogan 'Macron *démission*', calling for the President's resignation, ever-present during demonstrations, was accompanied by no programme for who would succeed him as head of state. Every attempt to label the movement as a revolutionary one is at best rhetorical. The gilets jaunes are thus a *social movement*, and not a revolutionary committee. It could, of course, still evolve into something else – and we will come back to its future in the Conclusion – but there are no signs of a mutation into something resembling the revolutionary potential of the past.

The workers' movements, notably those of the Paris Commune and the large strikes of 1936 and 1948–49, initiated a period of working-class action that has parallels with the current gilets jaunes movement. When the Prussian armies defeated French Imperial forces in 1870, the Parisian people revolted against their leaders and proclaimed a Commune in the capital. The short-lived insurrection, lasting a mere 72 days, saw the creation of a direct form of democracy in Paris. Among the rights guaranteed by Commune were the right to insurrection, the election of civil servants and judges, the right to recall representatives, a minimum wage, women's right to work, and equal pay (Noiriel, 2018: 369–70). The new French government, having ousted Napoleon III and surrendered to Prussia, quickly mobilized its troops against Parisians, retaking the city by force. Between 5,700 and 7,400 *Communards* died in the fighting, 43,000 were arrested, and a further hundred condemned to death, with 3,800 deported to New Caledonia. This bloody episode of French history shares some of the hopes of direct democracy of the gilets jaunes. But the comparison ends there. The workers' movement was urban and organized, seizing power, if only locally, rather than being dispersed throughout the country. While violence was present on the streets of Paris on both occasions, one can hardly compare the skirmishes of 2018–20 with the scenes of carnage of the spring of 1871. Similarly, during the large strikes of 1936 and 1948–49, workers organized themselves, this time to negotiate with the authorities over working conditions. In May–June 1936, following the electoral victory of the coalition of the three left-wing parties in France, a series of strikes made demands from employers. The newly elected government seized the opportunity of a popular movement on the streets to ratify the Matignon accords, which instigated paid holidays, the 40-hour week, and a pay rise of 12 per cent for workers. Perhaps the most successful of French strikes, it cemented workers' rights and secured important concessions for the least advantaged. Similarly, after the war, the national unity government collapsed when the communists resigned their ministerial posts in 1947. Freed from its governmental role, the French Communist Party (PCF) organized a series of strikes. In total, over three million strikers took part, and many small-scale battles occurred between protesters and police. At Villerupt, miners and metal workers fought the newly created Republican Guard (CRS); at least six lost their lives and many policemen were wounded. The CRS were reorganized by the government following the strikes, banning communists from their ranks. Reservists were called to action, and tanks sent in for reinforcement. Portrayed as a communist coup by its opponents, the strikes were brutally put down by the coalition government, including its socialist ministers. The severity of the repression resembles that faced by the gilets jaunes, as we will see. But the similarities end there. Unlike these workers' movements, the gilets jaunes are not part of trades unions. They are often independent workers or even business owners, employed in the services industry or caring for family members. Noiriel (2019: 46–47) puts it succinctly, showing that the gilets jaunes are the independents against the employees, and have chosen yellow over red, an end to taxes over wage negotiations, and the *Marseillaise* over the *Internationale*, the revolutionary chant written in 1871 to support the Paris Commune and a symbol of workers' struggles worldwide. The movement is thus a *non-unionized* protest, falling outside the remit of traditional industrial relations.

The trades unions were also left behind when students took control of their Parisian universities and took to the streets in 1968. Simply referred to as 'the events' (*les évènements*), the protests that took place in May and June 1968 changed French society forever. Étienne Balibar (2019: 211) equates the two crises, those of 1968 and 2018–20, to the collective voice coming from below, a grassroots movement that aims to disrupt social relations. Starting in the new university at Nanterre, where students were jam-packed in poor learning conditions, the protests spread like wildfire in the spring of 1968. Daily battles between students and police ensued, and students in other cities joined the movement, notably in Toulouse, Lyon and Strasbourg. Barricades were erected, and protesters used paving stones as projectiles against tear gas. Cars were set alight, shop windows were broken, and hundreds were injured in the fighting. When put in the context of previous social struggles, though, this violence was relatively moderate. But the media was ever-present, with radio commentators present on the scene 24 hours a day, and the tales of daily clashes were reported live into French homes. Trades unions, particularly the CGT under the control of the Communist Party, were reluctant to join in. But their base outpaced them, and against the wishes of its leaders, unionists took to the streets and started a general strike (Noiriel, 2018: 654–63). The whole country was then involved. Unlike in 1968, the gilets jaunes have not benefited from the support of French workers. The much weaker unions of the twenty-first century pale in comparison to the negotiating power of those in the 1960s. But, like the events of 1968, the gilets jaunes protests were born outside of the trade union movement. Unlike the *bourgeois* students who took to the streets then, it is a working-class movement (albeit not that of an industrial proletariat) that erupted in November 2018. Not widely helped by other sections of French society, even when polls suggest French people largely supported the movement in its initial weeks of action, the gilets jaunes are an isolated movement. Attempts to combine forces with other movements, notably Extinction Rebellion and the trades unions, have been made since, but these pale in comparison with the solidarity of 1968.

The gilets jaunes movement can thus be understood as a *sui generis* movement that has no immediate parallel in France's past. Although it certainly shares common features with some of the past movements – it is in the differences with the past that the movement comes to light. It is a national movement by its very scope, a popular movement in that it has affected every sector of French society, a working-class movement as its members were primarily drawn from the lower-middle classes of French society, a non-revolutionary movement that has not sought to take over the functions of the state, a non-unionized movement that has bypassed the social struggle around employers and trades unions, and finally an isolated movement that, despite its relative popularity among the French public, has not enjoyed a significant show of solidarity from other social forces in French society. What the movement has done, consistently, is provide a challenge to existing social relations and structures of power within French society. As such, it is a challenge to the existing social contract in place at least since the creation of the France's Fifth Republic in 1958. Whether this challenge results in a new constitutional compromise or not remains to be seen, but the questions raised in terms of liberty, democracy and economic justice merit serious intellectual reflection.

Towards a new social contract

What I suggest in this book is that we should read this movement as a challenge to the notion of the social contract. The movement demands, more than any specific request such as the resignation of the French President or the institution of a citizens' initiative referendum, a profound rethinking of what unites us all — rich and poor, city-dwellers and peripheral or rural workers, the politically active and apathetic or disillusioned voters. By reading the gilets jaunes as a challenge to this venerable tradition of the social contract, I will show that they have much to offer us from a philosophical perspective. I have chosen to address this challenge to the social contract through a series of theoretical concepts that are made accessible to a wide audience, and which concern us all as citizens of modern states. The issues of political violence, liberty, democracy and economic justice will form the backbone of this challenge to the legitimacy of political power. It will be my goal to show that this crisis of the social contract is an incredible opportunity to revive a debate about the role of citizens in politics, and to defend a renewed vision of democracy for the twenty-first century. I will argue that this process will need a renewal of the social contract, and provide a sketch for the steps we need to take to make this happen. Thinking about politics provides an exhilarating avenue of change, and although few saw the movements of the gilets jaunes coming, analysing their roots will enable a deep reflection on the very foundations of our practice and thinking about what constitutes the political.

Structure

A word about structure is necessary here. The first chapter will propose a theory of the social contract, in the context of the gilets jaunes. This theory will be detailed in the five chapters that follow. Chapters 2 to 5 are organized along the lines of a concept, and all five will focus on a particular thinker. The second chapter deals with the questions of *violence* and Hobbes' theory of the state, the third chapter with the problem of *freedom* and Spinoza's call for a free state, the fourth chapter with *democracy* and Rousseau's participative polity, and the fifth chapter with *economic justice* and Rawls' difference principle. Chapter 6 provides a reflection on the new social contract, taking Diderot as dialectician of change, and offer ways to think about the *future* of the tradition. Finally, the Conclusion will use Burke's theorizing about the social contract, as well as his reflections on the sublime and beautiful, to show how ugliness (as a concept) has seeped into political life, as well as offering reflections on some international comparisons, by showing the links between the gilets jaunes and the Brexit and Trump votes, as well as providing short comparisons with Poland and Chile.

1

Critical Times for the Social Contract

On 17 November 2018, a mass protest of people wearing yellow jackets, known in French as the gilets jaunes, started in France. What has become the largest social movement in post-war France, overtaking the events of 1968 in size and intensity, started as a protest against fuel tax increases, a 'green' carbon tax and the lowering of the speed limit on French national roads to 80 kilometres per hour (50 miles per hour) from 90 kilometres per hour (56 miles per hour). A grassroots movement, outside of traditional political parties and unrelated to trades unions, has caught the political and industrial establishment by surprise. Immediately labelled as populist, reactionary and violent by its adversaries, the movement has been linked to the election of Donald Trump in the United States, the Brexit vote in the United Kingdom, and the rise to power of the Five Star Movement party in Italy. While some of this is accurate – it is populist as opposed to elitist, reactionary as opposed to proposing a concrete political programme, and violent in its response to the repression of the French state – the movement will be shown to have much more potential for intellectual challenge than these immediate reactions suggest. The theory I propose here is that the movement itself is best understood as a fundamental challenge to the existing social contract in France – and by extension to other social contracts throughout the world – and its history is not limited to the months of political turmoil it engendered in France or even to the past couple of years of political upheaval in the wider world, but poses a challenge to the very future of our political order. A rethinking of the social contract is necessary given this crisis and framing the present political turmoil in philosophical terms will help shed some light on the opportunities for change that are arising, in part thanks to the movement.

The early days of the movement

Emmanuel Macron had the vision and the cunning to see the crisis of the gilets jaunes as an opportunity for political change. In his New Year's message to the nation on 31 December 2018, after weeks of civil unrest at home, he announced the beginning of a *grand débat national*, a great debate throughout France, to rethink the terms of the social contract. Detailed in his 'Letter to the French people' published a couple of weeks later, the initiative inscribed itself in the social contract tradition. Macron affirmed that suggestions made during the two-month debate would have a direct impact on his exercise of power.

> "Your proposals will therefore allow us to build a new contract for the nation, to give structure to the action of the government and Parliament, and also France's positions at European and international levels. I will report back to you directly in the months following the end of the debate." (Macron, 2019)

The promises were clear, the tone serious and hope was raised for those wanting a way out of the impasse of political representation. Having engaged almost two million people, this exercise in contractual theory can be seen as an attempt to replicate the democracy of the ancient Athenian Agora, made possible by the digital age. In practice, because the debates Macron took part in were limited to contact with locally elected mayors and officials, as opposed to the citizen body as a whole, it was more reminiscent of the Roman Senate and its political machinations than the direct democracy of the Greeks. The goal of this book is not to assess the effectiveness of this new contract as Macron implemented it – it would make for a short and dismissive assessment – but rather to use this opportunity to reflect on the theories that help us understand the contract and what it could have been. We will see that the idea behind Macron's debate was brilliant and ingenious but, in practice, it fell far short of expectations. Together with theorists of the social contract such as Hobbes, Spinoza, Rousseau, Rawls, Diderot, and Burke, we will see that the exercise is worth the political effort, and that it can provide a valuable contribution to life in a complex political association.

The yellow vest itself emerged as a symbol of resistance to state power. A legal requirement for all motorists, the high visibility jacket has to be kept within reach of the driver's seat in all vehicles in circulation in France, to be used in case of an emergency. As the protest started as a revolt by commuters against rising taxes on fuel, it was the obvious symbol for all those who rely on their own means of transport to get to work, go to the grocers, or take their children to school. Symbol of the further intrusion of the state into each and every vehicle, its use was subverted to reflect the needs of everyday working people and of those marginalized in French society. It also acted as a powerful reminder of the movement's working-class roots, those for whom working outside often means wearing similar 'high vis' jackets on a daily basis. The movement started not as an urban revolt, but as a rural or peri-urban plea for higher purchasing power and fairer taxes. It soon spread well beyond these narrow confines, and at first enjoyed enormous popularity, with 83 per cent of French people, according to one poll (Clavel, 2018), finding the movement to be justified at the end of the first month of protests. By contrast, the popularity of the French President, Emmanuel Macron, fell to record lows during the same period, to below 20 per cent in approval ratings. It is of little surprise that an overwhelming majority of French citizens would recognize the calls of the protesters for increased purchasing power as their own. After a decade of austerity under both right- and left-wing governments, the centrist party that surrounds Macron has not delivered on its promises for most citizens, who continued to see their own economic situation deteriorate and a decline in social services through the retreat of the French state.

The protesters who took to the streets, going every Saturday to the roundabouts of rural France, the town centres and metropolitan areas, have shown tremendous determination and tenacity. Although the numbers of participants fluctuate widely from week to week, even the most conservative estimates number from 282,000 during the first Saturday of protests to 18,600 during 'Act 26', six months later. For the one-year anniversary of the movement in November 2019, the Interior Ministry reported 28,000 participants – the highest level since March of that year – showing that the movement was diminished rather than dead. The last protest took place on 14 March 2020, mobilizing only a few hundred participants, as France was preparing for a national lockdown to fight the COVID-19 pandemic, marking an end to 70 consecutive Saturdays of protests. The protesters themselves claim much higher numbers, and notably over a million protesters at the first occurrence of the protests. In any case, spread over the time period of the movement, the participation is extremely high, and overtakes the numbers involved in the last large-scale mobilization in France, *La Manif pour tous*, the protests organized in 2012–13 against gay marriage. More importantly, the gilets jaunes are not themselves concentrated in the capital city. In the centralized country that is France, the movement appears as much a protest against Parisian elites as it does an attempt to curb the rise in fuel taxes. The anger against those centralized elites is seen in the opposition to the new nationwide speed limit. Parisians, who never need to drive on national and departmental roads, are seen to be dictating a policy of blanket reduction of the speed limit regardless of particular circumstances. One of the targets of the protests has therefore been speed cameras on French roads. On a visit to France in 2019, I was surprised to see that all the cameras I passed on the motorways had been vandalized rendering them ineffective. It is estimated that about three quarters of these cameras nationwide have been damaged in some way (Philippe, 2019). Outside of Paris, large cities such as Toulouse, Bordeaux, Lille and Marseille were also the theatre of protests. Even more surprisingly, smaller cities, with around 100,000 inhabitants, saw wide support for the movement despite relatively little press coverage. Rouen, Caen, Dijon, Besançon, Toulon, Perpignan and many other medium-sized cities saw thousands of protesters at one stage on their streets. Even in the streets of Paris, one could see regional flags flying as proud symbols of local identities and characteristics. Alongside these, many French flags also adorned the processions, signifying a return to a defence of French particularities against a wider world. A number of European flags were theatrically taken down by protesters, and replaced by French flags – and in at least one instance a European flag was burnt. Although anecdotal, these instances of pride in regional identity, of reclaiming the national flag, and of hostility towards supranational entities is, at the very least, a feature of the movement that we will explore in Chapter 4.

The *visibility* of the yellow vest is of further importance to understand the current malaise. Where liberal theories of the social contract, such as Rawls' (1971), have emphasized the blindness of justice and the abstraction of particular interests, the popular movement has been explicitly visible, audible and palpable. With an explicit desire to be seen, the gilet jaune acts as a form of political awareness-raising, an act of interpellation of the political class by those they are supposed to represent. The plight of the low-earning, struggling members of French society, previously invisible to metropolitan elites, is brought to the fore of the political scene. No longer able to turn a blind eye, the French government has had to backpedal on a number of policies, notably the proposed tax on fuel, but also a continued policy of austerity affecting those whose end-of-the-month struggles have become increasingly difficult. Gilets jaunes protests have often been loud, with street singing, chanting and the invasion of public and semi-public spaces such as roundabouts, shopping malls or airports, disrupting the quiet lives of the urban centres and their immediate periphery. The *Marseillaise*, in particular, became a rallying cry of the movement, along with calls for Macron's *démission* [resignation] and shouts of "*Ahou! Ahou! Ahou!*" – a chant accompanied by clapping, originating from the blockbuster film *300*, and having been popularized in football circles in the *Olympique Lyonnais*, and *Les Bleus*, the French national football team (LCI, 2019). This chant, a signifier of the importance of popular culture in the movement, is at odds with the purifying demands of the modern high street, where shoppers quietly roam the boulevards to run their errands on Saturday afternoons. The contrast between the loud, disruptive movement and the peacefulness of ordinary life is an act of interpellation for the current political order. The movement has also left its mark on French cities, with makeshift barricades erected, yellow vests covering statues, including a giant vest adorning a replica of the Statue of Liberty on 2 March 2019 (*Euronews*, 2019). A desire to be seen, heard and felt is thus at the forefront of the movement.

Much media coverage has focused on acts of violence by the protesters during demonstrations. Clashes with police near the Arc de Triomphe, the burning of several buildings, including banks, newsstands and the terrace of the chic restaurant *Le Fouquet's* on the Champs-Élysées, all provided dramatic scenes of unrest on the streets of Paris. Over 8,000 arrests occurred during the first six months of the movement, with quick trials and sentencing for many protesters. The case of Christophe Dettinger, a former boxing champion, illustrates this violence well. As a participant at a demonstration, he reports being sprayed with tear gas and seeing a woman being hit with batons while on the ground. Perceiving an injustice, he began hitting two *gendarmes* in front of him, with the skills of his former career coming into full force. At his hearing only five weeks after the incident, he admitted being ashamed of seeing himself on the footage of the events, and of having committed an injustice to redress another one. He was sentenced to 30 months in prison, 18 months of which was suspended. Beyond this particular example, the most dramatic scenes of protester violence are attributed to the 'black blocs', a loose term to qualify groups of protesters, not themselves wearing a yellow vest but rather covering their identity and dressed in back. The black blocs, not a recent phenomenon or particularly affiliated with the yellow vest movement, can often be seen on the margins of large demonstrations, irrespective of the particular agenda of the day's protest. Although there is little agreement about their political motives, they are generally committed to anti-establishment actions, notably through the destruction of property and symbols of power and wealth such as banks and multinational corporations, and attacks on police forces. More widely, it is estimated that the gilets jaunes movement has already claimed the lives of a number of people, up to 15 depending on sources. Most of these were the result of traffic accidents at the various barrages erected by the gilets jaunes early on in the movement. They have included both drivers in collision with one another, and protesters being run over by motorists forcing their way through. The movement has been violent, as we will see in Chapter 2, but this violence is relatively small compared with other violent demonstrations. The most dramatic of Saturdays was on 1 December 2018, when 55 vehicles were reported to have been set alight in the capital city (*Autotrader*, 2018). By contrast, a typical New Year's Eve sees around a thousand vehicles being set alight in France, and on average over a hundred vehicles are set alight every day throughout the country. While clearly dramatic when these scenes happen in the main arteries of the capital city under the spotlight of television cameras, the phenomenon is not unique, nor is it particularly large scale in the wider context of urban violence and given the history of social protests in the country.

In contrast to these acts of violence on the side of protesters, which remain relatively isolated considering the breadth of the movement, police repression has been systematic and well organized. In addition to tear gas and use of batons during police charges, the weapons of state control of the protests have come under increasing scrutiny. Three weapons in particular have raised concerns, including at the level of the United Nations, with Macron having to defend the heavy-handed approach of his security forces against international criticism. Among the three weapons in question is the LBD 40, a 'ball-launcher' exported by its Swiss manufacturers as a weapon of war but considered 'non-lethal' by French security forces. The launcher is particularly effective, as it propels its 40 mm-wide projectile at great speed towards its target in order to stop a potential aggressor from reaching the security forces. Although designed to be non-lethal, the weapon has claimed at least one death back in 2010 in France, and has been blamed for many permanent injuries during the gilets jaunes protests. Security forces are forbidden to aim for the head with this weapon, due its power; however, many instances of head injuries, including at least 24 protesters losing an eye, have occurred through the use of the LBD 40. Two other weapons, both grenades, have also been criticized as showing excessive force from the security forces. Known by the acronyms GMD and GLI-F4, these grenades contain an explosive charge equivalent to about half that of the iconic World War II US Army 'pineapple' grenade. These weapons, designed for crowd control but containing a clear risk to the public, have produced horrific injuries since November 2018, notably the loss of a hand by at least five protesters who had either picked up the projectile or been too close to it during detonation. Zineb Redouane, an elderly woman living in Marseille, was notably hit by a projectile from one of these grenades while she was closing her blinds on the fourth floor of her building. She later died in hospital, being the first fatal victim as a consequence of the use of police force. David Dufresne, an independent journalist who kept track of injuries to protesters, bystanders and journalists, has numbered over 860 cases of police violence during the gilets jaunes protests between its inception up to 30 June 2019 (Dufresne, 2019). His documentation includes detailed accounts and pictures of the results of police repression, including wounds typical of war zones rather than of the streets of Paris. Both the interior minister, Christophe Castaner, and the President denied any excessive use of force by security forces. Emboldened by public outrage at the destruction of property during some of the protests, and themselves attacking the violence of protesters, French politicians in the French Parliament strengthened the powers of the security forces, and weakened judicial accountability for state violence by passing a new law early in 2019, which notably gave unprecedented preventative powers to the *préfet*, the administrator who is the official representative of the state at the local or regional level. The consequence of the protests has already been a degradation of civil liberties, a quasi-criminalization of demonstrations, and a sense of impunity for the excesses of security forces, with few investigations into police brutality leading to any sanctions. By the end of 2019, only two police officers had been convicted, for their use of force against demonstrators on 1 May in Paris – a demonstration organized by the trades unions and only partially attended by the gilets jaunes (Chevillard, 2020).

Even though support for the gilets jaunes movement has fallen since its inception, it still raises the important question of what citizens can do when they are unable to secure any advantages from the main political parties that have been in power, despite a turnover of those in political office. While trust in politicians has not been particularly high for some time, with a crisis of representation since at least the 1970s being theorized by Rosanvallon (2000), the office of the president had, until recently, still been shielded from popular anger. Since Nicolas Sarkozy's presidency (2007–12) at the very least, presidents have had record low approval ratings, with François Hollande reaching the all-time low of 12 per cent approval ratings in 2016 (Clavel, 2016), illustrating that the last bastion of Gaullist political legitimacy is no longer considered sacrosanct by the French people. Emmanuel Macron himself has been the target of anger by protesters, with calls for his resignation being widespread in demonstrations, and it is clear that he is blamed personally for many of the shortcomings of the French state by gilets jaunes protesters as well as the larger public. The political crisis is deep and enduring, and a reframing of the political contract is an important step to take during such critical times.

One of the most consistent demands of the gilets jaunes has been the establishment of the power of referendum. Calls for a *Référendum d'Initiative Citoyenne* (RIC), or citizen-initiated referendum, have been seen as a way to further the claims of the French Revolution, symbolized in Article 6 of the Declaration of the Rights of Man and of the Citizen of 1789: 'The law is the expression of the general will. All the citizens have the right of contributing personally or through their representatives to its formation.' This call has shown that the gilets jaunes themselves are able to put together demands for change, and propose concrete solutions to the problems they perceive in the French social contract. Although there are issues with such referenda, as we will see in Chapter 4, there are no good theoretical reasons why they could not be used meaningfully to instigate change. Understandably, the current establishment is highly sceptical of such initiatives, with concerns around the phrasing of questions and the implementation of decisions cited most often. The French media in particular reacted with open hostility to this demand, ignoring the fact that out of the eleven candidates for the French presidency in 2017, six had proposed a similar referendum in their political programme (Hayat, 2019b). The French protesters' call for such an instrument of policy may not solve the crisis of political representation, but it does introduce an element of initiative that is clearly missing from modern polities.

The social contract

The concept of the contract, of an agreement that resembles a legal document made between individuals, is a modern concept *par excellence*, and was born at the beginning of the modern era. The golden period of social contract theory, roughly stretching from 1650 to 1800, saw the flourishing of various works on the origins of society, the state of nature that preceded it, and the legitimacy of political rule. The social contract tradition is often associated with the philosophy of Thomas Hobbes written in the middle of the seventeenth century, when the English state was consolidating itself. This is a convenient historical shorthand, as the publication of Hobbes' *Leviathan* in 1651 is also the historical birth of the modern state as we know it, distinct from its medieval incarnation. The Peace of Westphalia of 1648 enshrined the concept of sovereignty in a distinctly novel manner. Although these peace treaties that ended the Thirty Years' War were not without their medieval oddities – for example, Article 73 of the Treaty gave the town of Brisac (modern-day Breisach) to France, but maintained the city's privileges acquired when it was part of the Holy Roman Empire – they also put forward the notion that a ruler had ultimate jurisdiction over their territory, ending the claim of others, notably the Emperor and the Pope, to dictate terms on the small principalities of central Europe.

Thomas Hobbes' work acted as the philosophical justification of the rise of this modern political entity: the state. The state had already existed in practice since the Renaissance period, when the courtly manners of the medieval kingdoms and the individual fealty and loyalty of local lords to their feudal superiors had slowly given way to the rise of professional administrators, permanent and far-reaching taxation systems and standing armies under the control of a monarch. France's ultimate victory in the Hundred Years' War was made possible by such changes in administration, and notably the ability to raise taxes on a continuous basis, but other countries in Western Europe had similar developments. What started as wartime necessity ended up being the model for peacetime, making changes permanent that could only have been justified in the first place in times of emergency. In some cases, parliaments had also started imposing limits on the authority of those monarchs, further institutionalizing decision-making power in a complex apparatus of power. The ultimate victory of Parliament over the monarch in England, which concluded the English Civil War, coincided with the rise of a (nation) state on the British Isles. All of these changes rested on the ability of particular powerful actors within these states – German princes, the French King, the English Parliament – to deploy force against their adversaries. Political violence was always there at the beginning of the rise of the state, and it was ultimately the state's ability to effectively deploy violence that made its claims to be the sole legitimate source of the use of force successful.

This concept of state sovereignty is today taken as a cornerstone of the international order, and the theory of the social contract acts as its legitimating basis in philosophical terms. If the modern state claims a monopoly over the legitimate use of force within its territory, as Max Weber (1919/2009) pointed out, this claim cannot be accepted by the population of that territory without some justification for accepting this use of force without resistance. As we will see in Chapter 2, the use of violence by the state is a central question of its legitimacy, and the social contract offers a plausible set of answers as to what is acceptable, and what is not acceptable, for a population to endure. At the very least, the question of state violence requires a social contract to justify obedience. It would be theoretically possible for a state to impose its rule exclusively through the use of violence against its citizens, but in practice this has never happened. Even the least popular regimes, or the most brutal states, have offered forms of legitimation to their citizens and to the outside world to justify their rule. It may even be true that the more a particular regime, ruler or party has had its legitimacy questioned, the more it engages in acts of social-contract legitimation. In 1936, at the height of its repression of its citizens, during the most brutal of purges, Stalin's Soviet

Union was nonetheless publishing the most accomplished and progressive constitution the world had ever seen. The process carried forth by the constitutional convention at the time was possibly the most widespread use of public debate and popular participation, and probably holds the record to date. With 42 million citizens participating in the debates that preceded the drafting of the Constitution (Siegelbaum, nd), the Stalinist attempt at establishing a social contract dwarfs the exercise carried out in France in 2019, with its two million participants (Blondiaux, 2019).

Even when it does not engage millions and when it is limited to an elite, the social contract is still a vital part of the establishment of the modern state. The writing of the American Declaration of Independence and the French Declaration of the Rights of Man and of the Citizen provide two clear historical examples from the late eighteenth century. The two documents owe much to the philosophies of Locke and Rousseau in particular, as foundational tools for what to include in the formal contract-like statements of purpose for a political entity. The American Declaration of Independence of 1776 claims that 'all men are created equal', that they have 'unalienable Rights […] Life, Liberty and the pursuit of Happiness', that 'Governments are […] deriving their just powers from the consent of the governed', and that when people are reduced 'under absolute Despotism, it is their right, it is their duty, to throw off such Government'. One could not formulate more clearly the social contract of Locke put into practice. Article 3 of the French Declaration of the Rights of Man and of the Citizen of 1789 makes explicit the central claim of the social contract: 'Sovereignty lies primarily in the Nation. No corporate body, no individual may exercise any authority that does not expressly emanate from it.' Rousseau would have largely agreed. Although drafted by a small number of representatives, both documents illustrate the need for the wider nation to accept the terms of the contract. The legitimacy of the political order rests on its ability to convince the wider social body that it is acting in the interests of all, not just of the few.

More recently, one can see the Treaty establishing a Constitution for Europe of 2004 as an attempt to frame the legitimacy of a political entity with the formal structure of a social contract. It is particularly revealing that the Constitution failed as a political project, after the French voted '*non*' in the referendum for its ratification in 2005, quickly followed by a Dutch '*nee*'. Although most of the 2004 treaty's provisions were then integrated into the Treaty of Lisbon, the Constitution itself was dismissed on that basis. I only use its example here to illustrate what happens when a social contract is rejected on a political basis – it makes legitimacy of the political project dubious at best. The social contract is a necessary feature of any modern polity, in the sense that some of the functions of the modern state, including its most important one – that of the use of force – would not be tolerated without proper justification.

Economics in the social contract tradition

The theory of the social contract is not limited to the formal constitutional arrangements of the modern nation state, and although this has only been a minor part of social contract theory, the economic arrangements are no less important to the tradition. Nation states that established themselves from the eighteenth century to today have used the basic tenets of the social contract, yet the philosophical discussion of the social contract soon fell into disrepute. No doubt Jeremy Bentham had in mind the wider social contract tradition when he attacked natural rights as being 'nonsense upon stilts' (Bentham, 1795/2002). The comical image this conjures is a damning attack on the philosophy behind the establishment of rights, which formed the cornerstone of liberal regimes (as well as many illiberal ones) that used the language of universalism to defend their policies, and their use of coercion. Philosophers and political theorists in most of the nineteenth and twentieth centuries were reluctant to engage seriously with the tradition, even as it was growing in political importance. The social contract was, however, rehabilitated as a philosophical project by John Rawls, when he published his *Theory of Justice* half a century ago.

Rawls had supported the primacy of political rights in his *Theory of Justice*, first published in 1971. As a good liberal philosopher, he could not let go of their uttermost importance. But he nonetheless also argued that economic rights were essential, even if they were subservient to political rights. Rawls illustrates with his philosophy the two meanings of the word 'liberal'. On the one hand, his philosophy is liberal in that it is dedicated to the safeguarding of individual rights, putting the preservation of private property, individual enterprise and political rights above all else. But, equally, he is liberal in the political sense the term has in the United States: he is attached to the redistribution of wealth to favour the least advantaged members of society. This reflects in many ways the post-war Keynesian consensus: that free market capitalism is to be supplemented by a variety of social rights including accessible (and often free) healthcare, education and unemployment insurance and benefits for all. Although the precise nature of the consensus varies deeply from one country to the next, with Scandinavian countries on one end of the spectrum of capitalist economies and the United States on the other, there was nonetheless an attempt to bring economic concerns into debates on the political legitimacy of the state. As we will see in Chapter 5, even those who contest the legitimacy of economic redistribution, such as Robert Nozick, have to jump through hoops to do so. The basic consensus is that citizens deserve economic safety, and the onus of proof largely rests on those who disagree.

Crawford Macpherson understood more than anyone the challenges faced by the social contract in the Cold War. His *Democratic Theory* is an attempt to make the Western, capitalist system of production more palatable in the face of the competitive threat offered by the socialist block in the East. Highlighting the tension between the individualist and egalitarian bases of the liberal tradition, he shows that no democracy could hope to survive the challenge posed by socialist states if it did not treat the well-being of all of its citizens seriously, in particular those who have to sell their labour for a living. Against Rawls, he argued for a redefinition of our notions of property to include a right of access to both the means of labour and the means to a fully human life (Macpherson, 1973: 122–3). While traditional trades union movements in France and elsewhere have focused on the right of workers to access and negotiate their employment conditions, clearly the gilets jaunes, who by their varied occupations and social position lie outside the social democratic framework, are still demanding the means to a fully human life. A social contract is not simply a replication of an employment contract, but is also about the institutions, rules and opportunities to take part in political decision-making. What Macpherson saw in the 1970s is even more true today; but we no longer have the competitive socialist states pushing liberal democracies to move closer to these ideals. In the absence of an external stimulus to drive change, the gilets jaunes are providing an internal demand for change, one where the contract is wider than an arrangement between labour and capital, but about the general conditions of living a fully human life.

If the Cold War provided a clear challenge to a free market laissez-faire capitalist model, the events of 1989–91 heralded what some thinkers in the West called the 'End of History' and the triumph of liberal capitalism (Fukuyama, 1992). Although this picture is highly contested, it acts as a powerful reminder of the *Weltanschauung* of post-Cold War politics. The fall of the Berlin Wall and the dismantling of the USSR were used as vindication for the policies of Reagan and Thatcher, and the dismantling of the welfare state consensus in particular. Although the welfare state has largely survived these challenges, it is still under attack and on the defensive, facing widespread privatizations of former state-owned enterprises and the weakening of the social safety net. Leaving aside the excesses of the 1980s in the United States and the United Kingdom, even countries run by socialists began to feel the bite of neoliberal regimes. In France since 1986, under the leadership of then Prime Minister Jacques Chirac, and then under both left- and right-wing governments, the state has sold assets in banks, insurance companies and building societies; electricity, gas, and oil companies; the construction industry; telecommunication companies and televisions channels; car manufacturers; airlines; parts of the aerospace industry; motorways; logistics companies and airports. Although the French state maintains a stake in a number of companies, the trend for the past 30 years has clearly been towards the decline of state ownership, and nationalizations are few and far between.

The economic story behind the involvement of the French state in economic life goes back to the measures proposed by the Resistance during the Second World War. Often called 'the French social model', it formed part of the new social contract established after liberation of occupied France, and grew in the *trente glorieuses*, the 30 years of economic growth that followed reconstruction after the war. The French Fourth Republic was established on these principles, and the Fifth Republic, although it altered the political balance by strengthening the executive to the detriment of the legislative branch, largely replicated the social model promoted by the Fourth. The central pillar of the French social model, without a doubt, is the institution of the *Sécurité sociale*, the social safety net that extended protections afforded to workers in numerous professions from the early nineteenth century to a wider population (Garner, 2016). Initially open to wage-earners in 1946, it was gradually extended to cover their dependants and those lacking employment, finally covering the entire population by 1978. Covering a multitude of risks, such as illness, childbirth, inability to work, death, workplace accidents and illnesses, old age and family dependants, it is complemented by protection against the risk of unemployment, managed by a separate body called Unédic. The social model covers a very wide range of issues, and provides the foundation for the economic social contract between citizens of the French state. This contract is based on the ability of the *corps intermédiaires*, the middle-level bodies of social relations, to negotiate and guarantee the advantages of their constituents. These bodies include the trades unions, as well as associations representing employers. This has become increasingly problematic in sectors where trades union membership is low, such as in small and medium-sized businesses in the private sector, where the bodies that are meant to guarantee the rights and advantages of workers are either weak or not present. The gilets jaunes themselves have shown little sympathy for trades unions, in particular, as most of them come from sectors where unions have little traction over the economic conditions of work. Outside of the public sector and large industries, where trades unions still have significant membership, trades union membership is extremely low in France, compared to its neighbours and countries using a similar social model.

Emphasizing the specificity of the French social model is a mistake. It is clear that linking causally the social model and the woes of the French economy is a ploy by those who wish to do away with social and workers' rights to promote an increased liberalization of the French economy. Blaming high unemployment and low productivity on the existence of the French social model obfuscates the fact that the model is shared by some of its European counterparts, notably Belgium, Austria, the Netherlands, and, most importantly, Germany. The Bismarck social model France employs can and does lead to other economic outcomes in other countries, and one must differentiate between the guarantees of the rights of workers and citizens it provides, and the economic woes in the French case. The discourse over the decline of the French social model dates back to a shift in the French right from a Gaullist model that accepted the existing social contract under Chirac to a model of reform and liberalization under Sarkozy (Lebaron et al, 2009). Instead of looking to Germany for solutions to the ills of the French economy, the emerging *doxa* became to look for solutions across the Channel to the United Kingdom, or across the Atlantic to the United States for inspiration. As we will see in Chapter 5, the Thatcher-Reagan social model would be the inspiration for Macron's reforms, bringing about a liberal-libertarian ideology at the very top of the French state that led to the gilets jaunes protests. The attacks on the social model in France were coupled with a retreat of the state more generally, as the Bismarck social model demands a strong state to guarantee the smooth functioning of the cooperation between employers and employees. Under Macron, the selling off of the *Française de jeux* [the French lottery operator], ENGIE, EDF, the French railways (SNCF), as well as the project to privatize ADP, which manages French airports including the iconic Paris-Charles de Gaulle hub, is a clear sign of the desire to withdraw the state even further from economic life. Although as this book goes to press there have been signs of a freeze on some of these privatization projects due to the fight against the global COVID-19 pandemic, it is doubtful that this will result in a complete reversal of the trend.

This is not a uniquely French story, but one which is more widely visible throughout the developed world. It is easier to consider the exceptions to this general trend, notably Norway, whose sovereign fund, created in 1990, had a value above $1 trillion in early 2020. Like many other oil-producing states, this form of investment is aimed at lessening the dependency of these states on fluctuations in price of this precious commodity on the world market. It can hardly be a model for other countries who do not share this affluence in natural resources. China, under the leadership of its communist party, has largely transitioned to a model of state capitalism as well, both at home and internationally, with its total assets estimated at about $18 trillion in 2015 (Tang, 2017). Both Norway and China have their own particularities and are not meant to be seen as models for the rest of the world. They do, however, show that something could be otherwise in political economical terms, where the benefits of a free market economy are integrated into state finances, and where a part of the wealth created is maintained under public ownership. But both countries are very much the exception, in a world where public assets are auctioned off to finance pensions, provide tax relief or for ideological reasons. During the gilets jaunes protests, Macron's government has continued this trend of selling off state assets, notably with the controversial plan of the sale of French airports, in which the French state still had a controlling share.

The fall of the lead climber

Emmanuel Macron has been personally singled out as an ideologue of the neoliberal laissez-faire economics of the type advocated by the Chicago school. The gilets jaunes often attack his past as a banker for the Rothschild group, but it is his ideological positioning that is more interesting for us here. A fervent believer in trickle-down economics, he chose the metaphor of the *premiers de cordée* [the lead climbers] for his model of economic growth. The mountaineering term is all-the-more powerful as an explanation for Macron's vision in that when the lead climber falls, it is up to those below to provide support and insurance. The lead climbers seem to take the risks, collect the benefits, but are supported by the others when a fall occurs (Bloch, 2018). Reminiscent of the response by world governments to the financial crisis of 2008, this metaphor justifies the use of public funds to save businesses deemed too big to fail, while simultaneously withdrawing state involvement from the economic life of citizens. Macron's first act as president was to reverse the ISF (*l'impôt de solidarité sur la fortune*), the solidarity tax on wealth for those whose assets are valued at over €1.3 million. The government's argument was that those with wealth could choose to leave the country and become fiscal residents elsewhere, as evidenced in the very public example of Gérard Depardieu becoming a resident of Belgium and then a Russian citizen to avoid paying the tax. Instead of closing the legal loophole, Macron opted for abolishing the tax altogether, replacing it with a much more generous tax on real estate, with the loss to the French treasury estimated at €3.2 billion a year (Garcin-Berson, 2018). Much more important than the precise cost of the change in taxation was the message it sent at the beginning of the first legislative session under Macron's presidency: the richest will get the first share of tax breaks, with others to get benefits only if the budget allows. Such a benefit for low-income workers came at the height of the early gilets jaunes protests. Forced to come up with concessions following the breadth of protests, Macron announced a rise in the minimum wage (SMIC) of €100 in 2019. But the rise itself, based on the 2018 rate of €1,184.93 for full-time employment, included a pre-planned inflation adjustment of €21, a lowering of charges to the employer of €20, with the remainder coming from a revaluing of an employment bonus (*prime d'activité*). Thus, 21 per cent of the rise was pre-planned just to keep up with inflation and is not a rise in purchasing power, 20 per cent is actually given to the employer to redistribute to their employees, and the remaining 59 per cent of the rise will only be available to those in full-time employment, with part-time workers ineligible for it. A real improvement for some workers on the minimum wage, Macron's refusal to put the cost on employers and to use public funds to improve the conditions of those on the minimum wage has dramatic consequences for the most vulnerable of workers, notably those with caring responsibilities or working part time (Le Gall, 2018). As with his analogy of lead climbers, businesses are sheltered from the cost of the policy, with the wider taxpayers footing the bill for the much-needed revaluation of the minimum wage.

Against this type of free market capitalism, the call for fiscal justice is at the centre of claims of the gilets jaunes. Not satisfied with perceived inequalities in taxation regimes, street protesters are seen brandishing placards asking for the reinstatement of the ISF, with lower fuel taxes that impact on the self-employed, small business owners and commuters, and higher investment in public services. Ridiculed as contradictory by their adversaries, these demands are not in themselves absurd. Advocating for higher quality public services and a lowering of the tax burden on lowest earners is only an absurdity under very specific ideological conditions. The arguments against such measures usually rely on: the above-mentioned tax evasion by the richest, who can simply move elsewhere to avoid paying higher taxes; a firm belief in trickle-down economics, which argues that only those with high levels of wealth create wealth for others, notably by providing them with jobs; or a comparison of taxes on highest earners and corporations with rates in other countries, providing a competing advantage alongside a race to the bottom in tax rates for those with international mobility. The social contract has hitherto failed to address these economic concerns to a serious degree, and apart from Rousseau's critique of private property, or Rawls' difference principle (neither of which addresses the concerns of a modern post-industrial economy particularly well), questions of economics have been divorced from the tradition. Chapter 5 will explore an alternative to this lack of economic social contract, notably by putting back the state at the centre of the tradition.

Rethinking the contract

The modern conception of the state's legitimacy is phrased in terms of a contract. As the rising bourgeoisie from the seventeenth century onwards wanted as much security as possible in economic profits coming from their corporate ventures, it sought security in political terms as an essential condition for the safeguarding of its commercial activities. Even the most democratic states were run along the lines of a corporation answering to shareholders, with only the propertied able to cast a vote. France is one of the exceptions here, with male universal suffrage established as early as 1848 during the liberal revolution that established the second, short-lived Republic, although suffrage excluded women, military personnel, the clergy and Algerians. Most other democracies had to wait until the early twentieth century to grant the vote to non-propertied males, let alone grant women the right to vote. The language of the contract thus resembles the economic relations between two actors – two individuals agreeing to deliver services to one another – or the bond between a shareholder and a corporation. The political realm of the modern state is run on a similar basis to the corporation, and some argue that public administration is a copy of corporate governance altogether. Any new theory of the social contract has to take this dual nature of the contract – private and public – seriously, and make provisions for the interaction between the political and economic realms.

Other political theorists have already shown the importance of using the social contract as a critical tool. For Carole Pateman (1988), the sexual contract has remained the hidden patriarchal assumption behind social contract theories. The contract, she claims, is concerned with more than the story of origins that many have focused and commented on. It also provides a framework for how social and political institutions are to be conceptualized and understood. By hiding away the role that sex has played in the formation of the contract, theorists have often obfuscated the power that men have exercised over women in their own quest for power and legitimacy. By relegating matters of sex to the realm of the family and to private life, for example, men have been able to take part in political life and free themselves from particular tasks such as child rearing that would have made participation in politics much more difficult. The social contract has resulted in some social institutions replicating the relationship of master and slave, notably the relation between husband and wife. This mode of subordination may have been hidden away by the social contract, but Pateman exposed it clearly in *The Sexual Contract*. In a similar vein, Charles Mills has shown that the racial contract has been a prominent feature of European and then world history, coming hand in hand with the development of colonialism and capitalism in the modern era. White supremacy has imposed conditions on non-whites since at least the colonization of the Americas began in the fifteenth century, and has continued in various forms ever since. What Mills shows well is, as he says, that the 'classic social contract, as I have detailed, is primarily moral/political in nature. But it is also *economic* in the background sense that the point of leaving the state of nature is in part to secure a stable environment for the industrious appropriation of the world' (Mills, 1997: 31). What both Pateman and Mills have done, in their different manner, is to show that the social contract is alive and kicking and that it is intimately related to often hidden and obscured economic relations that have made the grand talk of equal rights and political participation possible at the cost of ignoring a significant proportion of society. The gilets jaunes have done very much the same for us here: they have shown that the poor, peri-urban and non-unionized working class and lower-middle class – or the *small-mean classes* – have been left out of the social contract as we know it.

The social contract has three important features that I want to put forward here, and the previous discussion should help the reader conceptualize its importance. In the first instance, it is a *necessary* feature of our modern political lives. In the second place, it is an *impossible* ideal to attain. And finally, it is a concept in need of renewal, as it is always *becoming* something other than what it was. These three features of the social contract – necessary, impossible, and becoming – need some unpacking.

Much of the discussion above about the social contract has already assumed that the social contract itself is necessary. It is necessary in the historical sense: it acts as a form of legitimation of the rising power of the state; it is necessary politically: no state can hope to maintain its structures and institutions without engaging in some form of contractual theory; it is necessary economically to cement the link between the private and public sectors; and it is necessary socially as the sheer size of modern polities makes it impossible to engage in many other forms of social organization. This necessity is itself contingent – upon the historical setting we are in, the political institutions we have inherited and are fashioning, the economic arrangements of today, and social norms and expectations – so the argument here is not that things cannot be otherwise, or that they always have been as they are. Clearly there are times in history when things were otherwise. The feudal arrangements that preceded the rise of the modern state had vastly different modes of organization. Then and there, the social contract was not necessary. But here and now, it remains necessary for the reasons given above.

It may be argued that the state is on the decline, and that perhaps the time of the social contract has passed for this precise reason. This is doubtful, however, for a variety of reasons. First, the state remains the most important unit of political organization. While there are clearly other forms of political agency, both on a larger scale than the state in the form of multinational institutions, and on a smaller scale than the state in the form of non-governmental organizations, both of these are heavily reliant on states for their operations. One can hardly discuss the United Nations or the European Union without mentioning the five permanent members of the Security Council or the workings of the European Council on which leaders of member states sit. Nor are multinational corporations a more likely successor to the nation state. Corporations have risen simultaneously with the nation state, and the existence of one historically relies on the other, as we will see in Chapter 5. One could, however, imagine a world where corporations have taken over some of the major functions of the modern state, in particular welfare, healthcare and private security for their employees. In some cases, this scenario of a world run by corporate entities can already be observed today, with healthcare provisions largely dependent on employers' benevolent whims in the United States. But to think that corporations will eclipse the state is to engage in science fiction. There is a large gap between this reality and the fiction popularized in the role-playing game *Shadowrun*, where players join rival corporate groups in their quests for power and influence. Set in the near future (the first edition, published in 1989, foresaw that this corporate dystopia to be in full place by 2050), this is an unlikely scenario, if only for the fact that corporations seek to maximize their profits and not take over costs of administrating entire populations associated with welfare politics. Only a complete collapse of the welfare state could foreshadow the rise of this corporate dystopia. Even *Shadowrun* had to resort to magic to explain the origins of its alternative universe. Nor is there a sense that the social contract would disappear with the rise of the corporation. It is already the case that the employment contract has become increasingly like a social contract, and it is likely that even a marginal rise of corporate power would further increase the need for contractual theory. Nor is anyone really suggesting that not-for-profit organizations can offer a model for future world governance, despite their crucial role in providing services and fulfilling the caritative needs of a market-driven economy. The social contract is not going anywhere, and any changes in political organization to happen in the future will likely lead to the reformulation of the social contract, not its disappearance.

In many ways, the attempt by the European Union to formalize a constitution, and by the United Nations to establish frameworks for the working out of differences between states have already expanded the social contract to the international sphere. Many scholars have taken it upon themselves to show the potential of this international social contract, further helping my argument here that the social contract is necessary (Rhodes and Mény, 1998; James, 2012; Weatherall, 2015). Even in a globalized world, where states interact with one another on an increased basis and institutionalize these relations, we cannot do without a social contract. Thinking about the international social contract lies outside the scope of this book, although its limitations will be briefly explored in Chapter 5. In a world where the use of violence is still one of the main features of the state, attempts at coercion by international institutions are highly problematic, and at best show the limits of cooperation beyond the level of the state.

The social contract, despite being necessary for the reasons given above, is also impossible. It is impossible in the sense that it is not a contract, in the sense of a legally binding document established between two individuals or even between groups of persons or corporate entities. Demographic reasons alone should suffice to convince any sceptics of that fact. With the possible exceptions of the smallest states (Tuvalu, the smallest member of the United Nations, numbers 10,000 or so inhabitants), an actual contract would be an impractical document to sign to begin with. A contract, at least in theory, is an agreement that can be amended if both parties agree. It would be impractical for the social body to renegotiate the terms of the contract on the eighteenth birthday of all of their citizens. Even in a small country like Luxembourg with 600,000 inhabitants, there are about 20 people turning 18, on average, every day. Let us not ponder what would happen in India, with its 1.3 billion citizens.

Traditionally, social contract theorists have sidestepped this issue by saying that the contract is implied. Yet even if this is the case, the question of what happens if one refuses to sign the contract, when they are legally entitled to enter into contractual obligations, remains open. Even the refusal of an implied social contract would at least include the duty of those who refuse it to leave. This is, to my knowledge, not the case anywhere and nor is it a desirable thing. Consensus should not be expected of a large-scale polity (even one as small as Luxembourg), and part of the discussion of the new social contract will be to consider the provisions under which contestation of the contract is possible. The social contract may be impossible to sign, but even an implicit social contract is impossible if it does not allow for contestation. In Chapter 3, I will argue that without this basic freedom, the benefits of the contract are not justifiable.

The social contract is also impossible in the sense that the origin stories often told by authors of the golden age of social contract theory – those writing from 1650 to 1800 – are impossible to believe nowadays. We will see in Chapter 2 that human beings did not start out as scattered individuals who, through their power of reason, decided to create states, as Hobbes had speculated. Nor are they isolated individuals that rarely meet other members of their species, as put forward in Rousseau's argument, which we will come back to in Chapter 4. We now cannot de-historicize the social contract as a typically modern phenomenon, one that arises in the early modern period to justify the state. Mills shows this clearly by showing that the racial element of the social contract is always present historically. In order to justify its rule over colonized peoples, the European states used contract theory as a mode of legitimation with an overtly racial subtext to justify exploitation (Mills, 1997: 63). The history of the rise of the state is much darker than some of its proponents have wanted us to believe. The subjugation of women, people of colour or the working poor has always been part of the creation of the state, and this book will follow the critical line of inquiry into the social contract started by Pateman and Mills.

The becoming of the social contract

The social contract is not impossible in the sense that we cannot think about it, but rather it is impossible in the sense that we will never have a finalized, finished and polished version of the contract that we cannot think about, change and (hopefully) improve on. This is because the contract is always in becoming, not in its being. On the one hand, we have a social contract tradition, which has justified the state as a political entity since at least the seventeenth century. At the same time, this social contract tradition has failed to convince that we *really* have a contract, that we are parties to it, and that it is a worthwhile way to think about politics. What I propose to do in this book is to formulate a sketch of a new social contract, not because I think the previous one has failed or is outdated, but because we *always* need to rethink the social contract. My hope is that this book will be saying something worthwhile about our contemporary political position and what we can do with the social contract to improve it. It is a book about a theory we have inherited from past thinkers – the social contract – and thus engages with some of these thinkers. But it is also a book about the present, and a movement that has questioned the foundations of this contract – the gilets jaunes. Finally, it is a book about the future, in that it proposes to look at possible alternatives for the contract we now have, and argues for a reshaping of social relations based on this philosophical engagement.

The social contract is necessary, not inevitable. We need to constantly rethink it anew in order for it to fulfil its purpose. We could do away with the contract altogether – say, by a return to feudal relations, or a futuristic mode of collective decision-making other than its current form. At the moment, alternative modes of political decision-making are either regressive or part of science fiction. There is today a monarchist party in France, called the *Alliance Royale*. Although it numbered only 3,393 votes in the European elections in 2019, and is by no means a potent political force, it shows a very weak will to return to a Capetian principle in politics, and a resistance to France's republican order. Equally implausible is the ideal of a fully participative democracy, with the fictional example put forward in *Star Trek*'s 'Borg' mode of organization, where all consciousness is linked via a neural network. Even within this model, a queen is still posited as necessary by the show's writers. This may say more about the limits of their imagination than about the future of human consciousness, but in any event remains an exercise in science fiction rather than a roadmap for the future. Without a clear path for either a return to previous, pre-contract institutions, or a mode of organization where political legitimacy is no longer a question the public asks of its leaders, the social contract remains a necessary feature of political life in the twenty-first century.

2

Violence

When the gilets jaunes first occupied roundabouts on 17 November 2018, in what was to become known as 'Act I' of the weekly Saturday protests they embarked on for 70 weeks, they were exercising an act of violence on their fellow citizens. In Savoy on that day, a motorist panicked as protesters tried to stop her car, and she ran over those in her way, fatally wounding one of the protesters. This 63-year-old lady, who was a novice to street protests, was the first accidental victim of the movement, with more to come over the next weekends. The very acts of standing on a road, marching through a city, occupying buildings so that their daily functioning cannot continue, are themselves acts of violence. Although at this particular roundabout in Savoy the use of physical force, to break one of these roadblocks, was limited to the motorist forcing her way through a crowd, I argue that violence was also exercised by the protesters, and moreover that it was legitimate.

Violence refers to a variety of different types of action. For the purpose of this analysis, I draw an important distinction between two main types of violence: physical violence (often referred to as simply 'violence'), and moral violence (often qualified by other terms, such as 'spiritual', 'structural' or 'psychological' violence). I will come back to the differences between physical and moral violence in a moment, but let me say first what they share in common. Both physical and moral violence are *coercive* and engender *resistance*. They are coercive in the sense that they seek to change the behaviour of others. Whether you are occupying a roundabout to stop commuters from getting to work (a physical type of violence), or using guilt to stop people from crossing a picket line (a moral type of violence), both forms are attempts at coercive behaviour. But violence also has a subjective element. For it to qualify as violence, it needs to be perceived as such by others. Typically, violence needs to be recognized as such by those on whom it is exercised. Let us stick to our examples above to illustrate this. If you were to stand alone on a roundabout, it would not have the violent outcome you perhaps intended. Motorists would be able to easily manoeuvre around you and in this scenario you are merely endangering yourself and not exercising violence on others. Drivers passing you would see you as a danger to be taken into account, as an obstacle, but not as someone exercising violence upon them. Perceptions are important, and here they make an essential difference between violence and non-violence. Equally, if you were to stand on a picket line with little or no support from the rest of your fellow-workers, and they were to feel no guilt, unease or even annoyance at having to cross your picket line, your action would not be perceived as an act of violence, not even moral violence. Hence, violence needs these two features: coercion and resistance. Without them both, violence cannot exist, whether in its physical or moral manifestation. Even symbolic violence, which I will come back to, shares these features of coercion and resistance with other types of violence.

The term 'violence', when used on its own, implies that there is a physical aspect to it. Non-physical uses of the term 'violence' need it to be qualified, typically, for interlocutors to make sense of what type of violence is being discussed. When we say that the gilets jaunes started their protests because of 'structural violence', we understand that this violence was not exercised with batons, LBD ball-throwers and grenades – at least, not initially. When I use the term 'violence' I will thus keep to this convention. Violence refers to physical violence, while non-physical violence will be qualified with appropriate adjectives.

Now that we have a sense of what all violence shares in common, let me differentiate physical from moral violence. Physical violence is material in that it uses material means to achieve its ends. Those material entities are varied and complex. They range from weapons of war (tanks, planes and warships) to the use of our bodies as means of coercion. While demonstrations and forms of social protest that refuse to use physical force are often labelled as non-violent, I argue here that they are non-forceful at best, and do in fact use forms of violence dependent on physical coercion. Simply blocking a road with a group of protesters' bodies is an act of violence, which uses material means to its end. When the iconic anonymous Chinese man stood in front of a tank in Tiananmen Square in 1989, he exercised violence – albeit without the use of physical force. Physical force was then used by Chinese authorities to break up the protests, with the dramatic consequences that ensued. But that does not absolve the anonymous man from taking matters into his own hands and exercising an act of violence himself. While there are important differences in the scale of violence used, depending on how much physical force is exercised, my argument here is that a non-force-using protest is nonetheless violent, provided it aims at coercion and engenders resistance, as I have argued above. It remains to be seen what would count as non-physical violence in this sense. I have used the example of moral violence in the form of guilt-inducing behaviour, but one could also think of speed cameras on roads as a form of non-physical violence. Although speed cameras have an obvious physical existence, they are also a moral force in that they aim (and often succeed) in changing the behaviour of motorists even when they are not physically present. We will come back to the concept of fear later in this chapter, as an essential bridge between moral and physical violence, but suffice to say here that speed cameras embody the moral authority of the state to regulate the speed of motorists on its territory. It is of little surprise that they have been targeted with physical violence by the gilets jaunes in the form of destruction and vandalism.

Before I come back to moral forms of violence, I want to stress that the gilets jaunes protests have used physical violence from Act I of their weekly protests, and to an extent have escalated forms of violence throughout the weeks. While there is a difference in degree between the blocking of a roundabout, the vandalizing of the Arc de Triomphe and the burning of newsstands or the terraces of chic restaurants on the Champs Élysées – physical violence is what is at stake here. This poses an important challenge to the claim of the state to have a monopoly over the use of physical force within a given territory. The state may well have this monopoly, although even for Weber it always remains at the level of a *claim*, and not necessarily a reality (Weber, 2009); but the state may not have the monopoly on the use of violence. It is a widely accepted right in modern democracies to be able to stage peaceful protests, and since these are coercive and engender resistance, they are violent without necessarily using physical force. The tension, between the (Weberian) claim of the state and the reality of modern democratic politics is essential and will be explored further in Chapter 4. For now, I do not shy away from calling the protests violent. The French government, President, and the bulk of the French press are right to point out this violence. Where they are wrong is to assume that this violence has no basis for legitimacy, as I will demonstrate, first and foremost by showing that physical violence is often reactive to other types of moral violence that are much more pervasive and systematic.

Moral violence and bureaucracy

Moral violence is no less important than physical violence. There is nothing today that exercises non-physical violence in a more effective manner than the bureaucratic state. The very machine of the bureaucracy is at the heart of the rise of the modern state as we know it today — as opposed to the non-bureaucratic world of the feudal political order. It is no wonder that two of the most important characters in the fictional medieval-fantastic world of *Game of Thrones* are Petyr Baelish and Varys, who symbolize the power of the rising bureaucracy over the dying feudal order. The real struggle for power is not the one between the various noble houses that captivates the audience, but between the two conceptions of power embodied by these two sides of the bureaucracy. On the one hand, Baelish seeks to accrue personal power — he describes power as a ladder that you can only keep climbing until you reach the top — versus Varys' obsession with the 'good of the realm' that makes him side with any person strong enough to hold the regime together. They both attempt to achieve their ends through blackmail, spying and manipulation, rather than force of arms — moral rather than physical violence. This bureaucratic violence, as a form of moral violence, is the one that is characteristic of the modern nation state and largely explains its successes and failures.

The bureaucracy, in fiction as in reality, is always a utopian vision of what the political order can be. David Graeber makes this point in his *Utopia of Rules* (2015), which shows the importance of moral violence in modern politics. What defines a bureaucracy, over and above its claims to rationality and impartiality, is its systematic threat of violence pervasive in everyday activities. The moral violence exercised by the speed camera may be couched in road safety arguments, scientific data and statistics about the numbers of deaths lower speed limits could prevent on the roads, and a plethora of other expert analyses to justify the coercion, but it is also backed by the threat of physical violence if one fails to comply with the moral order. Fines, late-payment fees, court orders, and imprisonment for non-payment of debt are ultimately the ever-present threat that backs up the otherwise immaterial violence of the fully automated camera system. When we obey the speed limit, it is a complex apparatus of state power, using moral violence in the form of a bureaucratic structure, and the nevertheless real threat of physical violence for non-compliance.

The story of Jerome Rogers provides an illustration of how moral violence turns into physical coercion. The young man, who took up a self-employed job as a courier in 2015, quickly fell into a vicious cycle of debt due to traffic violation charges. Already having to pay back a loan for his bike, petrol and insurance without which it was impossible for him to perform his job, Rogers had a very modest take-home income which would barely cover paying off a fine in any given week. As the fines issued by his local council began to pile up, the council outsourced the recovery of the debt to a private bailiff agency. Following numerous threatening letters, a bailiff finally visited Rogers' home asking for £1,019 to be paid on the spot. Rogers' family helped, but paid off only half the debt, leading to a another visit from the bailiff a few weeks later. Rogers watched desperately as the bailiff clamped his bike, without which he could not work anymore. He left his home that day, and took his own life never to return (Nagesh, 2018). Ken Loach's *Sorry We Missed You* (2019) similarly illustrates the plight of a delivery driver crumbling under debt after he gets fined by his employer for not showing up for work due to family emergencies. The vicious cycle of debt proves too much to bear for the main protagonist, Ricky, who sinks deeper into a personal crisis as events unfold to nullify his earnings. More than a mere statement about zero-hours contracts or the gig economy, what these examples have in common is the very real threat of physical violence that hides behind bureaucracy. The fines, whether they are imposed by a council or an employer, are enforceable by law, and the actions of private bailiffs have often taken the use of force supposedly reserved to the state into private hands.

State violence today relies mostly on this type of moral violence to create compliance. When, at the height of the gilets jaunes protests, the French parliament passed a law strengthening the bureaucratic power of the *préfet*, the administrator in charge of local governmental business, making them responsible for the banning of demonstrations without judicial oversight, they were creating a form of moral violence more potent than that which existed beforehand. The administrators who have used this power, and those who will use it in the future, are making decisions to ban demonstrations, to ban citizens from walking in the streets, that are not subsequently open to appeal, review, or contestation.[1] When we think of the state as claiming the monopoly on the legitimate use of force within a given territory, we often forget that most instances of violence are moral, not physical. No body that represents the state actually needs to be present for violence to occur. A simple letter often suffices to create a situation of violence that one has to comply with. Of course, as I have argued above, the moral threat is all the more effective if it is backed up by a physical threat. But physical violence need not be actualized – its very potential is enough for moral violence to be effective. At least in most cases. To understand the justification for this type of violence, let us turn to the most notorious theorist of the state, Thomas Hobbes.

Leviathan

Hobbes remains the foremost theorist of the state and the social contract, and any justification of state violence, or violence in order to resist the state, passes through his monumental work on the topic (Hobbes, 1651/1996).[2] It is a well-known thought experiment that leads Hobbes to justify the need for a social contract theory. In the state of nature, Hobbes speculates, human beings are in a situation of constant war with one another. Without political authority above them, human beings resort to all of the means at their disposal to achieve their ends, in particular their quest for self-preservation, but also their attempts at bettering their material conditions. They believe that they have a right to all things, including things that others also claim to have a right over. Concerned with their material well-being, they enter a condition of enmity and war against others, using violence, both physical and moral, to achieve their ends. The result of this situation is a state of fear and a constant danger of violent death, in which our lives are solitary, poor, nasty, brutish and short. These five adjectives put the fear of the collapse of social order in us. I have argued elsewhere that the state of nature is not as hypothetical as some have suggested, and that Hobbes, as well as other theorists of the state of nature, believed it a real situation that – if never quite present in its ideal form – pokes its head above the barricades in times of social or political conflict (Devellennes, 2013). But the threat of descent into a state of nature works perhaps better as a fiction, as a harrowing tale of the consequences of the collapse of the state. The gilets jaunes have certainly been accused of precipitating one such collapse when they engage in demonstrations and acts of violence, and it remains a powerful argument against them to date.

The popular television drama *The Walking Dead* illustrates the Hobbesian state of nature perfectly. In this post-apocalyptic wasteland set in the southern state of Georgia in the United States, a handful of survivors fight zombies to survive. Leaving alone the fantastical elements of the fictional universe based on a comic book by Robert Kirkman, it is other living human beings that are the single greatest threat to the group of survivors. They battle each other for scarce resources including food, shelter and weapons, and many of the plot lines revolve around the need to protect one's band from other groups of survivors on top of the existential threat posed by the unleashing of the power of death itself – the zombie (Kirkman, 2010). Never mind the argument that any such biohazard would likely result in the strengthening of the state, a plethora of regulations regarding every aspect of everyday life, and increasing concentration of power (as has happened in response to the COVID-19 pandemic); the creators of the show focused on the total collapse of society and the vanishing of state power as the only possible outcome of a (super)natural disaster on such a scale. In this fictional world, there is no agriculture, navigation, construction, knowledge, letters or other social goods – precisely as Hobbes had argued in *Leviathan* in 1651. The fear of the state of nature is as present today as it was in the midst of the English Civil War, when Hobbes' book was written.

But Hobbes' story does not end there. The state of nature may act as a powerful warning, but it is not the end of Hobbes' political theory. For Hobbes, human beings are not only desiring creatures that want to preserve themselves and acquire material goods.[3] They are also rational beings, capable of thinking about their situation and thinking of ways to move past dilemmas they face. And the state of nature poses one such catch-22, the fact that using all possible means, including violence, to acquire the material goods necessary to our self-preservation also has the negative effect of endangering our lives, as others also use similar means at their disposal. A profound believer in human equality, Hobbes argues that even the weakest of us has a hope of defeating the strongest, as we are able to use cunning and exploit others' weaknesses. At the very least, we can attack others in their sleep, and no one is immune from the ultimate threat of death. But we are also equal in possessing reason, and thankfully this provides us with a way out.

Thinking about our condition, we will come up, Hobbes claims, with 19 laws of nature – no fewer! But what does Hobbes mean by the laws of nature? He means rules acquired by reason, not rules existing independently of it. He is under no illusion that these rules are followed all the time, but rather argues that all rational beings can agree that living by these rules will result in a better state of life than living without them. A law of nature differs from a right, particularly the right to all things we have in the state of nature, in that a right is something we have irrespective of the circumstances, whereas a law is something we ought to follow to achieve our ends. Today, we would not call these 'laws of nature', but rather something akin to social rules, based on rational discussion and justification. Nevertheless, Hobbes makes a powerful case for them. Let me just discuss the first two, as the other 17 are less important – even by Hobbes' own account. The first law of nature, or social rule, is peace. It may be surprising to note this for those who have heard of Hobbes but have not read him in any detail. First and foremost, if we want to preserve ourselves, we ought to strive for peace. Part of the ambiguity is owed to Hobbes' formulation, for he immediately qualifies this first law of nature to include a recourse to war if others refuse to follow peace. But when he comes back to this law later in *Leviathan*, he simply refers to it as the law for peace. Hobbes' social contract is not one of the war of all against all, but a contract for peace as a remedy to the threat of war. In order to cement this peace, we need others to also strive for peace, and thus the second law of nature is to accept limitations on one's rights, in the interest of the preservation of the law. This is the mutual transfer of rights, where we give up our natural right to all things, and agree to limit this right in ourselves as it is limited in others. In short, the second law of nature is to form a contract with fellow human beings.

This peace-seeking contract, Hobbes points out, will fall apart unless we can trust others, and in a sense we can never maintain full trust that others will not break their word when the conditions seem advantageous to them. The contract itself is insufficient, as it needs to be backed up by the threat of violence for those who break it. This is Hobbes' justification for the state, and his theory is one of the necessity of state power. We need all parties to the social contract to be held to their word, and what better way than to invest a person – or a body of persons, as Hobbes was hedging his bets on a republican victory in the Civil War – with sovereign authority to enforce this peace? The *Leviathan*, as Hobbes names the state, is thus responsible for physical violence against those who may break the social contract, but is also responsible for moral violence in the form of fear and terror. Just as the state of nature is only a potential state of war of all against all, the peaceful order established by the state only uses violence in potential most of the time. The threat is real, but most of the time fear and terror are enough to act as deterrents.

Fear and death

Although we have qualified Hobbes' rather drastic transfer of all powers to the sovereign authority, and other social contract theorists – notably Locke – have added provisions to this concept, we still largely accept that if we have consented to state power, it is because it offers goods that we otherwise cannot achieve. For all the centrist rhetoric of Macron's government, and his supposed liberal (or neoliberal) background, he and his government have maintained a rather Hobbesian account of state power and the legitimate use of violence. Against forces that attack social peace, violence is justified, including, if necessary, lethal force. Continuing the policies of French left-wing and right-wing governments before him, Macron has attempted to strengthen the fear and terror instilled in his own citizens. One decision stands out, above all others, to make this case. On 23 March 2019, for the first time since the beginning of the protests some four months previously, the French army was deployed to secure important sites during gilets jaunes demonstrations. *Opération Sentinelle*, an anti-terrorism unit created in 2015 in the aftermath of terrorist attacks in the Parisian area, was deployed at key points throughout France. This use of military forces – limited to surveillance of important monuments

– sends a clear message to protesters. Unlike their police or *gendarme* counterparts, the specialized army unit has no riot-control equipment or training, and as damaging as the weapons of the security forces have been, they pale in comparison to the threat posed by the assault rifles carried by soldiers. Anyone who has visited French cities over the past years could not have ignored the presence of the army on French soil in key strategic locations. This drastic deployment of troops, which goes even beyond the use of troops during the Algerian war, sets a dangerous precedent for civil liberties and freedom of assembly. I will come back to this in Chapter 3, but for now my argument is limited to the analysis of state power and violence. What I aim to show here is that the use of force, even lethal violence, against protesters is fully within the power of the state, and is, at least to an extent, legitimate.

Although I will qualify this argument later in the book, I argue that states can be, and are, legitimate in killing their own citizens. One always hopes that this scenario does not happen, and important limits are put on the ability of states to do so, but ultimately the power of lethal violence remains in the hands of state officials, and is there by design. In Hobbes' account, it is clear that fear and terror cannot be fostered without the threat of death. This threat was ever-present in the state of nature, and it needs to be present in the social contract. Without it, the very structure of the social contract, and the rationale for the existence of the state, disappears. Machiavelli, a century and a half before Hobbes, had already supported this power. Not only is it better to be feared than to be loved, he claimed, but it is better to kill someone's father than to deprive them of their patrimony (Machiavelli, 2008). We are, thankfully, far from this use of lethal violence in France, but the threat remains real and is at times acted upon. I did not bat an eyelid when, on 9 January 2015, French security forces shot dead the two French terrorists who had attacked the *Charlie Hebdo* offices two days before, and in the process had murdered 12 people. The reason why I, and, I suspect, many of my readers, will accept this use of lethal force is that it was proportionate to the risk. Faced with armed and determined assailants, the state can and does use lethal violence. Had the terrorists surrendered to security forces, their summary execution would have provoked very different reactions. Although extreme, this example is not an isolated case: the effective deployment of state violence is an important part of the functioning of the state. The decline in support for the gilets jaunes from the general public can be partially explained by support for the law-enforcement aspects of the French state from the majority of the population. After the first month of protests, public attitude towards the movement shifted from being broadly supportive of its aims to being broadly hostile to its means. Part of the contract is to create peace, and it is legitimate for the apparatus of the state to be deployed to that effect.

Let us focus a little on actual acts of physical violence by the French state during the gilets jaunes protests. After all, French soldiers have yet to use their weapons against protesters, so their violence is at most moral, according to my own definition set above. Out of the 860 injuries suffered by protesters and bystanders from November 2018 up to June 2019, 315 were to the head. During the writing of this book, I dreaded opening up my Twitter account over the weekend, as videos of police brutality were being circulated with the hashtag of police violence (#ViolencesPolicières). Not being an expert on social movements or a veteran of street protests where police violence had occurred, the images went beyond my wildest imagination. Beyond the use of specific weapons detailed in the Introduction, it was the viciousness of some of the attacks that attracted my attention. Often cornered against a wall, blinded by tear gas, or simply standing idly by, protesters were routinely hit on the head with batons, inundated with pepper spray even when in a wheelchair, or dragged by the hair while on the ground. These images, captured by video amateurs, semi-professional or professional journalists, hardly ever made it to the official news outlets, despite the severity of the attacks. Attempts to capture the famous *casseurs* [wreckers], often members of the black bloc, are thus overshadowed by the hundreds of others injured in the process. There is no doubt that these images are not themselves representative of the majority of police or *gendarme* forces' behaviour during the protests. One often sees police officers themselves distraught by the actions of their colleagues, and attempting to help protesters who have fallen to the ground following a blow from a baton, providing them with eyedrops to treat tear gas, or having to protect their most aggressive colleagues from retaliation by protesters. Those images where protesters had lost a hand or been shot in the head with an LBD 40 may have been the most spectacular, but they were still acts of remote action, and thus paled in comparison with those where the injuries were inflicted *à bout portant* – in a mêlée attack on unarmed and unprotected civilians. But in many ways these images reinforce the psychology behind the use of state violence: that fear is central to the maintaining of order. Part of the decline in attendance at weekly demonstrations by the gilets jaunes can be explained by this successful use of fear and targeted violence by state officials.

This level of police violence is not an unfortunate consequence of state power. It is a direct consequence, and a necessary feature of it. In his *Critique of Violence*, Walter Benjamin (cited in Larsen, 2013) introduces the concept of *mythic* violence as the principle of lawmaking, the creation of boundaries, the use of threat and retribution, and the spilling of blood. Benjamin contrasts this mythic violence (which he perceives as unrighteous) with divine violence (itself righteous). I will come back to this in Chapter 4, but for now I am more interested in the mythical aspect that justifies the state as we know it than in the proletarian revolution Benjamin wanted to defend. At the centre of the creation of the state is a myth that creates order – law – and it does so through the spilling of blood. In the French case, this myth is very clear: it is celebrated every year in a ritualistic manner on 14 July, to commemorate the events of the Revolution. Of course, every myth chooses certain aspects to emphasize, and the fall of the Bastille (itself a bloody event) is the event the French republic chooses to commemorate over, say the reign of Terror later in the revolution. Itself a law-destroying event, the French Revolution abolished the last remnants of the feudal order to replace them with something resembling the modern French state we have today. Or so goes the myth.

The difficulty for the myth of the creation of the Fifth Republic in France comes with the status of the events that unfolded in May–June 1958. Faced with a military takeover in Algeria and Corsica, self-designated as a Committee of Public Safety in true Robespierrean manner, and the threat of a descent of the army on Paris, the Fourth Republic bowed to military pressure and abdicated power to De Gaulle, who quickly established the Fifth Republic in response to the political crisis. Opposed by some of the centrists, socialists, and communists, including the then-future president François Mitterrand, De Gaulle's accession to power is characterized as a military coup by those on the left, and a legal change in constitutional practice by those on the right – a divide that survives to this day. Perhaps the only reason it has not made its way into the mythical founding of the current French republic is that the events were bloodless, and that the very real threat of deadly violence posed by the French military was never actualized. De Gaulle himself later noted that he needed to achieve the ends of the 2 December 1851 coup by Napoleon III – the last use of military force to seize power in France – without using its means. He masterfully managed to keep his hands clean, riding on the coattails of the military leaders that had taken matters into their own hands (Sowerwine, 2009: 283–286). Nevertheless, it was physical violence – according to my definition above – that was used, with material means (planes, guns and soldiers) deployed to effectuate a change of behaviour in the French parliament. The myth of the French state is carefully crafted, around the fall of the Bastille, a symbol of royal absolutism, rather than around the Terror or the founding events of the Fifth Republic. But violence is nonetheless celebrated, and the fall of the previous order – whether it is the reign of Louis XVI or the Fourth

Republic – celebrated as a source of legitimacy for the new order. This raises the question of whether the gilets jaunes will ever be able to claim that their violence was a legitimate use of resistance against a repressive state, or whether their movement will fail and be seen as a mere thorn in the side of the French state in the late 2010s.

Resistance

When I discussed Hobbes' two laws of nature earlier, I skipped over an important detail which is now relevant. At the end of chapter 14 of *Leviathan*, Hobbes notes an important exception to the establishment of a contract (the second law of nature) to guarantee peace (the first law of nature). He argues that no one may contract away their right to resist. We can contract many things away, including most of our rights, but the potential for resistance is not eligible to be given away. Any contract which gives up this right is void. One may accept entering a contract under the threat of death (as Hobbes argues is the basis of the state), but one may never accept entering an agreement not to resist those who come to take away one's life. This important distinction, between the right of the state to kill its own citizens, and the right of citizens to defend themselves when the state comes to kill them, is crucial to understanding the gilets jaunes. If, as Hobbes argues, the right to resist is inalienable, unlike the right to liberty, which we have agreed to alienate in favour of peace, it poses an important caveat for political process.

Resistance to state violence is legitimate under very specific circumstances. For Hobbes, self-preservation is the only case that is convincing, and I will not deviate much from his sentiment here, although my conclusion will be somewhat at odds with his (that self-preservation is only exercised when the state comes to kill you). The potency of my argument will only be made in Chapter 5, when I discuss economic justice, where I will address the existential threat posed by economic injustices. Let me for now stick to the issue of citizen violence. We no longer accept the Hobbesian argument that the state merely kills us through the use of direct force. Whether it is the failure to curtail the use of dangerous chemicals, the premature deaths of the elderly living in poverty, the threat of climate change – pick your poison – we accept that death comes in many ways, with state officials having a more or less important role to play, from lack of adequate knowledge about an issue or outright negligence, all the way to active participation in the demise of their own citizens. Let me use a French example to illustrate how negligence kills. In the summer of 2003, a heatwave spread throughout

Europe. France, particularly hardly hit by the phenomenon, saw an intense and enduring rise in temperatures, higher than anything recorded since records began in the nineteenth century. The French statistics agency estimates that 15 thousand people died as a result of the heat, which reached a record high of 44.1 degrees Celsius (111 degrees Fahrenheit). In a country where air conditioning is rare and a luxury, it is of little surprise that the weakest suffered disproportionately – with people aged over 75 the most vulnerable to the dangers of overheating. The event was statistically significant, in that it actually lowered life expectancy in France, the first time this calculation had gone down rather than up since the 1950s (Guay, 2019). It was also a political event, in the sense that the role played by the government in reducing spending on social care was brought into question (Gaudin, 2003). It is clear from this example that the state can kill by negligence, when its policies have known consequences that lead to individual deaths.

Some gilets jaunes make similar arguments about the lowering of their economic power and the retreat of the state from investments in social services. If the consequences of a policy that the government puts into force lead to a lowering of life expectancy, it is not unreasonable to see the extension of Hobbes' argument about resistance to areas other than self-defence under the threat of immediate death. Hobbes' argument is, indeed, itself grounded in self-preservation, not merely self-defence. If the preservation of our 'selves' is threatened by particular state actions, resistance is a possibility – even under Hobbes' premises. A gilet jaune slogan encapsulates this call for self-preservation. While Macron insisted in November 2018 that the measures taken by the government were necessary due to the impending doom of climate change and the 'end of the world', the gilets jaunes were arguing that they were worried about the 'end of the month' (Masse-Stamberger, 2018). The end-of-the-world/end-of-the-month dichotomy is a powerful reminder of the pressing necessity for protesters to be seen and to have their cause heard. They are legitimized, even by Hobbes (reread with a contemporary twist), in challenging and resisting state power when it seeks to enforce measures that affect their lives in such existential ways.

If the above argument is correct, and self-preservation needs to go beyond the realm of self-defence, it raises important questions for the social contract and the possibility of resistance. Bearing in mind the importance of proportionality, I now want to argue that resistance to state power, when it threatens self-preservation now understood more widely, is legitimate – even if it involves physical violence. The central question then is: what would count as proportionate violence on the side of protesters, as in the case of the gilets jaunes? There is already a legal framework that allows citizens in democratic states the right to peacefully assemble, even if such peaceful assembly causes disruptions and changes the behaviour of others. I will merely assume that these are legitimate forms of resistance, as they do not pose obvious ethical or political issues for most citizens. The question then is: which, if any, forms of political protest are legitimate, even though they may be at the margins of legality, or sometimes overstep that boundary? At the beginning of the gilets jaunes protests, when protesters were primarily occupying roundabouts, the violence exercised by demonstrators was palpable. Getting up early on Saturdays, many protesters would be there by the time people were going into work, and were still present later when shoppers were making their way to the industrial estates or town centres to do their weekly errands. The disruption to economic life, in order to draw attention to the plight of those hardest hit by an economic model that favours inequalities, seems to meet the demands of proportionality. Yet it was also the deadliest period of the movement, as it was the time when motorists were involved in the most road accidents. Out of the first 11 victims of the protest movement, five were gilets jaunes hit by vehicles, five were motorists involved in collisions due to a blocked road or blockade organized by the gilets jaunes, and three died as a consequence of police action (Coquaz, 2019). These deaths are all deplorable, but none of them was deliberate, resulting from acts of violence seeking that outcome. It could still be a foreseeable consequence of the action by the gilets jaunes, and they may still have a share of responsibility in the deaths. It is reasonable to expect disruptions to traffic to endanger the lives of others, just as it is reasonable for motorists to act with care when there are pedestrians on the road. Emmanuel Macron deplored the deaths of the first 11 citizens in a speech given in Cairo, blaming 'human stupidity' for the accidental deaths. It did not seem to cross his mind that these deaths were the predictable consequence of his own policies that engendered popular outrage and one of the largest social movements of post-war France. Yet Macron clearly shares in the responsibility, at least inasmuch as his deliberate targeting of some of the poorest in society with increased taxes and lessening the tax burden for the wealthiest was predictably going to create social unrest.

Disruption seems a proportionate price to pay to bring attention to what is perceived as widespread injustice and social inequalities. Had these disruptions been more drastic and effective, it may have raised questions about their proportionality – but, as they stood, they hardly caused a dint in French economic activity (Alemania, 2019). The destruction of private property such as the iconic Fouquet's restaurant terrace burning during a gilets jaunes protest (or the setting alight of cars during protests) fails to meet the criterion of proportionality. It may be a symbolic act of violence in that it targeted a restaurant whose menu is beyond the economic reach of the protesters, but it hardly represents a systemic or structural issue of the French state or its policies that has endangered the self-preservation of protesters. As one act of gratuitous violence among others, it shows that protests have limits – many of which are already set in law – and the protesters caught with items or debris from this particular restaurant were quickly sentenced in French courts. It seems that the French state has been extremely effective in sanctioning those who broke the law during the protests, although it also issued many proceedings against protesters on lesser charges, such as participating in a demonstration that had not been officially registered. This is in stark contrast with the slow pace of the justice system under normal circumstances. It will probably be years until we hear back from most of the investigations into police brutality during the gilets jaunes protests, and if a recent case against police violence in France by the European Court of Human Rights is a good estimate, it might be 19 years until the state is formally sanctioned (European Court of Human Rights, 2019).

Conclusion

We will come to the issue of freedom, which better deals with these examples, in Chapter 3 but suffice to say for now that political resistance on the side of protesters is legitimate, and that this legitimacy is limited by appeals to proportionality. The limits of proportionality are not set *a priori*, but are decided by society as a whole – and are thus an essential part of the contract. Although the state has the power to impose restrictions on its citizens (and to enforce these decisions by the threat of death), it also cannot take away the right to resist, when resistance is conceived as a defence of self-preservation. This much has been sufficiently argued, for now, and will form the basis for a further deviation from the theory of Thomas Hobbes when we look at Spinoza's social contract in Chapter 3.

3

Liberty

If the state has the power of life and death over its citizens, and if we accept that, at least under specific circumstances, this power is even legitimately exercised, we are left to determine the limits of this use of state violence. In Chapter 2, I have already argued that there is an internal restriction to the legitimacy of violence. Any use of violence needs to be proportionate to the perceived threat and the ends to be achieved. Violence may be used, I argued, to oppose other types of violence, and in particular when the safety and security of those involved is threatened. But the use of physical and moral force is also limited externally – that is, by reference to another important concept of political thought: liberty.

Two liberties

In 1819, Benjamin Constant (1819/2010) proposed to introduce a recent distinction between two types of liberty. The ancients, in a few words, considered liberty to be the ability to rule over a common polity collectively, to legislate and judge, to condemn and absolve. But, as Constant points out, this collective liberty was not only compatible with, but dependent on the subjugation of the individual to the collective body. The collective body was free, but the citizen had to be subjected to its judgement. The most iconic example of such subjugation is the acceptance by Socrates of the death sentence assigned by his peers. Socrates felt compelled to accept his fate, and refused the opportunity to turn against his city and flee to save his life (Plato, 2003). By contrast, the liberty of the moderns, which is still our form of liberty today, is concerned with the fate of the individual. Liberty, since the rise of the modern state and its political institutions, is about freedom from arbitrariness (even from the arbitrariness of the collective), choosing one's path in life without restrictions, expressing one's opinion without fear of repression, and generally being limited by laws and rules rather than the will of those in power and their particular dispositions. This liberty, interestingly for Constant, is first and foremost a private enjoyment rather than a public good. Whereas the ancients thought that liberty was linked to a group's ability to rule over itself and make political decisions, for Constant the modern individual wants to be as free as possible from making political decisions in the first place. Freedom from politics is achieved through representation, by entrusting others to make decisions for us so we can devote our attentions elsewhere. We will see in the next chapter that this very individualistic conception of liberty is limited in scope, as the need for democratic decision-making has grown well past the stage it was at in the early nineteenth century.

Hobbes was already perceptive of this need for individual freedom in modern polities. A man is free, he claimed in chapter 14 of *Leviathan*, when there are no impediments to the action he has set himself to do (Hobbes, 1651/1996). If anyone were to obstruct the determined individual, say by putting up barriers in his way, then he would no longer be free. Let us get back to the gilets jaunes to understand this restriction on freedom. When the protesters were blockading roundabouts outside French towns, turning people away who did not display their own yellow vest on their car's dashboard as a show of solidarity, they were actively restricting the freedom of their fellow citizens. By preventing them from reaching their destinations, the freedom of the shoppers and commuters was being restricted, in order to raise awareness of the plight of the protesters. On the other hand, when the police set up roadblocks in the path of protesters, they were also restricting the protesters' freedom to reach their destination, or simply to continue on their way. Restrictions on freedom, in the Hobbesian sense, happen all the time and are not in themselves of much dramatic consequence. It is the point of the social contract, for Hobbes, to restrict freedom that leads to the unsustainable condition of the state of nature, where human beings are like wolves to one another. Having less freedom is a necessary condition of the social contract for Hobbes.

Individual freedom is thus defined, as early as the seventeenth century, as a condition of non-interference. When we are left alone to do what we want to do, we are as free as we can be in this individualistic sense. Freedom has enormous appeal precisely for that purpose: we do not like to be told what to do, to be stopped from doing things we like, or to have our life choices imposed on us by others. But that does not make it a purely individualistic good. We concede that some things we would like to do should be restricted, so that others will also be restricted in their ability to do the same things to us, for the sake of social peace. This makes freedom an individual good to be maximized at the political level, as restrictions on freedom typically require special justification, since the instinct of the modern individual is to keep as much freedom as can be kept. Our social modes of organization seek to defend a conception of freedom for all, and part of the spirit of modernity is to defend freedom against those who wish to restrict it. We are repulsed by previous social modes of organization, such as the feudal order that would restrict your life choices based on your birth (into slavery, bondage or serfdom), impose restrictions on you based on your religious beliefs or cultural heritage, or restrict your options in life based on your gender. Modern freedom is worth defending against its enemies, both in its individualistic version and as a social good to be maximized.

Spinoza's liberty

Spinoza has the most subtle and concise defence of modern liberty in both its individualistic and social variants. In the last chapter of his *Theological-Political Treatise* (1670/2007), abbreviated as 'the TTP' after its Latin title, Spinoza explains that even though it is in the power of the state to use all of the means at its disposal to support itself, a free state will be one where the maximum amount of freedom is allowed and where all are allowed to think and to say what they think. Although Spinoza argues his case more from the point of view of religious toleration, it is equally relevant to the contemporary context when there is political contestation, social cleavages and contestation over how to run the polity. His argument relies on two assumptions. In the first place, the state has the power to regulate what its citizens say and practise, but lacks the power to regulate their thoughts; and on the other hand, the state has the power to enforce its rule, but its use of violence to regulate thinking is counterproductive. Let me deal with these assumptions in turn.

Spinoza largely accepted the view that Hobbes had put forward a few decades earlier that the state has the power to regulate people's beliefs in the interest of peace. Living in a world rocked by religious conflict, Spinoza believed that the basic claim that the state can impose a version of religious peace on its citizens was not far-fetched or overstepping its bounds. But simultaneously, one person's mind cannot come under the full control of another: no matter how many regulations we put in place, we cannot control how others think. They may refrain from expressing their thoughts in public due to fear of reprisals, they may disguise their beliefs by acting in a prudent manner due to strict controls on what may or may not be said, but as long as they keep their thoughts to themselves there is little hope of the state changing their minds. This basic freedom, the freedom to philosophize, is considered a natural ability, and is impossible to regulate fully – although some have tried and failed. Nor is our ability limited to thinking *per se*. The freedom to philosophize will also include our emotional reactions to situations. We may be required to abide by the laws of the land, but when we perceive these to be unjust, when we have an emotional reaction to the unfolding of unjust events, we cannot be prevented from feeling what we feel and thinking what we think.

The freedom to philosophize does not stop at our ability to think for ourselves. The state may be able to stop us from acting on our thoughts and feelings, but Spinoza argues that a *free* state cannot do so. This is because a free state is one that seeks to maximize freedom for the individuals living within it. If security and safety are primary to the establishment of a social contract in Hobbes, the ultimate end of the social contract, for Spinoza, is to maximize freedom – without losing security and safety. A state can very well prevent its citizens from being free, but then it is no longer a free state, and it is unlikely to be one in which we would opt to live if we were given the choice. Reducing us to fear would merely turn us into beasts or robots, and surely this cannot be the purpose of the state. Allowing for a life of flourishing, providing the conditions for expanded reason, fostering a reduction of the feelings of anger and hatred are surely goods for any social contract worthy of the name. 'Therefore, the true purpose of the state is in fact freedom' (Spinoza, 2007). Clearly from Spinoza's own use of words, with reference to the development of the minds and bodies of the citizens living in a free state, it is the well-being and flourishing of the individuals that is at stake in his theory of the social contract. Such flourishing and freedom are only possible in a state that allows as much dissent and diversity as possible.

The freedom to philosophize and demonstrations

Although Spinoza never expresses it in these terms, it is fully compatible with his thought to argue that the right to protest is part of the freedom to philosophize. There are two reasons why this parallel is appropriate. In the first instance, as I have just noted, the freedom to philosophize is not entirely an intellectual exercise. It also relates to the realm of feelings and emotions – what philosophers today call *affect*. Spinoza's affective theory departs from many of his predecessors in the history of philosophy for not valuing reason above and beyond passion. Although Hobbes had also paved the way for such a theory, it is in the thought of Spinoza that it finds its most expressive formulation. In his *Ethics*, Spinoza had given a definition of the term: 'By affect I understand affections of the body by which the body's power of acting is increased or diminished, aided or restrained, and at the same time, the ideas of these affections' (Spinoza, 1677/1996). The body and the mind are not separated in Spinoza's thought, and the former has a decisive impact on the latter. Any freedom to philosophize is thus at the very least compatible with the expansion of bodily needs. In the second instance, the freedom of the body is also a pre-requisite for the freedom to think. A free state is one that allows the maximum increase in the power of body to act, compatible with the equal increase in power in other bodies. Spinoza's theory of affective freedom is thus one of a rise of power, an increased ability to do things with our bodies, and a social contract of empowerment. Although we will come back to the concept of power in Chapter 4, it is important to note here that Spinoza puts the body at the centre of his theory of ethics, and that ideas and rational expressions come as a consequence of the free body. The freedom to philosophize requires an expansion of the power of the body, and as large an area of freedom for bodies to develop as the state can allow and permit given that this freedom must be shared equally by all. When Spinoza includes within the freedom to philosophize the ability to talk and write about one's opinions, this must include the right to do so in public, including on the public square or in the street. Although Spinoza himself does not make this case directly, it is most likely because there was no need to make a separate case for freedom to assemble and talk in his time. There were fewer restrictions on the uses of public space than there are now, no administrative bans on demonstrations, or permanent police forces to enforce these in the seventeenth century. In France, although there had been police forces since the Middle Ages, they remained localized and sparse until at least the time of the Revolution (Rey and Féron, 1896). Spinoza had no need to make a case for public expression of one's philosophical opinions because there were so few limits to this type of expression in his day. In the present context, however, where police forces, mass mobilization and a right to demonstrate peacefully are taken for granted, the freedom to philosophize cannot but be extended to having the right to say what one wants in public spaces.

Nor is this controversial. Even the most vocal opponents of the gilets jaunes would not claim that they cannot demonstrate their discontent in the streets. They would, however, argue that the gilets jaunes are often acting outside the context of the law, by performing actions that do not follow the administrative procedures required in France today for lawful demonstrations to take place. These include providing in a letter contact details for the organizers of the movement; the goal of the demonstration, its location and itinerary; the size of the anticipated participation; and the demands of the protesters if they are seeking to speak to authorities. The letter, to be delivered to the authorities at least three full days prior to an event, needs to be signed by the president of the association organizing the event, and co-signed by three members of the said association (Service Public, 2019). Needless to say, in a decentralized and non-hierarchical movement such as that of the gilets jaunes, some of these requirements cannot be met, making any demonstration potentially outside the legal framework. By making the legal requirements for demonstrations so stringent, the French state is effectively limiting the freedom of its citizens to express their discontent through lawful means, and forcing them either into illegality or to abandon their freedom to demonstrate peacefully. The French state is thereby limiting the freedom to philosophize of its citizens, and to do so in public with their bodies as this freedom requires.

I have already discussed how the violence on the part of the French state has affected protesters in Chapter 2. The increased assertiveness of law enforcement forces is a deliberate policy of the French government. When the Paris police prefect was deemed too weak in his response to the gilets jaunes, he was replaced by Didier Lallement, who was well known for his harsh treatment of protesters. In February 2019, just before Lallement was appointed to his post in Paris, he came under fire from a civil liberties association in Bordeaux. The association, in a 60-page report, notes with widespread evidence that the prefect had used legal and illegal means to escalate tensions with protesters in 'the City of Wine', with dramatic consequences. Specifically, the report identifies the establishment of police files on the protesters, a practice legally reserved for terror suspects but now clearly used more widely by law-enforcement forces (Observatoire Girondin des Libertés Publiques, 2019). The choice of his appointment was a strong communicative message to the protesters: there will be more violence, fewer civil liberties, and the government is not scared of promoting someone who has been accused of using illegal means to support its repressive policy. The limiting of civil liberties is a direct consequence of this governmental policy.

This limitation of the freedom to philosophize has also spread more widely, beyond the attempts by the French state to limit the scale and intensity of the gilets jaunes movement. On 28 June 2019, a group of protesters staged a public action in Paris just as an all-time-record-high temperature for the month of June was recorded in France at 45.9 degrees Celsius (114.6 degrees Fahrenheit). The Extinction Rebellion protesters, sitting on the ground blocking traffic, were pepper sprayed and forcibly removed from the scene by riot police. On the videos, police are seen ripping off and destroying a protester's sunglasses, before spraying him in the face. The protesters had only given one day's notice to the authorities – making the demonstration illegal – and the police gave two warnings of their intention to use force, making their repression in accordance with regulation and procedure (Bouanchaud, 2019). There will be no appeal possible – one side followed dutifully the administrative procedure, while the other did not. During the night of the summer solstice, widely renamed in French the *fête de la musique*, a spontaneous (and thus illegal) street party near Nantes was broken up by police forces. Using LBD ball-launchers and grenades, the participants were violently attacked to break up the festivities. Fourteen protesters had to be rescued after falling into the Loire river, a wide body of water so close to its estuary. One partygoer, Steve Maia Caniço, never came home. The young man, who did not know how to swim, drowned as a result of police action. What these two examples illustrate is that civil liberties, and in particular the freedom to philosophize understood as the freedom to use your own body to express your opinions, are put under threat by the repression of the French state. Any state that poses increasingly restrictive conditions on the public expression of political opinions or even musical expression is bound to commit injustices far beyond the confines of what was intended. Much of the legislation used to justify these restrictions indeed started out as limitations for terror suspects, was enlarged to cover 'violent' protests, and is now clearly used widely on any and all who do not meet the restrictions of the bureaucratic state.

The exception becomes the rule

Macron had not waited for the gilets jaunes protests to start in order to attack civil liberties more widely. When he took office, he inherited a renewed state of emergency that had been declared during the terror attacks of 13 November 2015. The state of emergency, lasting 719 days, was the longest since the Algerian war. It widely transferred to the Interior Ministry duties and powers that typically reside in the courts. Although it ended on 1 November 2017, four of its measures had just been included into French law, rendering them permanent in the state security apparatus: those allowing for confinement to residence, administrative search warrants, security zones and the closure of religious sites (Adenor, 2017). All of these measures are now possible purely administratively, with no meaningful legal recourse. The onus of evidence is also set extremely low for justifying any of these measures: a perceived threat to public order suffices. Public liberties are easily taken away in times of perceived emergency, and there is little indication that these powers will ever be transferred back to judges rather than appointed ministers and state officials.

Giorgio Agamben was first to theorize the idea that the new rule of the legal order is a state of exception. With its modern inception found in revolutionary France under the measure of the 'state of siege', when responsibility for maintaining order is passed on to a military commander, the state of exception has now become the normal mode of conducting politics. This measure still exists under the current Fifth Republic in France, under provisions set by Article 36 of the Constitution. Whereas the state of exception existed in pre-modern societies, it was limited 'to justify a single, specific case of transgression by means of exception' (Agamben, 2005), whereas the modern version seeks to render the 'illicit licit', that is to create a space for law to be suspended by law itself. The state of exception is rendered paradoxical in the modern context in that it is used in permanence and has permeated politics in peacetime that would have typically been limited to wartime. To justify this, the rhetoric of the state is one of constant war against enemies within, and the use of 'state of exception' legislation to justify economic intervention and the restructuring of society. Christophe Castener, the French interior minister, said he had not ruled out calling in the army under the state of siege provisions of the French Constitution, after two police trades unions had called for the activation of the provision (*Le Monde*, 2018a). But the state of emergency is already present, with extraordinary security measures already passed into normal legislation since Macron's accession to power. It is visible in the extraordinary measures taken during the *grand débat*, when Macron visited the provinces and met elected officials throughout France. On 18 January 2019 in Souillac, a small town in my ancestral *département* of the Lot, Macron came to address 600 mayors of the region of Occitanie. A small town of 3,750 inhabitants, Souillac was turned into a military zone and temporary fortress. Demonstrations were strictly forbidden during the president's visit, particularly those of the gilets jaunes (L'Obs, 2019). A 10-kilometre perimeter was established around the *Palais des Congrès*, the local hall used for cultural events, with residents' houses requisitioned for snipers and an impressive deployment of armed guards stretching all the way to the Dordogne, the iconic river that borders the Neolithic caves of Lascaux and was home to literary figures such as Montaigne and La Boétie. The contrast between Macron and his predecessor Hollande could not be starker – Macron needs the entire arsenal of the state to safeguard him, while back in 2015 I had practically bumped into President François Hollande while waiting for boarding on the tarmac of Brive-la-Gaillarde airport, the local airport with 20 flights a week (16 of which go to Paris). The revision of the social contract was performed under a state of exception where the militarization of France is all the more apparent. The very weapons of social order discussed in Chapter 1 – the LBD and the two grenades used by French police – are testament to the ordinariness of the exceptionalism described by Agamben.

These limitations to civil liberties have gone well beyond the particular case of the gilets jaunes and are having a widespread impact on traditional workers' rights and the ability of citizens to organize themselves politically. On 1 May 2019, during the traditional May Day demonstrations, trades unions were the target of police brutality on a scale not previously experienced. The Confédération Générale du Travail (CGT), one of France's most well-known trades unions, was caught between police forces and black bloc protesters in Paris. Attacked by police, its president had to leave the demonstration and later denounced this unprecedented level of violence against well-identified CGT members in the demonstration (Bouchez et al, 2019). One of my cousins, Hugo, joined the demonstration to show his solidarity with those who had fought for workers' rights in the past, and described a harrowing tale. A self-described *bourgeois bohème* [the French equivalent of the hipster], he works in the technology industry in a management position, and is politically aligned with socialism. Every year, he goes to celebrate workers' rights on 1 May, in a festive atmosphere where solidarity with struggling industries is the caritative aim of the march. In 2019, however, the celebration march turned into a nightmare. He recalls seeing some gilets jaunes among the protesters, although these were in a small minority. A few had disposable masks with them, anticipating tear gas, but most were wearing shorts, skirts and T-shirts on this warm spring day. As the demonstration approached Place d'Italie, where it was due to end, Hugo heard screams coming from one of the side streets. Intent on staying out of trouble, he went another direction, only to be stopped by the mass of people ahead of him. The police had blocked their path, and were now closing the way behind them and cordoning the side streets. Blocked by thousands of other protesters, in a sea of human bodies, he then heard multiple explosions. Not being a veteran of violent demonstrations, he explains his astonishment at hearing the loud explosions, and that he began to panic. Then tear gas grenades started falling from the skies – one at his feet. People around him also began to panic, and ran back and forth to avoid the gas. A few veteran demonstrators managed to calm people down, but at this stage visibility was close to zero, with tear gas blinding the protesters and burning their respiratory tracts. He describes a situation of absolute fear, a terror for his life as grenades started falling at his feet. The fear was paralysing, freezing numerous protesters into place, unable to move, breathe or escape. Then the expected happened: the police charged the May Day demonstrators. For some time – perhaps half an hour, Hugo is not sure anymore as his notion of time is completely distorted at this stage – he heard things breaking around him. After the police charge, the infamous wreckers, some of whom may have been members of the 'black bloc', began their work around him: he heard a few pieces of glass break in the chaos of the demonstration. Finally, Hugo came face-to-face with the riot police. He, and those around him, raised their arms in a clear sign of surrender. The police ignored them, and moved past. It is then that Hugo realizes that he has passed the worst of the repression. But he was not quite out of it yet. He found himself in a no man's land, a zone between two police cordons encircling different areas of the demonstration. He rested for a bit, helped by street medics – volunteers who carry emergency supplies during a demonstration – before another grenade detonated in the side street where they were. Panic came back, this time not from being trapped in a human wave, but from the prospect of having a handful of riot police fall upon them with batons. He got up, ran, and found a way out of the police cordon. The horror was over. He admits coming out of this experience radicalized: he voted for Macron in the second round of the presidential election in 2017, but is now fervently against his president. The repression, he explains, is far from proportionate, and seems to be aimed at anyone who disagrees with the ideology of the government and the president. He also expresses his disbelief at reading nothing about it in the newspaper the next day – as if the repression of those who celebrate workers' rights is not worthy of the attention of the larger public. He had come to celebrate and to have fun, he came out shocked and motivated to change things. Beyond his particular experience, what this episode shows is that demonstrating for workers' rights has become increasingly difficult under the Macron *régime*. It also shows that the government is living in denial of what ordinary citizens experience – whether they are gilets jaunes or not. Treating all protesters as enemies has its price, and a generation of activists is getting radicalized by the repression. If there had indeed been wreckers among the protesters, they were few and far between. The mass punishment inflicted on all those who were there is beyond the scope of what should happen in a free country.

Liberal utopia

It is all the more surprising perhaps to most observers that these limitations on civil liberties are happening under the leadership of a liberal president, self-styled defender of the centre against the extremes. Not only was Macron elected in opposition to Marine Le Pen's far-right platform in 2017 but during the gilets jaunes protests he ran his party's European elections on a platform against political extremes. Playing on fears of the collapse of social order partly occasioned by the gilets jaunes protests, Macron clearly used the Great Debate, the public consultation he wanted to use as an occasion to rethink the French social contract, as an early campaign for his particular brand of centrism. As we have seen, however, his politics are accompanied by a rise in the power of the state, notably the police but also an increase in the power of administrative officials who are appointed to their post rather than elected. This bureaucratization of power will be further explored in Chapter 4, but it is clear here that it has limited freedom and led to the establishment of a strange combination of liberal authoritarianism. This marriage of convenience, between liberal principles and a rise in authoritarian rule, is neither new nor a contradiction in terms. It remains to be seen, however, how a supposed proponent of liberty can have such liberticide policies.

Macron is a liberal in the economic sense, but he does not hesitate to use centralized means, powers and ultimately violence to impose his economic reforms on French society. He has perhaps best been described as a liberal progressive – combining the economic needs of the free market and the progressive goals of social change and identity politics. As for the first set of these, the creation of markets and the imposition of privatizations has always necessitated the crushing of social forces and the use of state power to create the conditions of the type of liberal utopia which Macron defends. Whether it was Thatcher's iron fist, Pinochet's repressions, or the shock therapies of Yeltsin, the promotion of a liberal utopia does not necessitate the defence of civil liberties beyond the rights of property owners (Carr, 2016). The liberal order dreamed of by Macron is a utopia, therefore, in three senses of the word. In the first instance, it is a utopia in the sense of *u-topos* (nowhere), as it cannot exist and has not existed anywhere at any point. On the other hand, it is a utopia in the sense of its impossibility, in that it would require persons to act in ways that would violate their rights, liberties and inclinations. In the third sense, it is utopian in that it is in contradiction with itself. Let us deal with these three senses in turn.

When Thomas More wrote his *Utopia* in the sixteenth century, he chose the name of his fictional island based on the Greek word for *not a place*. There is no place like utopia, and the word has since become synonymous with fanciful thinking about an ideal society that cannot exist in practice. But utopian thinking is still as appealing as it was five centuries ago. We cannot but dream about what could be otherwise, how differently we could organize ourselves and our institutions, and attempt to bring those changes into being. That Macron's liberalism is utopian is not in itself that damaging to its claim to make the world (or at least Europe and France) a better place. Macronism, as Philippe Askenazy (2018) explains, is a movement that attempts to unite the forces of progressives and free-market political actors in France. As such, it is more reminiscent of the Blair and Clinton years and policies in the Anglo-Saxon world, than it is of anything France has ever known before. The strongest parallel, however, is with Thatcherism, though with a socially progressive twist. The freedom promoted by Macron has clearly been that of the entrepreneur, with a particular focus on start-ups and technology companies, tax breaks for the wealthiest (who often invest in these start-ups), and freedom for employers to dismiss their employees with as little compensation as possible. The French Clintonites and Blairites have been convinced that these measures are necessary to stimulate growth and redistribute wealth further down the line. This is in sharp contrast with the realities of the Clinton and Blair decades. Even in the years of boom and growth of the late 1990s and early 2000s, these reforms never did much to address social inequalities, which actually grew over the period. The golden days of progressive liberalism, that Macron symbolizes so well, are nowhere to be seen. They are clearly utopian in that even under the best conditions (global economic growth and prosperity), they have not delivered on their progressive promises. Given the economic stagnation of the past decade, the conditions are not ideal and are likely to lead to more dramatic consequences. The comparison of Macron's form of liberalism to the economic recession and rise of the oligarchs in Russia in the 1990s may be closer than the blue-sky thinking that his collaborators suggest. A return to the levels of inequality of the pre-First World War period, as detailed in Piketty's (2013) analysis of *Capital in the Twenty-First Century*, further corroborates this analysis of long-term economic trends. Social tensions, visible in the gilets jaunes protests, a lowering of pensions and benefits from the welfare state, and a spike in the net worth of the wealthiest, are more reminiscent of the darker days of economic liberalism than of the utopian optimism of the post-Cold War period. If Macronism is a utopia, the shadow of its dystopia is frighteningly looming over the future of France.

If utopias fail, so say the critics, it is because they ask of us actions that are contrary to what we do. Whether the argument is that they are 'contrary to human nature', 'unrealistic', or 'good in theory, bad in practice', utopias are attacked on the line that they demand particular behaviour that is not actually followed. Soviet utopia was thus demanding a level of self-abnegation and collective consciousness that, while beautiful in principle, simply does not account for human selfishness and desire for self-aggrandizement. The Macronist utopia similarly demands actions from human beings that go against what they do in practice. Since we are discussing freedom here, let us focus on this concept. In the first instance, Macron demands that, even though his citizens have the freedom to demonstrate and assemble, they do not exercise this freedom but instead refrain from resistance to his particular agenda for change. Under the rhetoric of the maintenance of the order of the Republic, demonstrators are grouped together as vandals and barbarians, wreckers and hooligans. This rhetoric has justified a particularly harsh state repression of their movement, in the forms of violence we have seen in this and the preceding chapters. As I have shown above, it is the freedom to philosophize that is being curtailed here, whether it is for the gilets jaunes, climate activists, defenders of workers' rights, or simply music enthusiasts.

But it is also the freedom of the 'lead climbers' that is being unrealistically constrained. The Macronist economic model, where tax breaks for the wealthiest make them able to reach new heights that elevate their fellow citizens, relies on a nationalist economic rhetoric simply not in accordance with international finance and business practices. The idea that the wealthiest, in particular those with millions of euros-worth of assets and more (the so-called 1%), will stay and invest their new tax breaks in the French economy seems naïve at best. It is unlikely that Macron – himself a graduate of l'ENA (l'Ecole Nationale d'Administration), the crème de la crème of public administration training in France, whose graduates form the bulk of senior civil servants, top politicians and CEOs in the country – would believe this to be the case unless he was attached to this utopian vision for ideological reasons. Freedom for owners of capital means the freedom to invest it where they please, and the highest returns are not to be found in the stagnant economies of Old Europe, not even in France under the leadership of a progressive liberal. Macronism demands just as much reform of the actual-existing actions of the lowest-paid workers as it does of the richest citizens. It is utopian in its demands that we forgo our self-interest, whether we are at the bottom and see our social advantages and benefits melt away, or at the top and see opportunities for growth outside the nation. For all the talk of trickle-down economics, such a model still is hopelessly utopian in that it does not account for the actual actions of the richest individuals and corporations when they benefit from tax breaks and other fiscal advantages.

Macron's particular type of progressive liberalism is also in contradiction with itself. One can point to a number of policies where this is the case, particularly in the reform of the labour market. The liberalizing of French employment contracts has had a direct impact on the most vulnerable of workers that Macron's progressive rhetoric had promised to protect. If it is easier for an employer to change contracts, get rid of employees without justification, or reduce social benefits such as parental leave and part-time working arrangements, there are fewer recourses for those who depended on those social benefits. Where the whims of the employer are the main source of employees' benefits and stability, a race to the bottom is the most likely outcome, particularly when economic growth is not strong, or when another recession looms. As Askenazy (2018) notes, the social groups Macron attracted during his campaign, such as LGBT groups and women, drawn by his socially progressive rhetoric promising identity-based benefits, have been sacrificed at the altar of his economic reforms, and are the first victims of the reform of economic policies as their stability in employment is the first to go. The promises of the reforms were 'equal opportunity, economic growth and low unemployment', while the realities are a precarious economic situation, rising inequalities and discrimination. As Askenazy (2018) argues, these nefarious consequences 'are not obstacles to equal opportunity, but rather, necessary conditions for attaining this objective'. When the consequences of reform of these protections are so well known, particularly in how it affects minorities and the most vulnerable workers, equality is not likely to follow, and Macronism is creating few big winners, and many losers.

Even though Macronism is synonymous with the retreat of the French state as an employer and as an owner of capital in key industries, it has also heralded the return of the French state as a provider of muscular security. The defence of civil liberties is a necessary sacrifice at the altar of liberal utopian reforms, as social forces will never accept a degradation of their conditions without fighting back. In order to turn France into a more attractive market for investors and international capital, Macron needs to repress his own people, who will fight for the preservation of their social advantages. The reform of pensions, the privatization of public assets, and the limiting of social protests all require a bigger state to enforce the measures – at least for the first few years of the reform process. As was the case with Thatcher's experience of enforcing privatizations and widespread social reforms, it came at a huge cost to the public purse, having to wait until 1986, seven years into the Iron Lady's rule, for public spending as a percentage of GDP to fall below the levels she inherited in 1979 (Rogers, 2013). Macron's reforms are likely to face similar upheavals, with clear signs that public spending is rising despite tax breaks, leading to higher levels of public debt. The retreat of the state from economic life will necessarily go through an increase in the role the state plays in the transition period. This contradiction is strong one, and will likely displease all those who support Macron today, both on the progressive and on the liberal side. Those wishing for a more progressive state will be disappointed at the curtailing of civil liberties and the rise of inequalities, and those wanting a stronger free market and lower levels of state involvement will be disappointed by the rising public debt that comes with the implementation of reforms. Macron will not be able to please both the progressives and the liberals that brought him to power. He is most likely to alienate both due to the internal contradictions in his politics.

Positive liberty

Liberty is about more than the mere freedom from non-interference for an individual. The positive right to take part in public demonstrations and express one's opinion publicly is taken as a fundamental right of a modern state. A state may limit this freedom, but it is correspondingly less free as it does so. Historically positive conceptions of freedom have been linked to the ability of a political community to rule over itself and make decisions. A state is freer, in the positive sense, if its politics are not dictated or limited by interference from outside powers. During the gilets jaunes protests, a recurrent theme was the sense that the French state was limited in its actions by multinational capitalism and its membership of the European Union. Both of these are claims I will come back to when dealing with economic justice, but they pose an important question for positive, national conceptions of freedom that need be dealt with here.

Even for Isaiah Berlin, perhaps the most vocal defender of the negative conception of liberty, positive liberty also had a role to play, notably in movements of national liberation (Berlin, 1969). When a people are under the rule of another, through either military, political or economic occupation and dependency, they lack a measure of freedom to act independently. The gilets jaunes clearly allude to this lack of freedom when they fly the French flag and take down European flags during their demonstrations. The idea that France is limited in its undertakings, either because of World Bank or IMF rules, or under the yoke of Brussels and the European institutions, is a popular belief within the social movement. It is of little surprise that this is the case, as French politicians have clearly made this case themselves in justifying austerity measures and degrading the state of public services. The Rassemblement National (RN), the rebranded Front National of Marine Le Pen, is the most popular political party among gilets jaunes supporters – with up to 44 per cent supporting the RN, according to one poll (Houeix, 2019) – although among the major figures of the movement there is more diversity in political orientation. The

RN is the anti-systemic party that plays most on this rhetoric of national liberation against international elites. Although by no means a majority in the movement, it manages to capture the feeling of distress against forces constraining the people as a whole. Importantly, the May 2019 European elections suggest that the gilets jaunes movement has contributed to repoliticization of abstentionist voters. Rural regions, which are really regions dominated by small cities (of fewer than 100,000 inhabitants), as Guilluy (2016) notes, are those most affected by the rise in fuel costs and where the gilets jaunes have the most support. These regions have seen record participation rates in the otherwise rather unpopular elections of Members of the European Parliament, which saw the RN arrive in first position ahead of the ruling party, *La République en Marche*. Freedom as a national liberation is a powerful motivator for social forces. We will see in the Chapter 4 how national elites have deliberately played on this national sentiment against international institutions in which they nevertheless actively participate. The dangerous game these European elites have played – blaming Brussels for their own policies – has dramatically backfired, with Euroscepticism on the rise in France in 2005 (Jeanbart, 2005), and with rumblings about the power of Brussels present within all the major political parties.

Collective identities are not limited to the national level, and the gilets jaunes are often very proud of flying the colours of their region during demonstrations. In the centralized state that is France, local governments in the regions play an important role but have comparatively little power. Split between four levels of governance – commune, intercommunal level, *département* and region – with often competing competencies, despite a recent restructuring of local government in 2015, local government is often divorced from local concerns and identities. Deliberately restructured into *départements* during the Revolution, in an attempt to break regional loyalties and medieval boundaries, and to rationalize the process of governance, France has seen a split between which region people feel a part of, and which administrative unit is in charge, with some talk of abolishing one level of governance still in vogue in some circles (Blairon, 2015). The *département*, the level imposed by a central Parisian elite during a period of revolutionary rationalization, is the obvious scapegoat. Certainly the commune, with its local and popular mayor, is not under threat and has fared well against the test of time. The flags of the regions of Britanny and Corsica have been regularly sighted at various demonstrations of the gilets jaunes. These two regional identities, the strongest surviving in France, with distinct languages that have gained in popularity over recent decades, are able to galvanize support. The freedom to have your own language taught in a public school is one example of the positive freedom that comes from the feeling of belonging. After decades of imposition of French as the language of all the French people, it seems a mark of political resistance against Parisian elites. Not all regional identities make this specific demand. Other marks of regional identity have also surfaced elsewhere – with the Occitan cross, a 12-pointed golden star on a blood-red flag; the checkered Picardy flag featuring the golden *fleur-de-lys* on azure and red lion cubs; and the two lions passant, attributed to William the Conqueror of Normandy, spotted on occasion among the gilets jaunes, but without clear demands for regional autonomy. It may just be that pride in one's regional origin is seen as a mark of defiance in a country where living in the capital is a mark of success, to study in one of the *grandes écoles* or to work at a prestigious company. Despite Article 1 of the French Constitution, which calls France a decentralized state, it is in practice one of the most centralized of Western democracies, and the resurgence of regional identities is also a form of resistance against an administration centred on metropolitan areas. Not particularly reactionary or wanting to seek independence from the French state, local particularisms are perceived as a rallying cry for those living in the periphery against the centralized rule of metropolitan elites. In regions where economic stagnation and lack of opportunities are the rule, the dominance of globalized capital and the major cities is perceived as an injustice for those who live *en province*, the French term that encompasses the entirety of the country outside of the metropolitan area of Paris. Regional identities are best perceived as a cry for help from the regions left out of the benefits of globalization, as we will see in Chapter 5 when discussing economic justice.

Conclusion

Freedom is an essential demand of the modern polity and its citizens. No longer content for security from external threats to be the sole concern of the Leviathan, the Spinozist social contract demanded that freedom be the goal of the state. This freedom, as I have shown, is the freedom to philosophize, understood as a freedom of physical bodies living in a social world. The bodies demand to be free to express themselves in public, through participation in social life and the ability to express themselves in social movements. Without this freedom, the state is merely a repressive machine, and any attempt to curtail freedom, however limited in scope, typically spreads to the whole social body. Limitations on freedom were first accepted under anti-terror legislation, but they quickly spread to the gilets jaunes and now threaten other activists, or simply those wishing to enjoy public spaces without filling in the required forms. The violence of the bureaucratic state is ever rising, with no end in sight for its totalizing demands. This raises the question of what can be achieved democratically in such as a state. The demands of positive freedom are also those of the political body, constituted of citizens, to organize itself. Chapter 4 will explore this ever-important notion. No freedom can be complete without a fully democratized state – and this includes the subjection of the economy to public rule.

4

Democracy

It is a truism of any discussion of democracy that our notion is heavily indebted to the ancient Greeks, and in particular to the Athenians. The word itself derives from *demos* and *kratos*, people and power, and is often translated as the rule of the people – or the rule of the poor, who formed the bulk of the people in ancient times. But this inheritance is more problematic than it seems. The term *kratos* itself can refer to might or strength, to acts of valour or violence, or to power or dominion. Who counts as the *demos* is equally fraught with disagreements and inconsistencies. For the ancient Greeks, only free (non-slave) adult males of local birth counted as citizens, whereas we have a much more inclusive notion of citizenship today, with women and some foreign-born citizens eligible for the same privileges and duties. We will deal with both of these concepts – power and the people – in turn, with a keen eye on what this means for the social contract.

The democratic social contract

Social contract theory, as a venerable concept in philosophy, claims its roots in ancient Greece. Socrates, in Plato's dialogue *Crito*, argues with his friend about the merits of accepting his death sentence, versus the merits of fleeing Athens, as is possible with the use of a few well-placed bribes. Socrates argues for the moral duty to obey the laws of the land, irrespective of the consequences for his own person. Socrates' argument binds the citizen to his community, and is perceived more as a moral duty than a political obligation. The city of Athens had made Socrates who he was, and he refused to betray it, even if it meant death. This moralism is hardly applicable to a modern polity, nor is it appropriate for the current crisis of the gilets jaunes. What Socrates' argument does show, however, is that democracy held a force over him beyond that of the power of legal or physical enforcement. Democracies claim a moral force over their citizens that often makes them accept conditions that would otherwise be against their interests.

It is in Genevan philosopher Jean Jacques Rousseau's thought that the modern conception of democracy has its clearest expression – after two millennia of dormant torpor. In his *Social Contract*, Rousseau delineates the limits of democratic power and couches these limits in contractual language. Unlike Hobbes or Spinoza, though, it is less the question of rights and the establishment of a zone of security that concerns the citizen of Geneva, but the moral standing of the state and the root of its power. As he put it, the question is to find a mode of association that preserves the rights of each associate as much as possible. Unlike more liberal theorists, such as Locke, who insisted on the defence of inalienable rights vested in the individual, particularly the right to property, Rousseau's solution to the problem of the social contract is the total alienation of each associate and his rights to the community (Rousseau, 2001). Rousseau raises the stakes of the social contract, by asking a fundamental question still relevant today. How can we preserve as much freedom and as many rights as possible whilst living together? Hobbes had answered that liberty needs to be sacrificed to security, so that we trade one good for another. Spinoza had concurred with Hobbes, adding the caveat that a state will not be free unless it safeguards as much liberty as possible. Rousseau takes the argument a step further by arguing that all rights are subordinate to the community, and that since the community will be run in a democratic manner, it is in the interest of all to not abuse this surrender of rights and to make the cost of the association as small as possible. Rousseau's argument for the social contract, thus, depends on his defence of democratic rule. Without it, the social contract is void.

The essence of the social contract, for Rousseau, is to create more power. Taken individually, the people have little power they can exercise effectively, as their particular wills, their desires and wants, oppose one another. Hobbes had already concluded that this was the dilemma of the state of nature, but for Rousseau it is more the dilemma of individuals living together in large societies. In his treatment of the state of nature, Rousseau had excluded elaborate modes of association from the history of humankind. He had speculated that human beings are solitary creatures and that even the family unit, often taken to be the most basic mode of human association, is itself artificial. The model human, he dreams, is more akin to the orangutan, the primate whose existence had been reported by European explorers to south east Asia in the eighteenth century, and who (supposes Rousseau) meets other members of its species only for reproductive purposes. The anthropology of Rousseau's speculations is not quite accurate, as our species, *homo sapiens*, seems to have always already existed in groups, but its conclusion is still relevant for us. Every form of association, from the most basic to the most complex, is constructed and can be reformed. The purpose of the state, as an association of modern humans, is to expand the power of the community to act together, and to direct its purpose for the common good decided in democratic terms.

This common good is phrased by Rousseau as a general will, an exercise of the desires of the people taken together. The concept itself is quite open to interpretation and misunderstanding. What Rousseau explains is that when the people come together in a democratic framework, they cede all of their particular rights and advantages in exchange for participation in the exercise of power. By coming together, the citizens establish a community, called a *republic*, that has ultimate power over all of its members. This is perhaps the most problematic part of Rousseau's formulation, as he insists that the community can force its members to be free, in order to conform to the wishes of the community. Taken as a foresight of the totalitarian regimes of the twentieth century, this enforced freedom is one of the most discussed formulations of Rousseau. Yet the idea is still with us today. Rousseau's argument is made in a chapter on sovereignty, the active part of the power of the political community, or republic. His main statement is that when the people assembled take a decision, when they exercise their common will and choose a path for the future, their decision is enforced with the full power of the state. The modern state, even in its most liberal of formulations, does not act very differently. Once a decision has been made by the sovereign, citizens are obliged to obey it, or face the consequences of sovereign power. When the French state decided to restrict the area where gilets jaunes protesters could demonstrate, by forbidding access to town centres or to the main *boulevards*, they were exercising sovereign power and forcing the citizens to be free – or at least enforcing the freedom of some by restricting that of others.

Herein lies the main issue with power as described by Rousseau. He had assumed that in order to force someone to be free, that person needed to have been involved in making the decision that is then later enforced upon them. If a citizen takes part in an assembly, which collectively makes the decision to impose limits on the freedom of all citizens, then that citizen is bound by the decision of the political body. What the gilets jaunes are contesting is the democratic nature of decision-making in modern France, and by extension in modern states. When a body of citizens have had three successive governments, from three different political orientations (right, left and centre), and those governments have taken no decisions that have improved their standards of living, they argue that it is legitimate for citizens to question their own role in decision-making.

Regaining the initiative

It is not without surprise, thus, that the RIC (*référendum d'initiative citoyenne*) has become the central demand of the gilets jaunes across their particular demands for social justice and Macron's resignation. A citizen-initiated referendum ticks all the boxes of Rousseau's demand for democracy in the republic. It is open to all citizens, not merely those in privileged positions or those already in power. It is an initiative, and thus opens an area of power and of will, as it transfers the agenda-setting power of the elites partly back to the people. And it is a referendum, the most direct form of participation in politics in a modern state. We will come back to the notion of citizenship later, so let us now focus on the notions of initiative and then referendum.

Initiative is a key term for what is happening during the gilets jaunes protests, as well as being a cornerstone of their demand for increased democracy. The power to begin something, to initiate a change, and to bring about a new manner of doing this is an appealing concept for those who feel disenfranchised. Initiative is also the immediate outcome of deliberation and of the will, as the driving forces behind both individuals and political associations. When the gilets jaunes protests began, the initiative came from online petitions and calls for a wide movement to protest imposition of new rules in citizens' lives. Against the French state's arguments that it was making its citizens safer, from road accidents when it lowered the speed limit on national roads, or from climate change when it proposed a new tax on fuel, the gilets jaunes took back the initiative by forcing the government to back down, and asking for other measures to be taken to combat these nonetheless very real threats. Where the gilets jaunes failed, in this respect, is by not institutionalizing their initiative in a manner that could have replicated it through time. But it is asking a lot of a grassroots social movement that sprang into existence in a few months. The initial impetus was reactive, to be certain, but could not have been otherwise. The power to propose initiatives does not currently exist, and the demand for the RIC is already the most pressing demand of the movement. One form of popular referendum already exists in France, and this was used for the first time in 2019. It is a shared-initiative referendum (RIP in French; *Référendum d'initiative partagée*), which was called following the vote by the National Assembly to privatize the Parisian airports. It currently requires the signature of at least 185 of the 925 members of parliament in France to initiate an official petition, which then needs to be signed by 10 per cent of the electorate – about 4.7 million people. At the time of writing, the first RIP had gathered just over 2 per cent of citizens' signatures (just over a million), making it unlikely to reach the target (Service Checknews, 2019). Needless to say, the current restrictions on the RIP are deliberately set to exclude any widespread use of the initiative, and they place the role of the citizens far below that of parliamentarians, who are responsible for setting the process in motion. The RIC, by contrast, would firmly set the power of decision-making in the hands of citizens, perhaps enabling them to propose decisions and reforms a little more pressing to their hearts and minds than who ends up owning airports.

The referendum itself is one of the rare ways we have found to engage the full citizen body in modern politics. Of course, elections are the most common and widespread way to demand citizen participation, but they are at best one step removed from the decision-making process. By selecting representatives to make decisions for them, citizens are not actively taking part in politics, but rather taking part in the selection of those who participate in politics. Modern politics at its best is not in itself democratic, but is rather a democratic election of an aristocracy – in the sense that the body of citizens selects who it thinks are the most competent (from the Greek *aristos*, the best) at making decisions in their interests. This system is not without its merits – taking part in all decisions to be made at the level of state would be time-consuming and often tedious – but it lacks the democratic element of direct citizen participation. Recourse to referenda has been commonplace in the French Fifth Republic precisely to bring about an element of direct citizen participation in politics – perhaps the only truly democratic element, where the will of the people is determined by their direct participation in the decision. Referenda can be called, according to the Constitution, for laws, changes in the Constitution itself or to approve membership of a new state in the European Union – although there are other possible procedures for all of these decisions rather than recourse to a referendum. The first referendum of the Fifth Republic was initiated by De Gaulle himself for the people to approve the new Constitution, and the last one was the failed referendum on establishing a Constitution for Europe in 2005. With ten national referenda in 61 years of the Republic, and with no referendum in the past 15 years, it is not a very widely used instrument of legislation for constitutional change. Most controversially, the result of the last referendum was largely ignored, as the provisions for the Constitution for Europe were rebranded but nonetheless integrated within the Lisbon Treaty, and passed through by parliament in 2008 without recourse to another referendum. When the people choose the wrong answer, political elites have ways of ignoring their will and taking decisions for them in their stead – forcing them to be free.

There are, of course, issues associated with referenda as an element of decision-making. Who decides on the question posed? How is an effective course of action determined after a referendum? How can technical issues be answered with a yes or no vote? Can a referendum be valid if turnout is low? Referenda are not a panacea for the political ills of a modern age, and some of these issues pose legitimate questions that need to be addressed if they are to acquire a larger role in political decision-making. Yet many arguments against referenda do not seem to revolve around these technical issues, which can potentially be addressed with technical solutions. There could, for example, be set procedures for deciding on a question, the use of more complex voting systems than a simple yes or no vote, such as preferential voting, and a minimum participation threshold for a referendum to take effect. Yet most objections to referenda seem to imply that they give too much power to the people. The people, it is often argued, cannot be trusted to make the right choice. Whether it is the decision by the French on a European Constitution in 2005, the Brexit vote in the United Kingdom, or the Swiss decision not to tax married couples at the same rate as cohabiting couples (BBC News, 2019), the assumption is that voters simply cannot understand the complexities of the modern world. This seems to be a particularly dangerous slippery slope towards less democracy. Rousseau's proposal that the citizens should take part in more decision-making rather than less seems to be a worthy rampart against the enemies of democracy.

The Legislator

Rousseau proposed that the origin of the republic, the beginning of a political community, needs to find its source in a great person, the Legislator. The Legislator is someone who is not a politician, or must at the very least resign from political office or be a foreigner in order to claim the title. The Legislator establishes a lasting political order, not because they are interested in the power, wealth, or prestige such a position holds, but rather because they are ready to sacrifice such worldly goods for the gratefulness of future generations. Divorced from the political process itself, the Legislator is thus a quasi-divine being, and possesses virtues beyond those of common mortals. Indeed, Rousseau speculates that recourse to the gods by the ancients was an attempt to ground the authority of the Legislator in the divine, and that we have lost this potential appeal today. Without divine status for its founding figure, the republic is doomed to question its origins and attempt to change its laws and constitution. But whereas Rousseau saw this as a threat, as only the Legislator could establish a firm republic, I propose to read it as an opportunity. Rousseau is correct that we need divine grounding for a stable republic, and that such a story is no longer believable in the modern world. Without the gods, we need a new process of establishing the social contract in the first place, and Rousseau's insight that democracy must be the cornerstone of political order is here the starting point.

Rousseau had compared the Legislator to a mechanic, who invents a machine that is then operated by others – statesmen. But this model is a hopelessly antiquated one for the modern world. Today, we no longer have a single mechanic, inventor or designer working on a new product. We have dozens, hundreds, or thousands of people contributing to the design and perfection of the products we use on a daily basis. To push Rousseau's analogy, we thus need a design team for the invention of the republic. The Legislator does not need to be a man, as Rousseau had assumed – they do not even need to be one person, but there is everything to gain from engaging a wider body of citizens in the process. Collective design of the republic can be a possibility for a renewal of democratic sentiment – and for a time it looked like the *grand débat*, the collective exercise of revision of the social contract proposed by Macron, could serve this function. But this opportunity was clearly missed. In the first instance, the debate only engaged mayors directly. Although mayors are clearly the most popular politicians in France, as they maintain local ties and are often voted in and maintained in office over and above party allegiances, they still hold a representative office and are not the people themselves. An appointment by lot, as was common in ancient Athens, or is still common in countries with jury duty, would have been a more direct involvement of citizens in the process. In the second instance, the outcome of the *grand débat* was condensed, selected and produced by the President and his office. Even by Rousseau's standards, this can hardly be how the Legislator operates. Independence from political office is a pre-requisite of the project, and its control by someone who is interested in pushing a particular policy outcome and particular legislative agenda can hardly produce what this attempt at a social contract requires. Third, and finally, it requires a vision of the future that is almost by definition incompatible with modern political life. Whereas political processes today are deeply concerned with the next election result, change of the party in power, and short-term gains, the process of the Legislator must by definition look towards the future. The Legislator, thus, can be a group of citizens, who are not themselves involved in politics directly and who are independent from the short-termism and party-political allegiances common of contemporary politics. They could, based on their work done on behalf of the whole state, propose changes to the constitutional arrangements, as Rousseau had envisioned was the remit of this privileged position.

Nevertheless, given the lack of divine authority of the people as a whole, even such an enlarged conception of the Legislator could not hope to have a permanent claim to establish a social contract. At best, this social contract would be temporary and open to revision, as the people, no more than the great statesmen of the past who have written our present constitutions, are not immune from human error or lack of foresight about the challenges of the future. As I argued in Chapter 1, it is impractical even for the smallest of states to get all citizens to literally sign the contract they enter when they become full citizens on adulthood. That is not to say that the social contract cannot be worked on, say, for every generation. Modern political organizations have elections every few years, typically every four to five years. Since the activities of the Legislator would be quite onerous – we can imagine thousands, if not more, citizens having to design changes to the constitutional order of their country over a period of several months if not years – it would be reasonable to assume that its activities would be undertaken less often. Why not speculate that once every 20 years, roughly the space of a generation, such a process is undertaken to revise the constitutional needs of the state? In France, under the Fifth Republic, this would have meant three Legislator processes: in 1978, 20 years after its founding; in 1998 and in 2018. The gilets jaunes protests, starting in November 2018, would have been drastically different if they had taken place in the context of a revision of constitutional powers rather than during the strengthening of executive and administrative powers under Macron. Giving the opportunity for the citizens to shape their state for the changing needs of each generation would at least give a feeling of participation in the political process. The new constitution itself, or changes to the existing one, could be voted on during a referendum, potentially with a separate ballot for each change. Rousseau's Legislator could turn from being a once-in-a-lifetime event for the existence of a republic, to a continual process that rejuvenates the political body.

Some may argue that this is already in the remit of politicians, to update and change political system as needed – changing and amending the constitution of the state with evolving situations. But this is to misunderstand the important point made by Rousseau about the nature of democracy and the general will. We cannot have a clear sense of what the people want if they are continually being represented by others and lack initiative in political life. Merely having more referenda will not quite resolve the issue of the nature of the social contract – while the institution of the Legislator as a permanent (if sporadic) feature of political life is a more inclusive mode of organization. Rousseau remained too aristocratic to contemplate such a democratic feature of political life – his model for the Legislator was Lycurgus of Sparta – but the situation has changed dramatically today. Mass, compulsory education, cheap and easy access to knowledge through online sources, quasi-universal literacy and mass participation in politics for the best part of a century have ensured that the situation of the modern state is very different today than it was in the late eighteenth century. Collective intelligence is not without its merits, and subject to democratic choice and control over changes in the constitution, would meet the criterion of non-arbitrariness. Provided the conditions are right – participants in the Legislator would need to be remunerated adequately, say at the level of politicians, selection by lot enforced strictly, voting on proposed changes done independently, public debate and media attention strictly regulated for fairness and impartiality – the process could change political life as we know it. It would certainly empower a group of citizens to effectuate change, and empower all citizens to decide on whether to accept or reject the proposals of the Legislator.

Power

One more consideration about power is important in our discussion of democracy. Power can be defined in a number of different ways. As Steven Lukes (2004) argues, there are (at least) three dimensions of power. In the first instance, power can be defined as the ability to get someone to do something they would not otherwise have done. This can apply equally to individual and to groups of people, so that this first-dimensional power can be seen when a group of riot police officers prevent a demonstration from going down a particular street. Without the police there, the demonstrators would have gone down the street, and they are thus being prevented from doing so, with power being exercised over them. The second-dimensional power is also concerned with getting others to do things, but adds that agenda-setting is another form of power that complements the first. When Macron and his team write the conclusions of the *grand débat*, they are engaging in agenda-setting. Condensing two million participations into a small document necessarily involves the setting of priorities, and is itself an exercise of power. Lastly, for Lukes, comes the third dimension of power. This third dimension builds on the previous two to add that some forms of power shape our very preferences, so that we are not necessarily aware of how we have come to value particular ideas, beliefs or material things that are actually against our interests. This form of power, often called *ideology*, is the one that is the most difficult to pin down. It is exercised in schools and universities: for example, in France there are citizenship lessons, grouped under the umbrella *parcours citoyen* [citizen journey] that takes place from kindergarten to the baccalaureate. It aims to shape young citizens to the values of the republic – with varying levels of success – notably liberty, equality, secularism and ecology. What happens, though, when one of these values clashes with your material interests? What happens, to take an example that sparked the gilets jaunes protests, when the government introduces a new tax on fuel, justified on ecological values, that will adversely affect your ability to get to work, go shopping or take your children to school? You can, of course, adjust your lifestyle to match the new restrictions imposed by the new law. But in rural or peri-urban regions, where there is no practical alternative to the personal car as a mode of transport, and where rent or the price of housing closer to work are not within the reach of many on a modest budget, the sacrifices must involve other areas of life, such as food, clothing, or the ability to go on holiday. When Lukes speaks of accepting an ideology that is against your material interests, this is what he means: power is being exercised over you in that you have internalized the ecological values to such an extent that you are willing for them to make your life more difficult and less wealthy. Needless to say, the inculcation of ecological values in the gilets jaunes had not produced the desired effect. Resistance is fierce, and opens up the road for considering a fourth dimension of power not discussed by Lukes.

For Foucault, the traditional analyses of power that see it as a fixture, a property that can be ascribed to institutions or persons, miss part of the dynamics behind the exercise of power. It is no longer the government, the educational system, or the prison that have power in his analysis of the phenomenon, but rather the relations between these and the bodies of those on whom power is exercised. In the context of the prison, Foucault (1991) had argued that he was conducting a microphysics of these relations between the bodies of the incarcerated, and the institutions in which they are located. Power is more akin to a strategy than to something we possess; it is closer to a plan of action than something vested in particular persons and political bodies. The exercise of power is not merely about making people do things, setting the agenda or forming an ideology, but also about the ways in which power is resisted by those on whom it is exercised. Power is thus not just something that those at the top of the pyramid have and exercise on others, but permeates through all levels of society and is also (though by no means equally) exercised by those at whom the strategies of surveillance and control are aimed. For the prison, Foucault argues, it is perhaps Bentham's panopticon that is the best example of such a mode of power. The panopticon, the all-seeing prison project the utilitarian thinker tried to sell to reform prisons, is an attempt to exercise power on the prisoners, but this is not all. It also requires that prisoners exercise power over themselves. The premise of the panopticon, where guards can observe all of the actions of the inmates at all times, is for the observed to change their behaviour out of their own volition. Power is not merely negative in this sense, it is also positive and creative. It creates discipline notably, and possibilities for modes of punishment that are less brutal and more humane than those that preceded it.

The panopticon is the architectural model of modern power relations for Foucault. The visibility of the inmate is key here, as the entire strategy of power rests on the potential to be seen at all times. It is quite prophetic, for Bentham, to have designed such a model which is widespread not in prisons, but in modern cities. The city with its closed-circuit television networks acts as the all-seeing eye of the panopticon writ large. The strategy of the gilets jaunes is unique in that respect, in that they do not hide, and in fact explicitly want to be seen. The perception of the yellow high visibility jacket is key. The attempt to use visibility as an instrument of power, as a strategy of discipline, is turned on its head by the protesters. Foucault had highlighted that those on whom power is exercised can always exercise forms of power back, and resist those who have attempted to discipline them. The *gilet jaune* itself, as a material object that creates a hyper-visibility, is used to subvert the strategy of power of those who think they possess it. MC Solaar, the French rap artist, had posited the possibility of blending in by wearing fluorescent colours in 1997 in his album *Paradisiaque*. In the urban chaos of the modern world, it is easier to blend in and to look inconspicuous not by attempting to hide and wearing black, but by wearing yellow clothing and making yourself seen. The visibility of the yellow vest is a subversive act of power, by those upon whom power is typically exercised, showing that power is not merely a one-way movement but engenders counter-forces and resistance.

The fourth dimension of power, thus, is one of resistance. Much as the microphysics of Foucault suggests, power works a little like electrical current. For power to exist, there needs to be resistance between two poles (negative and positive). Only then can electrical current actually move from one node to the other, for without resistance the current is inert. In social settings the analogy seems to work as well. Power is only exercised when there is resistance, no matter how ineffective such a resistance seems to be. Successful strategies of power engender little resistance, but if there is no resistance whatsoever, it is doubtful that what is happening is an act of power. We have seen in Chapter 2 that resistance is an inherent part of violence, and the same applies in the case of power. It is, in fact, often difficult to differentiate between an exercise of power, and the exercise of violence. Both are not the same thing, however, as power can be exercised without violence. Power only becomes violent the moment a coercion is enforced on bodies. When it is limited to the level of strategy and not yet enforced with physical or moral force, power remains distinct from its violent incarnation. To be effective, as I argued previously in Chapter 2, power rests on the threat of violence to come. But there is also power that does not rest on violence whatsoever. The power that comes from authority has an element of this. When we consult an authority on a topic, we are not giving them the possibility of exercising violence on us. We are nevertheless giving them power, in the sense that we accept that their advice, thoughts and wisdom is superior to our own and can sway us to act in a different way. But what is common in an intellectual setting – to ascribe power without violence, notably through the authority of the author – is without parallel in the political sphere. Where power can be exercised without violence, in politics the threat of violence is always already there.

It is all the more essential, in a political world where power is exercised, strategized on, and backed up by the threat of violence, to reflect on what are the acceptable limits of power, and when resistance is legitimate. Power, in a democracy, must reside in the people at least to the extent that they consent to the legitimacy of the decision-making process, even if they disagree with the outcome. It is commonly agreed that the fourth dimension of power, that which sees the capacity for resistance from those on whom power is exercised, has legitimate expressions. It is acceptable, for example, to withhold the fruits of your labour from your employers, by going on strike. It is acceptable to demonstrate your opposition to a policy or a government by marching in the streets. It is acceptable to wear items of clothing or carry with you objects that show your sympathy to a particular movement or its aims. Yet on 14 July 2019, in an attempt to protest the repression of their movement by the president and his ministers, some gilets jaunes defied the interdiction against demonstrating on or around the Champs-Élysées and attended the national celebration not wearing yellow vests, but carrying yellow balloons. They proceeded to boo the president as he rode a military command vehicle down the avenue, and some were arrested for organizing an illicit demonstration and for rebellion (AFP, 2019). It is difficult not to see these restrictions as attempts to silence political opponents who are not complying with the discipline imposed by the order in place. If the yellow colour itself is enough to see yourself get arrested, and if members of the public are forbidden to display political signs, the very freedoms of expression and association so dear to democrats are very much under threat.

A state for citizens

Who are the people that we have been discussing in this chapter on democracy? The rule of the people may be a truism of what democracy is, but the notion of the people itself, or of citizenship more widely, is not without contestation. As Gérard Noiriel (2018) argues, there is a difference between 'the people' and 'the working classes' (respectively, in French, *'le populaire'* and *'les classes populaires'*). 'The people' are thus not only the mass of the poor or the least well-off, but also those who are at the top and in the middle – in short, 'the people' is defined by the entire body of citizens. This thus excludes non-citizens – not just foreigners, but also those who have not yet acquired citizenship in the full sense, such as minors, and those who have lost their privileges, such as convicts. The body of citizens is, in the modern nation state, thus both inclusive, in that it encompasses all those who are considered to be citizens, and exclusive, in that it is defined against those who stand outside the state or have been for some reason excluded from it. It would be a mistake therefore to see the privileging of the nation in gilets jaunes protests, such as the singing of the *Marseillaise*, as a detail of the movement. It is a central part of the communal aspect of the movement. If anything, the gilets jaunes share very little in common – apart from being French. They believe in a system of national solidarity and redistribution, which they see as failing. Although they also have their local identities, they are citizens and nationals of a state that has responsibility over their well-being. This, of course, does not exclude solidarity outside the immediate (national) group, and on occasions solidarity has been seen between French and Belgian gilets jaunes, there could be spotted a Spanish flag flying in a gilets jaunes demonstration, and solidarity between different nationalities. We will see in Chapter 5 that internationalism is not excluded from the gilets jaunes model of economic justice. But the cement of the movement is national. They do not expect other states to come to their rescue, as the principal responsibility for citizens' well-being is still anchored in their own country. It is in this context that one can understand the scattered references to Frexit (a French exit from the European Union), or the symbolic taking down of European flags. Salvation is not to be found by recourse to more remote elites dispensing goods at their own volition from Brussels or Strasbourg, but citizens' rights and access to welfare are to be defended at the level of the state and with specific identification with the nation.

The gilets jaunes are thus a *popular* movement in that they have managed to engage all levels of the French people. From the low-earning workers to the small entrepreneurs that have formed the bulk of the gilets jaunes, there have been added the city-dwellers who have had their routines perturbed by the actions of these protesters, and the high-earners and chic upper-bourgeoisie, who have had their Saturday shopping on the Champs-Élysées interrupted by the outpourings of rage and the breaking of conventions about where it is appropriate to demonstrate. One of the largest problems with the movement, indeed, has been its refusal to accept police interdictions against demonstrating in the exclusive centres of towns and cities. Perhaps it was the desire of the movement to bring home to those who benefited from the abolition of the ISF (*l'impôt de solidarité sur la fortune*), the tax on wealth, that their actions have consequences, even for them, or perhaps it was just the will to disobey and show that they cannot easily be controlled – either way, the consensus that existed between the police and trades unions in the past about controlled and managed demonstrations has been shattered by the gilets jaunes. They have universalized their movement, in the sense that it touches upon each and every layer of French society – from the lowest to the highest.

There is one notable exception to participation in the movement: those from the infamous banlieues, the sites of social exclusion and often dominated by French citizens who are 'from a migrant background' [*issus de l'immigration*]. While a few of these citizens have participated on some occasions, notably in Marseille, many reported being afraid of participating, fearing being targeted by police during demonstrations because of their skin colour (Parikh, 2019). Noticeable by their absence, the youth from the banlieues are the big exception for the claim of the movement to be a true popular movement, in the sense that it engages (even if only in reaction) all sectors of French society. Often described as a group of middle-aged, white reactionaries, the gilets jaunes are much more varied than this cliché suggests. They are young and old, former activists and first-time participants, male and female, workers and bosses. The unity of the movement has precisely been its lack of distinction, and although they are clearly more working-class than anything else, this working class is by no means a homogeneous group that they have managed to capture, as we saw in the Introduction when we described it as 'the small-mean class'. There are also important differences between the various participants in the movement. The list of demands that were published for them – no one really knows how they came about, though the authors claim they were a collective effort among 30,000 people – illustrates this. They demand economic justice, which we will come back to in the next chapter, but also a new politics of immigration. The four demands on immigration are vague, but informative: to treat the causes of forced migration; to provide proper support for asylum seekers; to send back those who have been denied asylum; and to launch a policy of integration for those who stay

(L'Obs, 2018). Clearly, the emphasis is on the control of the in-group, the community based on national values, and although this control is not without openness, it demands acceptance of existing values by those who arrive, rather than a compromise or adaptation. The nation is here perceived as something worth defending, open to a point, but also without compromise for its own values and limits. One can clearly see that the issue of secularism, dear to the great bulk of French citizens, is at the heart of the concerns here. Integration is demanded of those who are given hospitality, and this includes accepting the secular nature of French society. Given the tensions in the banlieues, in particular, between secular forces and those wishing to retain their Islamic values, one can also understand the reticence of some to participate in the gilets jaunes movement. The fact that the first fatal victim of police violence during this time was an elderly Muslim woman of Algerian origin who was born in Tunisia, Zineb Redouane, who was closing her blinds in Marseille when she was hit by a grenade fragment, adds to the irony of the situation. The segment of the population she belongs to has been largely absent from the movement, yet it has not been unaffected by it.

The government's actions against the gilets jaunes were not the beginning of police repression in France. The youth of the banlieues have experienced it for decades, and are much more aware of the arbitrariness of those who have charge of public authority and exercise violence in the name of others. Many police strategies during the gilets jaunes protests have their inception in the French state's response to what happens in the banlieues. The motorcycle police units known as the *voltigeurs* used to carry batons to hit their target and drive away at high speed. They now carry LBD 40 launchers. Offensive grenades had also been used widely in the past, resulting the death of Rémi Fraisse, a green protester, in 2014 (*Le Figaro*, 2014). The now infamous *Brigade Anti-Criminalité* (BAC), who dress in civilian clothes and wear an iconic red armband for identification as police officers, are typically operational in the banlieues rather than on the Champs-Élysées. That they carry batons (and hammers, on occasions) and are known for particular ruthlessness is well-known in the suburbs of Paris, Lyon or Marseille. Police repression did not start in November 2018, at the inception of the movement. It has been endemic in the country, and its wider use against protagonists who were not typically targets of such acts of policy repression is a surprise only to those who have not been paying attention. The French state has indeed treated the inhabitants of the banlieues as second-class citizens – even though the great bulk of them are French, and now many are third- or fourth-generation 'immigrants' – and this attitude has now spread to others in society. When one begins to take away rights and privileges from one segment of society, it is without doubt a slippery slope for others who disagree with those in positions of power. As we have seen in this chapter, though, power is not unidirectional. The gilets jaunes are the potent reply to the exercise of power that has gone on for decades. Commentators in France had been warning that many situations – in the banlieues, in peri-urban areas, in factories, in inner cities, and so on – were reaching breaking point. That commentators are surprised now that the situation has (sometimes quite literally) exploded in places is ironic.

Commentators on the movement have largely been from the middle segments of French society. Journalists, politicians, intellectuals have often labelled the movement and attempted to put their own spin on it. As Noiriel notes, this is typical of popular movements in France since the high Middle Ages: it is often the dominant classes that have been able to put their label on them. Whether it is the characterization of the gilets jaunes as a jacquerie following the peasant revolts of the fourteenth century, as a *poujadiste* movement following the anti-tax protests of the 1950s, or simply calling the movement a populist right-wing uprising in the most pejorative manner possible, this process of labelling has been widespread. Needless to say, as Noiriel (2018: 35) notes, these characterizations are largely baseless and irrelevant. Even the most sympathetic of commentators, who see the movement as a type of revolution, miss out that revolutions typically involve the seizing of power (through the state and its institutions). The middle classes have been attempting to classify, analyse and define the movement, based on their particular affinities for or against its aims and goals. But they miss out that the movement itself has claimed its own origins in its own words. Though a few spoke of revolution, or wrote it on their banners, most speak of their action as a popular movement (Noiriel, 2018: 34). Who are we to undermine their own understanding?

Conclusion

The national dimension of the movement is clearly established. Although it is largely working class, it has involved many other segments of society and can best be described as a movement of the small-middle stratum of citizens – either lower-middle class or upper-working class – what we described as 'the small-mean class' in the Introduction. It has been foreshadowed by police tactics against the banlieues; it has involved the most modest parts of French society directly, who have largely contributed to the movement, the middle classes, who have been commenting on it and trying to portray it as a jacquerie, or peasant revolt, and the upper classes, who have seen their iconic boulevards closed off and vandalized.

5

Economic Justice

Economics has been at the forefront of social contract theory since at least the seventeenth century. When John Locke published his *Two Treatises of Government* (1689/1988), the English throne had just forcibly changed hands in favour of William III, the former president (*stadtholder*) of the Netherlands, in an episode of history worthy of the best of television dramas to date. Locke himself claimed that his book sought to justify the accession of William to the throne, although he had probably written most of it much before the Glorious Revolution. The dubious game of thrones that followed the invasion of England by a group of Dutch soldiers, the use of the Dutch fleet and the eventual accession of an Anglo-Dutch foreign leader to the throne, was not only like a medieval power play, but reflected the new realities of the land-owning classes of a growing empire. The invasion was justified as the preservation of the Protestant religion, liberty, property and a free Parliament (where these land owners were represented). Very concerned with establishing the rights of major property owners in his time, Locke in his *Two Treatises* defended a vision of private property which suited their needs perfectly. Those who work the land, or who invest in it to make improvements, he claimed, have a rightful claim to the ownership of the land, irrespective of customary rights to the land that had existed beforehand. Through a mystical and theological grounding, Locke created the modern theory of private property, which claims that God had given land to men in common, but that depriving others of the land was justified if you mixed your own labour with it. Its Protestant ethics – that salvation is to be achieved through labour – further strengthened the deposing of a Catholic monarch. The famous Lockean theory of property, thus, established the rights of major land owners both at home and abroad, as the appropriation of the commons – land of essentially communal usage that was quickly being privatized by major land owners – and colonial expansion into the Americas were ruthlessly defended against prior users of the land. Locke had himself participated in the writing of the Constitution of the Carolinas, essentially a (social) contract between the eight Lords Proprietors of the province of Carolina, promoting their territorial claims, reinforcing their aristocratic privileges, justifying serfdom and legalizing slavery. Coming from a founding father of liberalism, this may seem a surprise. But it is not merely accidental – liberalism in the Lockean sense, as in its contemporary incarnations, justifies extreme inequalities based on an absolute defence of private property. That Locke failed to challenge the accepted norms of his day in terms of servitude and slavery is not surprising: they reinforced the rights of land owners and he was committed to defending these rights in his works. In this chapter, we will see that liberalism of the twentieth century has not deviated much from these origins. Through Rawls and Nozick, we will see that large inequalities and an absolute defence of private property (especially of the wealthy) is still the dominant liberal model today in the twenty-first century. Macron will be placed precisely at the intersection of these two modes of liberalism: the Rawlsian justification of inequalities through an appeal to redistribution, and the Nozickean libertarian defence of private property. Macronism is a type of liberal-libertarian politics more widely characteristic of the post-Cold War consensus that attacks the economic role of the state, to replace it with a vaguely redistributive model for those at the lower end of the economic spectrum – let us call them the 99% – whereby the relatively better-off see part of their wealth redistributed to the least well-off. This is combined with enormous tax breaks and advantages for those at the top – let us call them the 1% – through corporate loopholes, where special tax exemptions and widespread privileged access to power are the norm. Such a model, however, is not inevitable. The economic role of the state was, for a good five decades, part of the post-war consensus. There is no reason why an increased role of the state in economic life is not possible. There is no good justification for the exclusion of economic life from the democratic input of the people.

It's the economy, stupid

Economic justice acquired a new meaning after the Second World War. Faced with the task of rebuilding devastated nations and the threat of the rising popularity of communism at home, Western European governments adopted a widespread palette of instruments to bring about social and economic justice. In France, the ordinance of 4 October 1945 established social security, universalizing for all citizens coverage that had only existed pre-war through trades unions or for civil servants. This predates the instauration of the Fourth Republic, which nonetheless includes social security in its Constitution the following year. In the United Kingdom, the creation of the NHS, voted for in 1946, answered a similar need for added economic justice and medical security extended to all – it had already existed in France since the late 1920s. These social and economic advantages available for all reflect the needs of a society that appeases its working classes, and offers them benefits in exchange for social peace and collaboration in the rebuilding effort. It is perhaps as much an artefact of the geopolitical realities of the Cold War, where these benefits (and more) were available on the other side of the ideological divide. It was difficult for Western capitalist economies to claim that their economic model was better than that socialist world if their own workers could not afford basic services available to all in the USSR. More fundamentally, the divide was not only between two conceptions of economic justice, but also between two conceptions of rights.

In 1966 at the height of the Cold War, the capitalist and communist blocks opposed each other on the subject at the United Nations. Two fundamental sets of rights were established as 'universals': civil and political rights were advocated by the former, while economic, social and cultural rights were put forward as primordial by the latter. The emphasis on one set of rights was clear from the start: for the 'democracies' of the West, the emphasis was on political contestation, freedom of political association, and individual rights. For the 'people's democracies' of the East, the emphasis was on economic growth, the provision of basic social and cultural services, and political unity behind these goals. While most countries in the world adopted both of the conventions that ensued, the United States never ratified the convention on economic, social and cultural rights, while China never ratified that on civil and political rights. The Western welfare state, although it had already secured advances before the Second World War, exploded in scope and strength in the early years of the Cold War. The social contract could no longer be contained within the realm of formal politics, constitutional arrangements and civil rights. The material needs of people and the distribution of wealth in society became central issues for the legitimacy of a country. The social contract was in practice taking an economic turn.

It is at the height of the Soviet-style challenge to Western capitalist economies that the philosopher John Rawls revived the dormant theory of the social contract. If talk of the contract that unites a people had fallen into disrepute among philosophers, it is not because it lacked relevance, however. Throughout the nineteenth century, and the first decades of the twentieth century, the social contract was in practice still very useful as a concept, as many nation states emerged after decolonization or the fall of empires, or through unification of old feudal lordships. It is ironic that as the world was going through hundreds of exercises in social contract practice, social contract theory was hardly discussed by philosophers. Perhaps it had become so commonplace that its purpose as a critical tool had lost its edge. In the next chapter, I will come back to the critical potential of the social contract, but for now let us focus on the return of the social contract as a tool of philosophical analysis.

The central figure of the revival, Rawls, remains a major figure of political thought today. His *Theory of Justice*, published in 1971, is still widely read, commented on, and forms the basis of many debates.[1] There is even a musical after the magnum opus of Rawls, which premiered in Oxford in 2013! To my knowledge, no other philosopher has had this privilege. What makes Rawls so special? Two things are important for my argument here. In the first instance, he revives the theory of the social contract at a time when political representation in Western democracies is entering a period of serious crisis – an epoch that we are still living through today. In the second instance, he manages to capture the post-war economic consensus in his work, and (re)introduces the notion of economic justice to the debate on the social contract. Let us deal with these two achievements in turn.

Rawls (1971) revives the social contract, which had largely become of historical interest rather than philosophical value. His theory of justice operates on the same level as previous theories, in that he is concerned with the legitimacy of particular constitutional arrangements, the provision of rights and duties, and justification for the modern state in its current form. Rawls notoriously avoids the concept of the state of nature, though, preferring a mind-game to the more problematic essentialist claims about human beings made by previous social contract theorists. He proposes that, in order to understand the justice of public institutions, we must place ourselves in the original position, behind a veil of ignorance. The original position – where we do not know any particular features about ourselves, such as our ethnic background, our personal wealth or level of education, our occupation, our conception of the good, or (as he later added), our gender – acts as a guarantee of the fairness of the institutions devised. The reasoning is that if we might end up anywhere in society, we would devise a system that is at least bearable for those at the bottom, those Rawls calls the 'least advantaged'. A theory of justice based on this original position would thus create a political system where all citizens are fairly treated, and in particular where you would ensure that wherever you end up, you could live a fulfilling life irrespective of what that life is defined as. It is a typical liberal social contract, in that it refuses to give a conception of the good based on a set of comprehensive principles, but provides a framework where individuals are left alone to choose for themselves what those goods are, and the role of the political community is merely to enable this choice.

Rawls' social contract is one where all actors in society accept that redistribution of wealth is in everyone's interest. But this redistribution also makes income inequalities legitimate. It is in fact part of Rawls' second principle of justice – the difference principle – that stipulates this. Inequalities, Rawls concludes, are justified as long as they benefit the least advantaged. It is perfectly acceptable, for Rawls, to have wide (even widening) inequalities in society, as long as everyone is trending upwards. It is, he hopes, a rather intuitive notion of justice. If everyone is getting richer, it is acceptable that those who lead the change get even richer than others. It is this liberal principle that drives Macron's 'lead climber' analogy, described in Chapter 1. The economic leaders are those who take the risks, and enjoy the rewards, of their entrepreneurial behaviour. They then also pull up all the others below them. Never mind the fact that this is not how climbing works (the lead climber does take the risks, but she does not pull others up the mountain), the message from Macron is compatible with a liberal contract such as Rawls'. Inequalities are not only acceptable, they are fully justified and even desirable. Without the incentive of vast economic wealth, creativity and innovation are curtailed – or so goes the liberal mantra. Any promotion of equality is a substantive good – that is, one that the liberal state cannot take sides on without overstepping its role. The liberal state thus makes other models of the state illegitimate: both the socialist version, for it seeks a substantive good of equality, but also the conservative state, which aims to preserve national values. Both socialist and conservative variants are *de facto* asking too much, and do not allow individuals to flourish among their midst. Macron's version of liberalism is closest to Rawls, although the libertarian challenge remains strong.

Robert Nozick, in his *Anarchy, State, and Utopia*, had argued that Rawls' principles of justice demand too much of the state (Nozick, 1974/2001). Redistribution of goods, even under the strict provisions set by Rawls, was too much for the libertarian thinker Nozick. Using Locke as a model for the defence of a notion of property based on ownership of one's body, Nozick claims that any transfer of property is an affront on the body of the person. Since we acquire goods by mixing our labour with the products themselves, as Locke had reasoned, anything we work on becomes our own and is thus considered justly acquired. We then enter in a series of contracts with others in order to trade goods we have produced with goods we need, and the role of the state is strictly to make sure these contracts are observed by various parties. Never mind the fact that this is not either how property, in the modern sense, is acquired or how wealth is created, Nozick remains adamant that his model of property is the most realistic. If all of our property has been acquired through our own labour, taking it away, even through taxation, is akin to forced labour. There is something intuitive about this model, too. When we work to acquire things, the act of taking those things arbitrarily does feel like forced labour. But applying this equally to the worker earning the minimum wage, to the landlord living off his rents, and the shareholder enjoying her dividends is odd at best. Although Nozick explains that any property justly acquired can be disposed of as one wishes, it still raises issues when it comes to inheritance, what exactly counts as just acquisition in an economic model where shares and rents generate enormous incomes for a few select individuals, and how economic actors at the highest levels are really independent from the machinery of government. When a major corporation secures a contract overseas with the help of its home government, can it really claim to have only acquired its wealth through its own merit and labour? Certainly, many questions raised by the gilets jaunes point to scepticism of such libertarian ideals, even if many of its participants seem on the surface to be close to Nozick's libertarianism. They proposed, for example, that large economic actors pay high taxes, giving the examples of McDonald's, Google, Amazon, and Carrefour [a French supermarket giant], while small economic actors (artisans, small and medium-sized businesses) should pay low taxes. Closer to Rawls than to Nozick, the gilets jaunes here demand that small businesses should be treated with the same level of care and attention that any relatively weak economic actor deserves. Their call for economic justice could not be clearer, and is pro-business and pro-individual choice, at least to the extent that it aims to favour local and national businesses against large and international competition.

The liberal-libertarian compromise

Rawls' model is not just opposed to Nozick's; it further stands in opposition to socialist ideals, where a notion of the good is put forward and priorities argued from a substantive position. More social protection, better healthcare, free and accessible education, control of the economic resources of the state are all assumed as goods to be promoted by a socialist model. Rawls, as a liberal, refuses this imposition of a social good. Only the individual, with their particular priorities, can set such a good, and society needs to stay clear of the path of its members. But Rawls also stands in contrast to the libertarian ideal, such as that defended by Nozick.

It was the hope of many French voters that Macron, the centrist who followed a socialist and a conservative president, would side with the likes of Rawls who seek to guarantee social justice as fairness. After weeks of gilets jaunes protests, Macron finally introduced the first measure that goes in this direction, with the revaluation of the minimum wage. This minimum wage will be paid out of taxpayers' money – not employers' pockets, as Macron announced – placing him closer to Rawls than to Nozick. The introduction of a tax on fuel further suggests that Macron is not against using taxes as a lever to achieve his goals, while on the other hand the abolition of the ISF suggests a much more free-market attitude. This has shocked many of the gilets jaunes, particularly those who are closer to the libertarian ideal than to the socialist one. The small entrepreneurs, artisans and self-employed workers who joined the protests at its inception are not close to the trades unions or other forms of public organization familiar with social protests. They are not the natural ally of the urban working classes who work in industry or construction, or as employees of the state. Yet they donned their gilets jaunes, occupied the roundabouts, and marched in the streets of the metropolises. What seems clear to them, and is certainly difficult to refute, is that Macron is stuck in a double bind. On the one hand, he supports a libertarian ideal for the richest in society, for the corporate boards and their owners, and on the other hand, he supports a more redistributive model *à la* Rawls for the rest of society. A liberal-libertarian mishmash, with hints of social redistribution and benefits for the least advantaged, but also increased freedom from regulation and taxation for those at the top. Needless to say, few are happy with such a mixture.

Neither Rawlsians nor Nozickeans would accept this as a worthy compromise. After all, in the 1970s, when they wrote their books on the social contract, the federal rate of income tax in the US was above 70 per cent for the highest earners. A real battle of wealth redistribution was at stake – one that Rawls lost to Nozick, with US tax rates for the richest at a bare 37 per cent in 2019 – and one that is still raging in France today. Rawls' liberal defence of inequalities has its faults, but it also defended the existing heavy taxation of the richest in society – the top 1 per cent of earners (those earning $352,000 and above in 2010 dollars, according to Piketty [2013: 468]). This level of redistribution was already on the decline at the time – the highest band of income had been taxed at between 80 per cent and 90 per cent from the 1930s to the 1960s – and Rawls can at least be seen as defending a fairness in taxation for those at the top. But revenues from work, as well as revenues from capital, are taxed relatively leniently at the moment, compared to their historical levels. In France, the top income tax bracket is currently 45 per cent, a little higher than in the US, but tax on dividends of capital is currently only 30 per cent. As the richest 1 per cent typically have an income comprised of both salary and the returns on capital investment, it means that on average the richest 1 per cent pay less tax than the disparity in income tax suggests. Supposing an equal split between the revenue from work and capital for someone situated in the top 1 per cent of earners (let us say, a €200,000 salary, and income from dividends on share investments of €200,000 a year), they will end up paying €64,200 of tax on their salary and €60,000 on their dividends – or 37.9 per cent tax overall – hardly a crippling level of taxation for the richest in society. Those with even higher revenues, the top 0.1 per cent of earners, typically have revenues coming mostly if not exclusively from capital, meaning their rate of taxation would be tending towards 30 per cent. Such a regressive taxation system, where the top 1 per cent pay less tax than middle-class professionals, and where the top 0.1 per cent of earners pay even less tax than these, is largely contributing to perceptions of growing inequalities today. Even the gilets jaunes have not fully perceived this level of inequality, often focusing their attention and criticism on those with high salaries. One of the demands of the gilets jaunes, indeed, was limiting salaries to €15,000 a month – effectively taxing any earnings above that rate at 100 per cent. In short, it is a call for economic justice that is at the forefront of the gilets jaunes' demands. That they have not made similar demands on dividends is perhaps a function of the lack of experience they have in this area – it is unlikely that many who took part in the protests have more than a tiny percentage of their income coming from rents and the revenues from capital.

The gilets jaunes' demands

Economic justice is the best summary of many of the 42 demands put forward by the gilets jaunes.[2] The measures themselves, the fruits of a collaborative effort that the authors say involved collaboration between 30,000 participants, are certainly not quite representative of what all the gilets jaunes would want to see change in present-day France. Yet, since they were published relatively early in the history of the movement (on 28 November 2018), and since they have been widely shared and commented on, they form a helpful basis for understanding what economic justice means for those who participated in the drafting of the demands. The measures themselves broadly refer to housing, tax, public finance, employment and salaries, health, transport, education, the political system and migration. The measures in all of these areas relate at least partly to demands for economic justice. Even the measures suggested in the document on changes to the political system relate to the pay of members of parliament and of former presidents (to limit the former to the median wage, and to end the latter). Demands for migration are equally couched in terms of economic justice: the demand that the causes of migration be addressed suggests support for economic aid, and that for asylum seekers to be provided with decent accommodation and access to social services is an explicit demand for international social solidarity. Many of the other demands are straightforward calls for more equality and fewer advantages for large economic actors. Higher wages for the lowest earners, a lower level of public debt, more and better public services particularly in rural or peri-urban areas, an end to corporate exemptions from taxation and to austerity measures are all demanded with equal force. The point here is not to treat each measure in turn, but rather to identify the trends that these measures reflect. And the overall sentiment is a call for economic justice writ large. Let us ponder what the principles behind such economic justice can be.

Neither Rawls nor Nozick are fully acceptable in the context of the gilets jaunes. The libertarian Nozick rules out the fair usage of taxation beyond the minimum state, and Rawls justifies wide inequalities as long as the least advantaged benefit. Macron's politics, which blends the two models together to defend a liberal-libertarian compromise, is the worst of all worlds – satisfying none, by further increasing already high taxes for those without income from capital, and by deepening social injustice. What the gilets jaunes are demanding is closer to the pre-modern demands of a moral economy than what the liberal consensus offers. The moral economy, historically, surfaced during popular movements in the eighteenth century. The rules are based on what was considered popular common sense: that the price of commodities be fair and not too far above the cost of production, and that norms of reciprocity rather than those of the market regulate exchanges (Hayat, 2019a). When these moral demands on the economy were deemed to be violated, the people felt the right to rectify these violations themselves. These two demands, for fair prices and norms of reciprocity, are completely antithetical to the demands of a market economy. The market, not a moral decision, is supposed to set the price, and reciprocity is by no means a requirement of a modern economy, let alone in the labour market where many of the demands of the gilets jaunes take place. Only the guarantee of a minimum wage in law meets these moral demands, and even then, the gilets jaunes' demands for a significant growth in the minimum wage (the SMIC) to €1,300 a month have not quite been met by Macron's public relations stunt of announcing a €100 rise in the minimum wage in December 2018. In practice, the SMIC for a full-time worker is still €1,202.92 after tax in 2019, or 7 per cent short of the gilets jaunes' demands. A lot can be done with an extra €97 a month, particularly for those living from paycheck to paycheck. Their moral outrage stems from the favouring of those at the top – with the suppression of taxes on wealth – rather than those who struggle with their end-of-month bills.

If Rawls and Nozick, despite discussing an economic social contract, cannot account for the demands of the moral economy of the gilets jaunes, what can provide a solution? One can substitute Nozick's fair acquisition principle, or Rawls' difference principle for the principles of fairness and solidarity. These are, I argue, the principles put forward by the gilets jaunes themselves in the list of demands they present, and reflect broadly the demands for an economic social contract based on core values. Let me deal with these two principles in turn. Fairness was already defended by Rawls in his *Theory of Justice*, but I have shown that it ends up by justifying large inequalities. Fairness, in this respect, is thus clearly insufficient for the demands of contemporary social movements, which all seek higher levels of equality. Whether it is the Occupy movement in the United States or the gilets jaunes, the opposition between the 1 per cent and the 99 per cent or the demands for strict national controls on wages, pensions and public finance, the demands are all aiming for higher levels of equality. The Rawlsian acceptance of unequal outcomes, in other words, is unacceptable in the current political climate. There are good reasons for this change of heart. Since the early 1970s, wealth inequalities have grown enormously (Piketty, 2013).

Economic fairness has been taken seriously by a variety of theorists of deliberative democracy. Brian Barry (1989) in particular has done much to address some of the shortcomings of Rawls and Nozick. Against the *a priori* social contract of these thinkers, Barry accounts for an empirical method of the social contract where the individual circumstances of various democratic practices matter in the quality of political deliberation. How closely a particular society fits the particular ideals of the social contract is a matter both for theoretical discussion and empirical investigation. Among the various criteria he discusses for such an empirical fit is the quest for sympathy engendered towards others living with us in society. As he explains, 'a society in which there is a good deal of fellow feeling for other citizens will be closer to the circumstances of impartiality than one in which many people are unmoved by the lot of sections of the population with which they do not identify' (Barry, 1989: 348). Together with other criteria for impartiality, including the ability of various sectors in society to articulate their own interests and participate in political decision-making, and where politics is a matter for debate rather than an electoral game, the list reads like a set of deficiencies all modern democracies face today. Without these conditions of impartiality *à la* Barry, the outcome of the purely procedural theory put forward by Rawls can lead to inequalities that are difficult to stomach for those at the bottom of the economic ladder.

Fairness of outcome, which includes higher levels of equality between poorest and richest, is now a pressing social demand. The erosion of the power of the state is often blamed for rising inequalities, where states compete with each other in a race to the bottom of taxation for the wealthy and for big business. But this obfuscates the deliberate will of political elites to promote such inequalities. In France, it was under a socialist president, François Mitterrand, that this trend became the most obvious. The 'liberal' turn of the socialist party signalled the end of an economic alternative, with socialist governments happily taking part in the sale of public assets, the lowering of taxes for the richest, and corporate-friendly attitudes to regulation and financial services. The issue is endemic to liberalism writ large, which now encompasses right, left and centrist parties, who all accept the dogma of a hands-off approach to financial regulation – despite popular demands for increased control over economic matters. The liberal social contract has come to exclude collective control over the economy, preferring a laissez-faire mentality, where businesses regulate themselves while citizens are expected to bear the brunt of welfare costs and responsibilities. Any social contract that addresses the principle of fairness of outcome must therefore include the possibility of increased state control of the economy.

Fairness, as a value, has never been and cannot be the outcome of market processes. If fairness is indeed a principle to guide a new social contract, it demands higher involvement of the state in market practices. The precise nature of this control is up for debate – and indeed should only be decided by democratic means. We have seen in Chapter 4 that the economic demands of a democratic system can only be seen as legitimate if they are decided by the people assembled. It may be the case that the people assembled leave a significant area of economic life free from state interference. Certainly, the composition of the gilets jaunes points at least partly in this direction, with a plea for a smaller state being central to many of their demands. Visibly, though, some areas of the economy lend themselves particularly well to public control. Education, healthcare and national insurance are all areas of the economy where public control is already in place. But in other areas, such as transport, infrastructure, utilities, low-cost housing, and more, the state has been on the retreat. The state used to own or have a controlling role in many of these industries, including electricity, water and gas companies, car manufacturers (a demand of the gilets jaunes for a French car industry illustrates this call), highways, airports and hospitals. Since the 1980s at least, the trend has been reversed, with the consequence that there have been increased inequalities of access – with the high costs of private services making them prohibitive for many.

Many gilets jaunes do not contest the liberal capitalist economic model as long as it is perceived as one that values hard work, small to medium-sized businesses and an entrepreneurial spirit. What is being contested in the demands that they put forward is the type of rent-seeking capitalism that is so apparently in contradiction with economic justice. After all, it may be valued as *fair* that an economic actor who has a successful business lives well from it. What the gilets jaunes are reacting against, however, is non-productive financial capitalism, particularly of the rent-seeking kind. Demand 17 on their list, in particular, refers to the end of illegitimate state-incurred debt. Those who have bought debt that is deemed to be unfairly acquired should, according to the demand, forfeit their right to that debt and the repayments be halted immediately. More generally, David Graeber has argued that our very monetary system is the cause of such a rejection of illegitimate public debt. Why, he asks, since money is chiefly created through the issuing of monetary IOUs, is that power not more widely shared or even democratically decided upon? Instead of financial institutions creating money through these IOUs, he speculates, the monetary system could be restructured so that when new monies are created, they are shared equally among all citizens. This revolutionary proposal, he accepts, is not quite the demand of the gilets jaunes (Graeber, 2019). But they are nevertheless demanding something quite compatible with a rethinking of the financial system. The point is that financial institutions, through their exclusive right to issue IOUs in the form of money, have a rent-seeking monopoly that could be shared democratically. French motorways, owned by private companies, are also attracting the wrath of the gilets jaunes for similar reasons. Since there is no practical alternative for many motorists but to use these motorways, it can be considered a natural monopoly, and profits extracted from it a form of rent. Demand 28 specifically addresses this point of highways, with a demand that no profit be extracted from them. But it is rent itself that is the single biggest cost the gilets jaunes are attacking. A call for rent control forms the substance of demand 25. It specifically asks for controls for the most vulnerable of renters: students and precarious workers. At the root of the demands, thus, is a demand for fairness to be applied to the bare necessities of life. These include access to roads, trains, hospitals, education (at all levels, including universities), accommodation, food, heating, proper insulation and psychiatric help. Any profiteering in these sectors, considered to be vital to the well-being of all, is grouped together as immoral. It is to all forms of rent – that is, all charges for the necessities of life – that special economic moral standards are applied. Anyone getting rental income from public debt, from shares in highways, from housing, or profiting from these, while citizens see their access to such goods diminish, is perceived as having an unfair advantage. The economic analysis may be a little simplistic – but the message is clear: the market should not apply everywhere. It is one thing to make money from selling products one can live without; it is another to profit from goods considered essential for decent material well-being and a life worth living.

Solidarity and dignity

If fairness of outcome, not merely of process, is required in the moral demands of the gilets jaunes, it is equally backed by demands for reciprocity. In the French context, reciprocity is often phrased in terms of solidarity – *solidarité* is, after all, one of the three core values of the Republic, though certainly the most forgotten one. Reciprocity and solidarity formed some of the demands of the gilets jaunes, such as demands 8 and 10 relating to pensions. Pensions are notoriously polemical in France, as the disparities between pensioners reflect class structures very heavily, and show large gender inequalities (Observatoire des inégalités, 2013). In a state pension system where middle classes are favoured over working classes, and men favoured over women, the gilets jaunes have perceived these inequalities very vividly. They call for solidarity within the system, which in effect would level the playing field between classes, and for a minimum pension to be set at €1,200 a month, which would largely benefit women, who typically receive 42 per cent less than men because of the structure of the pension system that calculates pensions based on trimesters of contributions in full-time employment. A doubling of the minimum pension (currently set at €636.56) would *de facto* ask for increased solidarity from those earning at the top of the pension scale – or increased contributions overall, with the same effect on solidarity. The gilets jaunes' call for pension solidarity is a demand for higher reciprocity, where those who have contributed less financially, but have often done manual or care work, be favoured over those who have been more economically successful, as demand 36 makes clear.

Reciprocity is also demanded from elected officials. Since they are representatives of the citizens, their wages should be set at the median wage – which forms demand 11. At €1,719 in 2019, the median monthly wage is far below that of members of the National Assembly, currently standing at €7,239.91. The point is clear: if representatives are meant to represent those who have elected them, they cannot be earning four times what the median worker earns – let alone those on the minimum wage. Public representatives would thus have a direct incentive to increase the median wage – as it would affect their own material well-being. Demand 40 also calls for the end of lifelong presidential indemnities. With a pension top-up of €6,000 a month, a right to sit on France's Constitutional Council with an attached salary of €11,500, and permanent security and secretarial staff, the cost of France's four living ex-presidents at the end of 2018 was estimated at above €10 million a year. A minuscule sum for the budget of the state, this demand from the gilets jaunes can only be understood as a moral demand for reciprocity. With no other position in life subject to a permanent salary, let alone the staffing costs associated with presidential indemnities, the principle of reciprocity demands a fairer system for people who have essentially ceased their official functions. These demands on reciprocity from elected officials also show that economic justice, as demanded by the gilets jaunes, is not purely about cost-cutting or motivated by the bottom line of the balance sheet. It is a demand for reciprocity based on an equal valuing of the moral worth of persons: their dignity. If an ex-president requires €2.5 million a year, or a member of parliament €7,000 a month, to exercise their function with the dignity required, how can an ordinary citizen be expected to live with dignity on less than €1,300 a month?

Economic dignity is the final demand of the gilets jaunes. If they have also demanded security, liberty and democracy, they have made it clear that respect and dignity are key to living a fulfilling life. In this respect, it is Emmanuel Macron who has provoked the wrath of the gilets jaunes beyond repair. Since his accession to power in 2017, Macron has been thoroughly disrespectful to those people who are economically unsuccessful, to those below him in social standing and to any who do not share his vision of an economic model where elites carry the rest of society behind them. A few examples will help to contextualize this, for those not yet familiar with the most important controversies over the words and actions of the French president. In a backstage video clearly choreographed to show a more humane and down-to-earth president, Macron is sitting at his desk and talking about money being spent on social security. Sitting on a rococo-style chair adorned with gold, reminiscent of the most ostentatious style of the reign of Louis XV, Macron deplores that we are spending 'crazy dough' [*un pognon de dingue*] on helping the poor – and asks for urgent reforms of state spending on the matter (Colin, 2018). Macron's public relations stunt, attempting to portray him in a more favourable light speaking freely to his advisors, backfired considerably given the luxurious surrounding of his office. He had, however, not waited to enter the Élysée Palace, the residence of the President, before making such disdainful remarks about struggling citizens. In 2014, Macron shocked the general public when, as economics minister, he called the female workers at a slaughterhouse which was closing down "illiterate" (Drillon, 2014). Not only were the employees of the workplace not mostly women, as Macron had claimed, singling them out in his criticism, but he clearly had amalgamated low-skill jobs with lack of reading skills – as if education alone could land you a well-paid job in the remote region of Finistère, in the western-most corner of France. The most revealing phrase of the president's attitude towards those deemed insufficiently successful was uttered at a speech given to start-up entrepreneurs following his election to the presidency. As a self-styled political entrepreneur, he created his own political brand, *En Marche!*, in 2016, using his own initials to create a party that is now in power (Ventura, 2016) – the very definition of successful start-up. According to Macron, speaking in a converted railway station turned into this new entrepreneurial hub, "a railway station is a place where those who succeed and those who are nothing cross paths". 'Those who are nothing': the expression has the merit of being clear. Either you are a successful entrepreneur, or are similarly self-made and economically well off, or you are not worth a mention, a thought or consideration. Coming from a president who had just been elected after gathering a mere 24 per cent of the vote in the first round of the election – when there were alternative candidates to vote for other than Le Pen – this episode did not set his presidency on a unifying path, and certainly did not exemplify a respect for the dignity of those who had elected him.

It would be a mistake, however, to see Macron's role in the rise of the gilets jaunes movement as more than a catalyst of the wider economic system which ignores the value of human dignity. Macron may have attracted personal antipathy from the protesters, many of whom now see his resignation as a necessary part of the solution, but this is merely because he symbolizes the attitudes of successful economic actors towards those who are less successful. Nowhere is this more apparent than in the rise of property prices in contemporary economic life. Considered by many as a sign of a vibrant and successful economy, the rise in house prices has had the unfortunate effect of pricing lower earners out of desirable areas, relegating many to the periphery (and not the desirable wealthy suburbs or upmarket villages), thus increasing the need for private transport as a necessity for economic life. Out of range of public transport, needing to commute increasingly long distances for work, far from family and other networks that provided care and other services, citizens are now often vulnerable to fluctuations in energy prices for a large part of their budget. Squeezed by green initiatives that target all energy consumers indiscriminately, by austerity measures which close down state aid previously available, and by a labour market which requires increased mobility, a perfect storm has been brewing for a while, as the geographer Christophe Guilluy has claimed. Contested for his broad-sweeping claims and the many exceptions to these that he does not address, Guilluy's analysis is nonetheless prophetic of the current dilemma. In his 2016 book translated into English as *Twilight of the Elites* in 2019, he equates our contemporary geographies to those of medieval citadels, but where city walls have been replaced with the price of housing per square metre, effectively excluding millions from housing in the cities. Going from €2,480 per square metre in the mid-1990s, by the mid-2010s a Parisian flat sold for over €8,000 per square metre on average, with some areas as high as €15,000 (Guilluy, 2016/2019). This was almost five years ago; the average has now surpassed €10,000 per square metre. Even for a non-luxurious one-bedroom apartment – say, at 35 square metres – the price tag is beyond the reach of most workers – let alone those who have families and would like their children to have a bedroom. This led Guilluy to warn that the dominant class, though it has little to fear from city-based movements, has everything to fear from a radicalization of those excluded from this economic miracle: France in its peri-urban dimension (Guilluy, 2016/2019). The tax on fuel was only the trigger for a wider social malaise and existential crisis among those who have been excluded from the benefits of globalization and the liberal-libertarian consensus. The pressure cooker had been close to exploding for some time, and it only took the particular tactlessness of Macron and his government to increase the pressure to breaking point. This discontent has been the focus of parties at the extremes, in a series of attempts to galvanize the angry population behind their programme. But neither the Rassemblement National, Marine Le Pen's rebranded Front National, nor La France Insoumise, Mélenchon's splinter party to the left of the socialist party, have managed to gather the support of the gilets jaunes. Though at times clearly anti-European and preferring national businesses over foreign ones, the gilets jaunes have not flocked en masse to the existing extremes. To put this in the context of their call for economic justice, let us look at the international dimension of their social contract.

International justice

In *The Law of Peoples*, John Rawls makes the point that a social contract can be extended to the international level. In an article that sketches out the book, he claims that 'though the idea of justice I use to do this is more general than justice as fairness, it is still connected with the idea of the social contract' (Rawls, 1993: 37). Part of the social contract tradition, for Rawls, must include its relation to other societies, and this is the task he sets himself to do in *The Law of Peoples*. Which societies, he asks, should we tolerate and work with to pursue our goals and interests? A corollary of this is to ask which societies we should not tolerate and are justified in fighting against, by a variety of different means – either economic, diplomatic, or military. While the latter question is important, it is outside the scope of the present argument on the gilets jaunes and the social contract. There is little benefit in discussing just war theory or the use of international sanctions – however important these may be in a different context. Yet the first question of what is to be tolerated in other societies is important for the present context, as some of the suggestions of the gilets jaunes clash with the institutional framework of the European Union and other international organizations and need to be placed in the wider context of economic globalization.

It is worth noting that Rawls' own conception of justice, using a constructivist framework, itself assumes that the debate about the notion of justice and the social contract takes place at a national level, in a closed and self-contained society (Rawls, 1993: 39). It is also worth noting that Rawls' Law of Peoples is precisely not the Law of Nations or a series of international treaties that regulate international behaviour (Rawls, 1993: 43). While the latter exists as a result of international conflict and cooperation, the former remains an exercise in political legitimation: an international social contract theory. This is precisely the appeal of Rawls' theory. It is both about international matters for a particular people, and rests on the ideal conception of how these people ought to treat other peoples they interact with at an international level. Rawls argues that democratic societies will agree to seven principles of justice between them: (1) the freedom and independence of peoples; (2) their equality; the right to (3) self-defence and (4) non-intervention; (5) the observance of treaties; (6) limits on war, and (7) honouring human rights (Rawls, 1993: 46). Without going into much detail on each of these, I only wish to discuss here a clash between two sets of Rawls' principles. On the one hand, (1), (2) and (4) demand the independence and equality of peoples, and respect for non-intervention, and on the other hand, (5) demands the observance of treaties. These two sets of rights clash in the present context of the European Union and, more widely, economic globalization such as membership of the World Trade Organization or the International Monetary Fund, as the independence of states is threatened by the wider context of economic institutional cooperation and treaties.

It is not so much the principle of the observance of treaties that is at stake here – and Rawls' conception of the Law of Peoples need not be discarded altogether – but rather the reality of economic justice at the national level putting in jeopardy the complex web of international agreements already in place that favour a particular conception of economic activity where the role of the state is curtailed and strictly controlled. In the context of the Eurozone, it is the ability of member states to raise public debt that is limited by international treaties, particularly by the Stability and Growth Pact (SGP), which provides a set of rules to be obeyed by members of the Eurozone. Specifically, member states with a budget deficit that exceeds 3 per cent of GDP fall under the corrective arm of the SGP and in principle end up in the Excessive Deficit Procedure (EDP). The European Commission then reviews the excessive deficit and makes recommendations to the country to remedy the situation. In 2019, following new spending measures, some of which were meant to address the protests of the gilets jaunes, France predicted breaking the SGP rule relating to the deficit, with a forecast of a 3.1 per cent deficit for the year. In addition, France has consistently broken the rule that overall debt should be at no more than 60 per cent of GDP, with debt in 2019 standing at 99 per cent of GDP. This breaking of the rules led to a European Commission report on France, which did not make recommendations for changes in policy, noting that the projected deficit for 2020 was below the 3 per cent threshold (European Commission, 2019). However, the EDP has led to severe economic restrictions in other cases. In Greece, Italy and Spain notably, following the financial crisis of 2008, large measures were imposed to reduce public spending and raise revenue, leading to austerity policies imposed on struggling economies. With the potential for punitive sanctions of up to 0.5 per cent of GDP following three consecutive years of breaches of the Pact, these measures can severely restrict the ability of a member state to raise spending in times of need. In fact, the Pact is designed to limit the fiscal policies of member states, and has had mixed successes in doing so, according to Jasper De Jong and Niels Gilbert (2019).

This restriction of fiscal policy at an international level, between democratic countries having signed treaties to that effect, raises an important question in the context of the gilets jaunes and the international social contract. The Pact described above, agreed in 1997, imposes limitations on fiscal policy in a member state under the threat of economic sanctions (the UK being the exception here, since it secured an opt-out clause for the sanctions, and has since left the European Union). Although these sanctions were never used, their very existence meant that recommendations could become binding, and this has generally led to at least some level of compliance. This effectively limits the scope of action for national governments, although it does not quite tie their hands completely. An increase in government spending to promote increased economic activity can thus be limited by the adherence to a previously agreed treaty, in terms that have made an important difference for the citizens of many European countries. In effect, the principle of non-intervention is not applied here, by adhering to the principle of observance of treaties. This would not be a very significant development, if European treaties were not notoriously difficult to revise; once agreed, it requires the approval of all member states to modify them. Of course, there are still policy alternatives within the treaties of the European Union that would have allowed France's leaders to address economic justice over the years. Any increase in spending can be compensated for by an increase in revenues, but this is easier said than done in periods of economic downturn. As successive generations of politicians have blamed 'Brussels' for the decisions they themselves, and their predecessors, took there, to tighten the rules that prevent them from easing the purse strings in times of need, it is hardly surprising that the gilets jaunes have at times expressed their anger at European institutions. This is not limited to the European Union, and although I will provide a short comparison between the gilets jaunes and the Brexit vote in the Conclusion to the book, it is the principle of international agreements that is at stake here. As these agreements are considerably more difficult to alter than national laws or even constitutions, it raises the question of their democratic validity decades after they were signed. Any democratic international social contract would need to address this question of international treaties, and the limits they impose on national democratic institutions.

Part of the limitation of a theory of an international justice such as Rawls', as with his theory of justice at the national level, is its proceduralism. The establishment of a just social order is predicated on the following of certain rules or procedures which seem to more or less guarantee the legitimacy of institutions established. If, to take the example above, European Union member states agree to procedures regarding fiscal policy, these are legitimate in establishing constraints on them in perpetuity – at least until they are revised. One of the issues with excessive proceduralism, however, is that it fails to account for the circumstances, some of which would have been unforeseen at the time of signing the treaties, or the power dynamics that exist between stronger and weaker states negotiating these procedures. It is unreasonable to expect Greece, for example, to have the same negotiating power as Germany when it comes to European Union finances. There are, however, alternatives to this model of thin proceduralism. One such model could be a thicker model of international solidarity. As with the international debate on economic justice in France where the gilets jaunes called for greater solidarity between social actors, a model of increased solidarity at the international level can be defended against the legalistic and rigid model that Rawls prefers. This is the argument made by Philip Cunliffe (2018) in relation to the European Union. Preferring a model of internationalism over cosmopolitanism, Cunliffe argues for the thickening of social bonds between states, without the creation of international institutions and structures. The absence of a sense of solidarity in Rawls' Law of Peoples is notable in this respect. Instead of enshrining rules of behaviour in institutions, a model supported by solidarity between states can be promoted as a viable alternative.

Three of the demands made by the gilets jaunes can be taken to illustrate this demand for international solidarity. Demand 14 asked for an end to work placements in other countries – sometimes called *social dumping* by commentators. While this demand can be interpreted as being against migration from other European Union countries, it clearly is not phrased in those terms. It merely asks that those working in France conform to French employment rules, rather than the employment rules of their employer's country. Read generously, this demand protects foreign workers in France, who otherwise may see their rights limited by their employer who is based in another EU state. Read less generously, it protects French workers and employers from competition from other areas of the EU where social protections are less expensive. Under both readings, however, the terms of solidarity are clear. On the one hand, it provides solidarity towards foreign workers in France, and on the other, it protects French businesses from what is perceived as unfair competition. Demands 18 and 19, that the causes of immigration be treated and that asylum seekers receive good treatment, both provide for international solidarity. Far from excluding foreigners, in this case including immigrants and asylum seekers from outside the EU, these demands ask for increased solidarity towards people in need in other states. For the gilets jaunes, the demands of international justice are ones of increased solidarity, coupled with a demand for political action at the level of the state. Although they deserve more treatment and detail than I can provide here, suffice to say that they depart in important ways from Rawls' more procedural approach. Notably omitting the duty to observe treaties of the past, the gilets jaunes' demands call for the revision of the terms of international justice. But it would take a particularly cynical reading of their demands to not see that their aim is towards increased solidarity, not closed borders and the end of all immigration.

Conclusion

Macronism is not a uniquely French phenomenon. Like Thatcherism and Reaganism previously, it reflects a consensus between the winners of globalization and the economic order of a post-Cold-War world. The small-mean class, comprised of the working classes as well as the lower middle class that largely form the movement of the gilets jaunes, has been sacrificed at the altar of austerity, privatization and the retreat of the state from social services. The particular brand of liberal-libertarianism being promoted by Macron is reminiscent of the worst aspects of Rawls and Nozick – with small amounts of wealth redistribution justifying large inequalities, and a laissez-faire economic model for those at the very top. A new social contract is desperately needed, one that gives economic concerns their proper weight and addresses the need for justice and solidarity discussed in this chapter. In the next, concluding, chapter, I will show that such a model is possible. A new social contract will take into account the need for liberty, democracy and economic justice which we have discussed in Chapters 3 to 5.

6

A Renewal of the Social Contract

Perhaps the most important lesson of the gilets jaunes and their challenge to the existing social contract in France is in their being and becoming. Who could have predicted in November 2018 that the movement would still be active, if somewhat diminished, more than a year later and that it would take a global pandemic to stop their weekly gatherings? Who could have predicted that some of these demonstrators would be present each and every Saturday during that time, in blazing heat and freezing cold, in peaceful protest and in violent interactions, in large numbers as well as small? The very being of the movement is in itself an achievement, regardless of its failure or success. Anyone who has participated in a social movement will know that it shapes your expectations, your interactions with others, and the social context around it. I participated in the Great University Strike of 2018, the largest strike ever seen in higher education in the United Kingdom, which culminated in four weeks of protests on campuses throughout the country. Of a much smaller scale than the movement of the gilets jaunes, it nonetheless changed relations on campuses in a meaningful way. It is fair to say that there is a 'before' and an 'after' the strike, and as such it constitutes an event. The event of the gilets jaunes is on a different scale of importance altogether. There is a 'before' and an 'after' the gilets jaunes crisis, and although the after is yet to be seen, time will tell how social relations changed and whether it was for the better or for the worse. Although the becoming of the movement is still uncertain, as we will see in the Conclusion, it is clearly an opportunity for change and for rethinking the terms of the social contract that shape how we interact with each other, and how institutions shape the type of outcomes we can hope for from the political process. As such, one of the greatest achievements of the movement to date has already happened: it has called for a renewal of the terms of the political association to include more participative democracy; it has called for a renewal of the social contract.

The gilets jaunes have achieved a change in the policies of the French government in the course of their first year-and-a-half of activity, and brought to the fore the question of inequalities in society. They have reversed the decision to introduce a green tax that would indiscriminately target all motorists. They have secured a pay rise for the lowest-paid workers in French society. They have alerted the general public to the inequalities of the suppression of the tax on wealth, and have called, so far unsuccessfully, for its reinstatement. They have shown that the state is ready to repress, maim and kill to enforce order against a movement that shakes its quiet consensus. They have slowed down the pace of liberal-libertarian reforms by the French president, Emmanuel Macron. They have galvanized opinion and forced everyone to side with or against their plight, in favour of or against the government's response and agenda. They have created a sense of political engagement that, even if only short-lived, will nonetheless cause many arguments and much discussion in the years to come, at the workplace, among friends, in the family, in cafes and with strangers on the streets and roundabouts. They have shown that the social body is ill, and in need of treatment. What I propose to do here is to offer a pharmacology of the movement: in the sense that the movement both represents a profound social malaise and demands an answer that needs to be thought through and discussed; and in the sense that the movement itself offers part of the solution to the disease it is a symptom of. I will show that Diderot, with his particular wit and fine sense of ambiguity, is best placed to give us an account of the social ill that is apparent in the current gilets jaunes crisis, and to phrase it in terms of a social contract problem. Diderot's metaphor of the healing knee in his posthumously published novel *Jacques the Fatalist* of 1796 illustrates a powerful alternative to the model of kneeling and crawling demanded by the authoritative figure of the state, in particular the president, and the social contract it represents.

Jacques and his master

'How did they meet? By chance like everyone else. What were their names? What's that got to do with you? Where were they coming from? From the nearest place. Where were they going? Does anyone ever really know where they are going to?' (Diderot, 1796/1986: 21). These opening lines from *Jacques the Fatalist* apply just as much to the story of Jacques and his master as they do to the gilets jaunes who have been out on the roundabouts of France since November 2018. Characterized as a jacquerie, a peasant revolt, by their adversaries, the gilets jaunes are the Jacques of the twenty-first century. Just like Jacques in Diderot's tale, they are insolent, disrespectful and at times violent, but their master, who remains nameless and thus could be anyone, needs Jacques all the more because of these features. Instead of a tale of Jacques' loves, which Diderot painfully unfolds with a thousand detours as they travel aimlessly through pre-revolutionary France, it is a tale of the gilets jaunes' anger that is at stake here. One emotion is swapped for another – love for hate, tenderness for social conflict – as the whole travel story behind Jacques and his master's wanderings further seems to be a roundabout *avant la lettre*. Much like a present-day motorist who might go round and round the poorly decorated central island of the roundabout without ever reaching its centre, Jacques' tale seems to meander endlessly around the story of his loves. The two protagonists err without a clear goal in the French countryside, never revealing the purpose of their travels or their destination to the reader. Jacques and his master are trapped in a large circle that goes round and round, touching upon the question of Jacques' loves and the affective dimension of their own existence. The gilets jaunes' choice of the roundabout, at the beginning of the movement, also exemplified the seeming fluidity of traffic in the modern urban space, which keeps going forward while going nowhere. Unlike other urban developments, the roundabout is not a destination in itself, it rarely features as an address to enter in one's GPS or as a place where one can stop for long. That they chose to express their anger there, in a public space where things seemingly go nowhere, where life never stops to reflect on the futility of the existence of this architectural oddity, is a poetic formulation of the movement as a whole. The affective dimension of the gilets jaunes' story, however, is not to unveil their loves – although love is not absent from the bright yellow roundabouts – but rather to share their anger and disillusion. Jacques, ever the fatalist (we would use the term 'determinist' to describe Jacques' philosophical outlook), believing that everything that happens is pre-ordained on a huge scroll in the sky, puts the problem succinctly: 'Are we ever the master of when we fall in love? And if we were, are we the master to act as if we weren't?' (Diderot, 1986: 36). Are the gilets jaunes masters of their anger, and if they are, are they expected to control or hide it? Emotions have power over us, and it is understanding their anger that is at stake here, just as it is understanding Jacques' loves that is at stake in Diderot's tale.

The first misadventure of Jacques and his master says volumes about Jacques' propensity to use violence to right an injustice. After a day of riding, the two protagonists stop at an inn, which has just been robbed by a group of bandits, who are eating and drinking the supplies they stole from the owners of the inn in one of the rooms. Jacques and his master are served a few scraps by their apologetic hosts, but the bandits, proud of their own achievements and of their feast, taunt them by sending chicken bones over to the protagonists' room. Jacques, angered by this personal insult, takes his master's gun, barges into the bandits' room, and takes all of their clothes at gunpoint. He then goes back to his master, after locking the bandits in their room, and barricades their own bedroom door, falling asleep unperturbed by the risk that they might knock down the door in revenge, while his master panics and fears for his life. After all, whether they take revenge or not is written on the great scroll up in the sky, according to Jacques' own fatalist philosophy, and there is little he can do to alter that. Jacques and his master escape unscathed the next morning, with the satisfaction that Jacques has taught the bandits a lesson. Justice has been served, if only from a personal standpoint. Indeed, Jacques' selfishness does not extend to helping others out of the kindness of his heart, as he did nothing to help the innkeeper and his family. Instead, Jacques saved face and his honour by replying to the insult with force, reinforcing his sense of worth and dignity. Impervious to the danger this desire for recognition made him run, Jacques shows the power that dignity can have as a motivating force.

The gilets jaunes also demand and claim their own dignity in the face of what they perceive as despising state authorities. Faced with the disdain of their highest elected official, the president of the republic, who sees them as unsuccessful victims of their own bad choices, they rebel against public insults and disdain shown by those in power. As we discussed in Chapter 4, power is more diffuse than is often expected by those at the top, and a revolt from the bottom has been a defining feature of the French republican tradition – and indeed, predates it, as exemplified by Diderot's book being written a few years prior to the French Revolution. The gilets jaunes are a form of jacquerie, but not in the sense meant by their adversaries. They are a jacquerie in the sense exemplified by Diderot in his tale. It is a revolt of those who have not been speaking out politically, who have not had the protection of social forces such as trades unions or political parties, and who are exercising their right to resist. This particular jacquerie is thus a tale of a renewal of the social contract, one that challenges the terms of the political association.

The metaphor of the knee

Diderot himself was no stranger to the social contract tradition. A personal friend of Rousseau and d'Holbach, both of whom are important social contract theorists, he contributed to the writings on the topic early in his literary career, particularly in his article on *autorité politique* [political authority] in the first volume of the *Encyclopédie*, the momentous project of universal knowledge for which Diderot was the editor for over two decades of his life. The article, a profession of republican radicalism, anchored in an uncompromising vision of social equality, and displaying a faith in the power of humanity to control its leaders, attracted the wrath of the political authority in power at the time. Diderot had spent weeks at the prison in Vincennes as a result of his subversive writings, and although it did not stop him from taking risks, as is evident in the first volume of the *Encyclopédie*, he became much more calculative in his writings, often obfuscating his own thoughts in dialogues and contradictory positions. A little literary detour will thus help explain the social nature of Jacques' loves in Diderot's *Jacques the Fatalist*. Itself a form of novel – although Diderot points out on numerous occasions that he is not indeed writing a novel but rather telling a true tale of actual events – the book is a masterpiece of hidden subversions not unlike the rest of Diderot's literary works. In the book, there is a double play on words by Diderot on Jacques' knee injury, which is the initial impetus for his love story, and forms part of the culmination of the novel – as the love story plays itself out around the knees of Jacques' lover, Denise (Breines, 2011: 122). The first play on words is with the English translation of Jacques' *genou* – the knee. Said with a French inflection and accent, 'the knee' become Denis, Diderot's own first name, identifying the knee in the text with the author of the book. The plural 'the knees', using the same Franco-English inflection, becomes Denise, the name of Diderot's sister to whom he remained close throughout his life, *and* the name of Jacques' lover in the book. Denis and Denise are both present in the book on numerous occasions, not least of which when the author interjects himself into the story, interrupting Jacques' tale to, for example, tell us that he is not writing a novel. As Diderot partly plagiarized Sterne's *Tristam Shandy*, which he himself freely admits in *Jacques the Fatalist*, the play on words with the English author is not a coincidence but is a wink to the story that inspired his tale. The knee, and the injury Jacques sustained from a bullet in a battle, which began the entire tale of Jacques' loves, is Denis [Diderot] himself, the author of the book. The author Denis begins the tale with an injury to the knee, and Jacques' long recovery from this initial gunshot wound will put him in the situation where he meets Denise. The knees, in their plural form as a pair of bodily parts used in the erotic play with Denise, is the culmination of the story and its final climax in the sensuous play between the two lovers. It is the interaction with the other that enables the knee to become the knees, that completes the pair that forms part of the social aspect of Diderot's book. Although the main thrust of the book is framed as a love story, the wider social implications of the transformation of the 'I' into the 'Us' (*le je devient nous*) is not absent from Diderot's tale. Not quite framed in terms of a social contract (the term does not appear in the book), the beginning of the tale with Jacques' *genou* (singular) and the ending of the story with the *genoux* (plural), the knees of Denise, is a tale of the I and its other, which completes it – just as the second knee completes the first and the lovers find each other.

This tale of the 'I' and the 'Us' is even more apparent with the second play on words, the *calembour* [pun] used by Diderot in the word *genou*. In French, the knee, *le genou*, is pronounced literally as *je-nous*, I-Us. The first-person singular and first-person plural come together in the knee, the I and the Us are literally the *genou*, the knee. Not only is Denis Diderot the knee, but the knee itself is a mixture of our self and others, which complete us. Diderot uses his literary play on words to confirm what he says about the complexity of the self in his other writings. The self is not given *a priori*, independently of social relations, but rather is constituted through these relations. This is further evidenced by Diderot's use of the reader in the tale, who constantly asks questions and interrupts the flow of the tale of Jacques' loves. Although these interruptions are clearly just a voice used by Diderot, the author, to tell his tale, this involvement of the reader makes 'us' responsible for the story and its many meanderings, just as much as the 'I' of the author is a starting point of the tale. The play between the I and the Us is thus an integral part of Diderot's writing strategy, and it forms part of his reflection on the social. The story itself could not have unfolded without both the reader's interjections in the tale and the author's attempts to resist these interruptions, and without the interplay of the characters of book, whose story Diderot claims to be describing as it happened rather than as a fiction made up by himself as an author.

The injury to the knee, which Jacques reports early in the book and begins the tale of his loves, is sustained in the course of a battle with an unnamed enemy. It is the fruit, in other words, of state violence. The knee injury is a direct consequence of the social and political contract that binds us all, in that the knee is broken for the defence of the realm, and the exercise of sovereign power. The state employs soldiers, who are used in a battle, and Jacques, one of the infantry grunts whose lives are so disposable, is the victim of such violence. Unlike others, who died, however, Jacques survives and has to suffer a knee injury, the worst of all injuries, according to him. Formed of countless bones, ligaments and other things, the knee is the most painful part of the body to injure, Jacques claims, to the derisive comments of his master (Diderot,

1796/1986: 28). Metaphorically, the social contract – what unites the I and the Us, is also the most difficult thing to repair when it is broken. The injury to the knee is akin to an injury to the tacit agreement we all observe in our social relations. The role of the servant towards his master, the respect for social hierarchy and relations of power, the limits placed on the free expression of erotic desire, are all torn upside down in Diderot's account of the adventures of Jacques and his master. The breaking down of the social, like the breaking down of the knee, is the focus of Diderot's fiction, as the set social roles of the protagonists in the tale are inverted and challenged by the unfolding of events. Jacques' master tells him as much when he compares Jacques with Socrates, and particularly with Socrates' most contractual obligation: his acceptance of his death sentence by his fellow citizens in Athens. As we have seen in Chapter 4, Socrates' death is often used as a tale of the ancient social contract. The master tells Jacques that he will equally die as a philosopher, even though he had never heard of Socrates or read philosophical texts – he accepts the consequences of his actions as necessary and does not shy away from their effects – be it his own demise or even death. Diderot, not unaware of his contractual argument, winks at us through his text, signalling that Jacques is in fact making contractual arguments throughout his tale. Just as Socrates is a type of social contract theorist *avant la lettre*, Jacques is a type of unaware social contract theorist – not educated in philosophy, he instinctively makes philosophical arguments without knowing their origin.

The repairing of the social contract, in Jacques' tale, operates through a reversal of social roles. The master is forced to reverse his role towards Jacques, when the latter falls from his horse and is knocked unconscious. Upon Jacques' awakening, he finds the master taking care of him, and asks him what he is doing. '*The Master* – I watch over you. You are my servant when I am ill or in good health, but I am yours when you are in distress. / *Jacques* – I am relieved to hear that you are human, it is rarely a quality of masters towards their servants' (Diderot, 1796/1986: 176). The subversion of social roles and expectations is an integral part of the tale. This particular episode is the most explicit one written by Diderot, but the entire story revolves around the fact that Jacques is smarter, bolder, and more assertive than his master. Jacques is, in many ways, the master of his master, having the intellectual cunning and genius his social superior so desperately lacks. Jacques is constantly challenging the authority of his master, as Diderot had warned us in his article on political authority in the *Encyclopédie*. Subversion of expectations, reversal of hierarchies, and events disturbing social peace all take place at a relentless pace while we wait impatiently for the unfolding of the tale of Jacques' knee. Can we even imagine such a tale during the gilets jaunes crisis? Could we picture the master, in this case, the President of the French Republic, taking care of those who are injured in his country, of his fellow Jacques? Can we imagine the reversal of social roles and expectations?

During their adventures, Jacques and his master are told the story of Madame de la Pommeraye and the Marquis des Arcis. The two protagonists had had an affair, but the Marquis had fallen out of love with his former lover. Feigning to have forgiven him, Madame de la Pommeraye puts together an elaborate scheme to get her revenge on the Marquis, taking place over months after much scheming and conniving, culminating in the Marquis marrying a young lady who was a former prostitute. After their wedding night, the young bride confessed her role in the betrayal, crying with her head on the Marquis' knees [*les genoux du marquis*] (Diderot, 1986: 417). The play between the I and the Us (*les genoux*) is again present at the moment of the inversion of social roles. Instead of crushing his reputation and ruining him, the marriage makes the Marquis subvert all social expectations and live a happy and loving life with his new wife. Social shame be damned, the long tale of revenge ends in a blissful family life and happiness, made possible by the Marquis' unexpected acceptance of social difference. For Diderot, the knees have a particularly curative dimension. The social order would have typically crushed the dreams of the young woman after her revelation to her new husband, and could have ruined the reputation of the Marquis forever. But Diderot sees it as an opportunity to invert the power that prejudice and social propriety have over our lives. If we are able to move past the moment of shame that comes from accepting having our social role reversed, there is space for redemption and a happy-ever-after ending.

The knee also has such a curative power in religious practice. The act of kneeling, of praying and professing your faith in God can have a similarly cathartic role. Diderot – himself either an atheist or a very unorthodox believer – could not have missed the irony of the situation. Far from being a signal of submission to divine will, the knee is used by him as a symbol of pleasure and erotic desire. Against the asceticism of the Catholic Church in Diderot's time, the libertine attitude to the knee itself reverses social expectations. Perhaps an atheist or naturalist form of prayer, the knee's erotic potential replicates the actions of kneeling in Christian worship. Of course, such a replication is highly unorthodox in Diderot's work, and is meant to shock, or at least challenge social expectations. A similar reversal can be seen with the art of crawling, a natural extension of kneeling, this time in front of the Sovereign. In his posthumous book on the art of crawling, d'Holbach – Diderot's lifelong friend, collaborator, financier and contributor to the *Encyclopédie* – parodies the manners of the Court towards the Sovereign. Only the courtier, d'Holbach claims, is able to silence the voice of reason, let go of every ounce of personal worth and dignity, and perfect the art of crawling in front of their master. It is a truly unique sacrifice they perform for the nation, when courtiers debase themselves to such an extent as to deny their own noble roots and proud nature (D'Holbach, 1790/1972). The submission to every one of the wishes of their master is no easy feat, and it takes years of training and practice to achieve a level of self-mastery that is strong enough to enable such lowly activities. Like kneeling of the religious variety, it is an act of submission and surrendering of the ability to think for themselves and use their reason critically. D'Holbach's playful short text confirms the flipside of the act of kneeling – where being on your knees is not emancipatory but part of replicating social order and hierarchy. Coming back to Diderot's use of the knee, it is thus clear that the very focus of the knee as a source of erotic desire thwarts expectations of the knee as a symbol of submission to religious or secular power. There are better things we can do on our knees, for Diderot, than praying or submitting.

Social malaise during the gilets jaunes protests

The knee has also acquired a significance during the gilets jaunes protests. On 6 December 2018, a group of *lycéens* [high schoolers] defied the authorities and entered a state of protest. When the police arrived, they lined up the pupils, made them kneel and place their hands on the back of their head, before arresting 189 of them, to the outrage of the wider public (*Le Monde*, 2018b). Here the knee is a symbol of submission to the sovereign authority of the state, with these dramatic images reminding us of the demand for obedience and the consequences of rebellion. As we have seen in Chapter 2, violence is an inherent part of the being of the state, and the violence of ultimate submission, through kneeling, is reminiscent of the medieval origins of the state and acts of fidelity due to one's lord, as was clear in d'Holbach's parody of the art of kneeling. The state, as I have argued above, is within its right to demand such submission, but if it uses this power without maintaining zones of freedom, it risks damaging the very social fabric that unites citizens together. Two days after this incident, the gilets jaunes staged a protest where they knelt in front of security forces in solidarity with the high schoolers arrested in Mantes-la-Jolie. They repeated this kneeling protest on numerous occasions, showing the power of the symbolism of the knee as a sign of submission. Unlike Diderot's use of the knee as a form of social bridge between different classes of citizens and a cure for social ills – Jacques the poor servant, his master, and the Marquis and his disgraced wife – the knee here is a symbol of repression and violence, and a symptom of wider social ills and inequalities. The knee here is akin to the bullet wound suffered by Jacques at the beginning of the book, and the healing process is the one that must follow for the restoration of a social contract following the damage done to the I-Us, *le genou* – the social knee.

The securitization of the gilets jaunes protests has been akin to asking participants to bend the knee to the figure of the sovereign, embodied in the institutions of the police and *gendarmerie*, the persons of the *préfet* and the interior minister, culminating in the figure of the president himself, Emmanuel Macron. The similitudes with royal authority have been manifold. From the '*Jupiterean*' presidency of Macron – the ostentatious displays of *ancien régime* historical wealth in Versailles and the Élysée palace – to the use of language – with Macron using the familiar *tu* to address citizens, but demanding the formal *vous* in response from them – the demands have been ones of respect, authority and sovereignty embodied in the person and the office of the president. Not themselves unique to Macron – Sarkozy still demands to be addressed as Mr President, as is the custom for *ex officio* presidents, and refuses to answer if addressed any other way – they are nonetheless particularly pronounced under the current office-holder, leading to a malaise and disconnect between him and the people. Perhaps exacerbated by his youth – Macron became president at the young age of 39 – and lack of political experience, the demands for respect from someone that does not afford his fellow citizens the most basic of human dignity has been rocking the foundations of the office he occupies. Under Fifth Republic presidents, the office was, at least until Sarkozy, somewhat removed from the everyday politicking of governmental business. But since 2007 and the accession of Sarkozy to the office, a new type of presidency emerged which was much more involved and present in everyday life. This new presidency is at odds with the office established by De Gaulle in 1958, who wished for a more modest, austere and removed role for the head of state – a more sublime form of presidency, as we will discuss in the Conclusion. Historically intervening in public only in times of crisis, the office of the president is now ever-present and surprisingly silent in times of crisis. It took Macron 23 days to comment on the gilets jaunes – no doubt hoping the movement would dissipate by itself before he had to become personally involved – even though he is otherwise quick to comment on any number of news items – from forest fires in Siberia or the Amazon to the passing away of former French CEOs.

It is through his use of Twitter that Macron has distinguished himself. In the first year after his election, from May 2017 to May 2018, he issued more than seven tweets a day from his personal account (De Fournas,

2018), more than his US counterpart Donald Trump – otherwise well known for his use and abuse of the social media platform. Less controversial than the latter, Macron has nevertheless broken the seal of a calm and reflective presidency, and become part of the 24-hour news cycle. He also became, in 2018, the most re-tweeted French person, and broke another national record with over 44 million tweets mentioning him. His communication strategy may be working – people are clearly engaging with it – but it has also spectacularly backfired when it comes to his popularity and capacity to engender respect and admiration. This use of social media, alongside the 24-hour news networks that have risen in the French audiovisual landscape over the past decade or so,[1] have enabled what Noiriel has called the phenomenon of *fait-diversion* (Noiriel, 2018: 721). Combining two French terms – the *fait divers*, a type of news story that is typically anecdotal and used to be added as a puff piece at the end of a news broadcast; and the verb *faire diversion*, which means to divert the gaze, typically as a method of obfuscation or subterfuge – the concept of *fait-diversion* describes the ever-more present anecdote that distracts the viewer and keeps them watching a channel that dispenses news on a constant basis – whether there are important news items to cover or not. Perhaps better translated as a 'distranecdote', the purpose of these *fait-diversions* is to distract the public (in order to increase revenues from advertising through large viewership) with anecdotal news items that would otherwise not have made it into the news. During the gilets jaunes protests, this phenomenon became increasingly visible through the use of a few images, often looped in the background, with pundits and commentators authoritatively describing the protesters as backward peasants rebelling violently against a political order they do not understand. The focus on the few scenes of violence during gilets jaunes protests, and their screening on BFMTV, attracted the wrath of the gilets jaunes, for whom it was perceived as a betrayal of the movement which encompassed much more than these few spectacular instances of street violence. Few news networks conveyed what was generally happening on the roundabouts, showing scenes of collective solidarity or pacific displays of anger, and it took news media months to report on the scale of police violence and brutality during the demonstrations – but all news outlets showed burnt cars and clashes between protesters and police, and deplored the material damage suffered during demonstrations. For those on the ground participating in the events, it was a display of media bias and unfair coverage of unfolding events, as their reality was nowhere to be seen on the silver screen. Further taking away from their dignity, the traditional broadcast media, in particular BFMTV, become synonymous with the domination of establishment forces, against which collective resistance was organized on social media, particularly Facebook and Twitter.

A counter-movement of news was created by the gilets jaunes themselves, with many taking to the new media technologies available to them as an antidote to the disease of media bias, as they perceive it. Facebook groups have proliferated over the weeks since the movement started to organize itself, with a national group numbering over 160,000 members, as of 2020, and dozens of local groups coordinating local action, sharing pictures, and starting conversations about the movement and its future. The groups, often relatively small with only a few thousand members, are nevertheless extremely active, with hundreds of posts each day, testifying to the activities of the protesters. Similarly, on Twitter, news is shared about events on a constant, immediate basis, providing an alternative vision of the situation on the ground to those portrayed by the main media outlets in France. Some newspapers have caught onto the phenomenon, for example the left-leaning *Libération* newspaper offers a CheckNews service that attempts to evaluate the quality of information shared on social media, and evaluates the data there on a regular basis. What is clear in the manner in which the gilets jaunes have used these new communication technologies is that they have found innovative and inventive ways to circumvent the limitations of popular access to mass media. More reminiscent of the spread of popular newspapers in the nineteenth century than the centralization of news in national – often Parisian – newspapers characteristic of the post-war situation, the ability to make, distribute and share news has been largely popularized and democratized – with all the challenges this poses for quality control and verification of information. Partly a cure to remedy the lack of accurate representation afforded them in traditional news outlets, social media use by the gilets jaunes has empowered them in ways that would not have been possible even a few decades ago.

Respect versus toleration

The willing participation of political elites in the phenomenon of 'distranecdote' (*fait-diversion*) has created a paradox in that they still demand respect despite partaking in the circus of the 24-hour news cycle. Respect for one's elders, particularly for one's parents, is a key demand of pre-modern societies. It forms one of the ten commandments, and is still an important social norm in many societies today. But modern politics is not based on such pre-modern principles, no matter how worthy they are. Machiavelli hit the nail on the head when he understood that it is better for the Prince to be feared than loved, better for the ruler to have authority than the love and personal attachment that comes with respect (Machiavelli, 1532/2008). During modernity, respect turned to toleration, and an important shift happened. Instead of inspiring strong personal ties, we expect from our political leaders a framework that allows all those living in society to be able to fulfil their own personal life goals and ambitions, as long as they do not threaten those of others. Spinoza's theory of toleration acts as an important reminder of this shift in perspective, building on his defence of liberty that we have seen in Chapter 3. For Spinoza, seeking toleration is a prudent and wise option for the ruler, as the state's exercise of oppressive means over the opinions of its citizens tends to breed a rebellious citizenry. Toleration makes a state freer, which is the true goal of the state for the philosopher of Amsterdam, and ultimately contributes to stability. When people's opinions are regulated by the state, the outcome is more often than not a failure of the state to effectuate the desired change in the hearts and minds of its citizens, and a growing resentment on the part of those targeted by this attempt at mind control and a growing desire to enter a state of resistance. Spinoza, forever a pragmatic in political terms, is essentially warning rulers to let their citizens be, not to attempt to morally elevate them, for these attempts will likely backfire and start a rebellion against the state. Tolerating the opinions of others is a much safer course – but this means accepting what – in one's own perspective – is supposedly wrong (Spinoza, 2007).

Toleration demands much of ourselves and little of others, as opposed to respect, which is demanded from others towards ourselves. When Moses came down from Mount Sinai with his ten commandments, he was one of the elders to be respected according to the stone tablets. This particular demand for respect was thus cementing social relations which favour the old and the wise over the young and impetuous. Respect is something you demand, based on an alleged superiority of one kind or another, from others who are made to appreciate the said superiority. Toleration, on the other hand, is a sign of inner fortitude and strength. This is certainly the sense ascribed to it by ancient philosophers, particularly Roman ones, for whom to tolerate something was a personal virtue worth cultivating. Seneca, for example, saw it as an essential virtue in the fight against ill health, as tolerance of pain can make the difference between life and death (Tønder, 2013: 84). The modern conception of toleration often obfuscates this role of tolerance as a personal virtue, but it is worth remembering it as a key differentiation from the concept of respect, which typically is closer to an entitlement than to a virtue. The President of the French Republic is entitled to the respect due to his function, the argument goes, because the Presidency represents a venerable institution that demands a particular type of genuflexion. But bending the knee is not the appropriate metaphor for toleration. The metaphor which is more appropriate to toleration is the one linked to toleration of pain. The person who has the virtue of tolerance is able to withstand the pain of the broken knee, and attempt to live through the healing process. Toleration is about living past the pain and the hurt caused by others, and finding ways to mend the (social) situation that created the injury in the first place. Any renewal of the social contract will need this virtue of toleration as endurance, and demand no genuflexions in attempting to heal the social pact.

What toleration does not demand, however, is passive acceptance of others' claims to truth. Chantal Mouffe (2005) has argued that democratic thought precisely needs to be combative despite the acceptation of the other as an adversary. This *agnostic* politics, based on the ancient Greek practice of *agon*, the competition between adversaries rather than the fight to the death between enemies, is the other side of the medal of toleration. Toleration as an active virtue demands that all sides be recognized as legitimate entities in a fair match between their respective claims. To put it simply, the claims by some gilets jaunes that the structural violence of the state, which culminates in depression, ill health and sometimes even suicide among workers who are on the receiving end of the liberal-libertarian policies described in Chapter 5, is worse than the street violence of protests are open for democratic debate. As we have seen in Chapter 3, however, the freedom to demonstrate and make the case publicly through social action and movements is being put under threat through the criminalizing of unorthodox political engagement and increased bureaucratic control of fundamental rights and freedoms. These measures essentially have biased the playing field of contestation, with ordinary citizens not able to compete with better-funded and more influential interests in society that can more successfully shape policies and decision-making at the highest level. Trades unions in France have been declining in power since the 1980s, with the lowest point being the defeat of the railway workers' movement in 2018. Faced with historically low membership numbers, with only around 11 per cent of French workers being members of trades unions[2] (compared with historic highs of around 30 per cent in the 1940s), there is little doubt that these intermediary bodies of political contestation have lost some of their fortitude and much of their bargaining power. Besides, with civil servants twice as likely to be members of a trades union than other workers, those working outside of public services are likely to see the successes of trades unions as little more than a corporatist defence of privileged working conditions for the few that benefit from them. This was precisely the line of reasoning of the French government during the pensions strike of 2019–20, when those who benefit from the numerous pensions regimes were portrayed as privileged and refusing a universal system applicable to all equally – when the reality of the reforms meant a lowering of pension benefits for all. Faced with union (in)activity that they see as taking part in the subterfuge of power and domination, it is unsurprising that the gilets jaunes have turned to direct action, and categorically refused forms of delegation and representation to negotiate a solution to the current crisis.

Combating the new orthodoxy

When Diderot and other radical French philosophers of the eighteenth century were advocating for toleration, they were butting their heads against the Catholic Church and its dogma. This battle was extended to all churches, including the Protestant ones, and Spinoza had already had to put together a radical theory of toleration in the Netherlands in the preceding century, despite that country's relatively lax laws and high levels of freedom of expression. The orthodoxy of the times was couched in religious terms, but today's ruling *doxa* is phrased in economic terms. As I argued in Chapter 5, Macron has been the foremost proponent of the liberal-libertarian consensus in France, with strong parallels throughout the Western world – and beyond. The idealization of market economics, couched with a thin layer of redistributive justice that justified growing inequalities, forms the backbone of this liberal-libertarian religion. This religion has the traditional characteristics of other religions. It has its texts, its theologians, its priests and its claims to universal truths. The only thing it lacks is a notion of God, but divinity is not fully excluded from it either. The holy texts of this religion are widely available. If we take only Rawls and Nozick as examples – though many other authors could form the canon of this liberal-libertarian religion – we can see the pervasiveness of their claims. Rawls' *A Theory of Justice*, according to Google Scholar, has over 82,000 citations, while Nozick's *Anarchy, State, and Utopia* has over 21,000. (Diderot's *Jacques the Fatalist*, by contrast, has 84.) There are, literally, thousands of books and articles discussing these canonical texts, and offering a wide range of interpretations of their prophetic message. These form the theology of the liberal-libertarian religion. Although both Rawls and Nozick stay clear of making theological claims, their philosophical foundations are deeply embedded in theology. Rawls' Kantian foundations rely on Kant's three postulates, despite the former's attempt to distance himself from them. Kant had speculated that his entire philosophical system would fall apart without these three postulates: the existence of God, the immortality of the soul, and free will. Equally, Nozick's foundations rely on a divine gift made to humanity by God, through Locke's theory of property. For what is the doctrine of the ownership of one's body about, if not a personal gift from an unexplainable and divine source? If that is not enough to convince the reader, the economic *doxa* of the free market is notoriously phrased in terms of Adam Smith's 'invisible hand' – one cannot think of a more theological metaphor to explain our economic system.

Macron appears as the high priest of the Gallican Church of this liberal-libertarian religion. He has fully internalized its claims, notably about the trickle-down nature of wealth, the essential role played by those with direct access to economic knowledge, and the need to use stately power to enforce such a vision. Those who do not share in his faith are illegitimate in their views, for they have not accepted the correct *doxa* – the orthodoxy of free-market capitalism. Just as the deists, atheists and unorthodox believers of the eighteenth century challenged the authority of revealed religion, a challenge to the authority of the liberal-libertarian religion is necessary today. The goal of these radical thinkers in the eighteenth century was not to get rid of religion altogether, but to put it in its proper place – in the realm of belief and faith, and not in a position of authority and social control. Their demands for toleration were made against the hold of religion on social and political life, and contemporary demands for toleration must equally challenge the liberal-libertarian consensus and relegate it to its proper realm: that of opinion and belief, rather than economic fact. The unorthodox challenge to the liberal-libertarian religion is to dispel the myth that economics should be a technical field with technical solutions, rather than a social and political field with social and political solutions. A pluralism of opinions about the role that democracy should play in economic life, the demands for economic justice and a rethinking of the social contract on economic life are the new challenge to ruling *doxa*, as we saw in Chapter 5.

Diderot was notoriously dismissive of the claims of revealed religion, and is often thought to be an atheist. His critique revolved around a scepticism for the absolutist claims of religious thought, and a preference for a more dialogical, if not dialectic approach. It is of little surprise that Diderot preferred fiction as a form of expression. It allowed him to engage in a dialogue between characters – Jacques and his master, for example – as well as between characters outside the book – the author and the reader. His thought relied on dialogues, on exchange of ideas, and these are difficult when one has a canonical text to refer to and to restrict debate. Dialogue implies openness to novelty, to ideas that rethink the personal and social links between persons, and to movement. A new social contract will, and must be, a dialogue between persons. The thought that one can find a technical solution to a social movement such as that of the gilets jaunes is utopian at best, and disingenuous at worst. Every social crisis is akin to a damaged knee – it is a painful and deep wound inflicted on society as a whole, that impacts on all aspects of the social body, not just the damaged part. Dialogue was, for Diderot, the way to deal with social ill – along with time, tolerance of pain, and the will to direct healing. One cannot heal the social body by repressing the illness.

Renewing the social contract

I have made the case that the social contract needs renewal, and have left the specifics of the new social contract deliberately vague, as I have insisted they must be subject to democratic decision-making – and thus not decided *a priori* by anyone, least of all myself. We can, however, ask the question of what a new social contract will look like in practice. In the first instance, it will demand the recognition that others' political and philosophical opinions are legitimate and worthy of protection by the (free) state in which they live. I have argued earlier, in Chapter 3, with Spinoza, that a state's role is not fulfilled unless it guarantees a maximum amount of freedom for its citizens. Clearly, the reaction of the French state during the gilets jaunes protests has gone precisely the other way, and its goal has been to restrict the freedom of its own citizens, applying increasing bureaucratic controls over their ability to express their political opinions, particularly through public gatherings and protests. The first step of toleration would be to remove these restrictions on freedom of expression, and to enable as much expression of civil discontent and unease about the current political system as possible. The French state is not under siege by its own citizens, and state of emergency legislation is not automatically warranted against those who take their discontent to the streets. This increase in the virtue of toleration will demand much patience and restraint from those on whom the violence of the gilets jaunes is being exercised. If one is stuck in traffic on a Saturday morning on the way to do the weekly shopping, or if one is inconvenienced by the public demonstration in a town or city centre in France, this seems to be the price to pay to live in a free state. It is not pleasant or desirable to live in a country where weekly protests take place, but if this is the price to pay to address social ills and to heal the metaphorical knee that is the 'I-Us', the social contract, it seems to be a price worth paying.

In the second instance, tolerance will require the establishment of long-term solutions to remedy the social ill at the source of the troubles. Clearly, the gilets jaunes themselves have made suggestions for long-term solutions that merit discussion. One of the most unifying demands is the resignation of the President of the Republic. This seems unlikely to occur, but with Macron's approval ratings falling below 20 per cent, it seems the sentiment is widespread in French society. What is at stake here is the relative unaccountability of the office of the President. With no recall mechanism, no opportunity for votes of no confidence, no effective parliamentary scrutiny, and little trust in opposition parties, the gilets jaunes are touching on an important problem of representative democracy. How can we, in a world where news is instant, commentary on political issues never-ending and ever-expanding, and involvement of politicians in our daily lives more apparent than ever, accept that our democratic will be consulted only at infrequent intervals every few years and will determine the future of the country from that point on? The gilets jaunes' desire for increased democracy, as opposed to a republican model based on the aristocratic elective principle, is their answer to the question. The precise form of this increased democracy is up for (democratic) debate, but should be made in a spirit of toleration. When democratic decisions are taken, no matter how ill-informed they might seem to political elites and experts, they need to be tolerated and implemented for the sake of establishing a long-lasting democracy. Toleration of the will of the majority is an important part of building trust between citizens and political elites, and all signs point towards a need for this trust to be rebuilt. Undermining democratic decision-making has long-lasting and deep-cutting consequences, which can be remedied by an approach of toleration, where elites accept the will of the majority and do their uttermost to implement it.

Conclusion

Although the gilets jaunes are a *sui generis* type of social movement, parallels with the past have been numerous and are used to prophesy the future of the movement and its impact on French society – and beyond. According to the reading proposed above, the gilets jaunes are best regarded as another challenge to the social contract that has, at least since the French Revolution, united those in power with those on whom power is exercised. One of the greatest failures of the social contract as it emerged in the time of the French Revolution was the compromise achieved between the bourgeoisie and the rest of the *tiers état* – the working classes. The bourgeoisie, which largely led the revolution from 1789 to 1792, and then again from 1795 to 1799, was opposed by the radical democratic ideals of the Jacobins who led the charge in the in-between years, opposing a representative model of democracy with direct democracy. At the time, as is still sometimes the case today, the justification for the representative model was framed on the inability of the working classes to rule themselves, to understand the complexities of political life, and to make the right decisions for the future. Part of this justification was provided by the radical philosophers of the Enlightenment themselves, notably Diderot and his close personal friend d'Holbach.

Diderot had himself pondered about the role of emancipation in pre-revolutionary France (he died in 1784). Along with d'Holbach, he thought that emancipation would come from popular ownership of the means of production of the time – the land. Favouring a model of land redistribution to guarantee for each farmer a plot of land that would provide enough to feed a family, the economic model they advocated was in line with the needs of their time, where the overwhelming majority of the population lived from cultivating the land (D'Holbach, 1773/2001: 488). Transposed in contemporary terms, the principles they advocated for are still largely relevant. They sought to instil in the citizen two fundamental principles: independence defined as a form of freedom from domination; and a personal interest in the defence of the common good, also called patriotism. Only those who have internalized these two principles could form the true citizen, they argued, and the redistribution of property in the form of productive land would allow the ticking of both boxes. Independence would lead to more time to spend on education and self-betterment, as well as protecting the citizen from domination by others. Without independent means of subsistence, they reasoned, one is always prey to the needs of their landlord and/or employer, and can never make decisions based on Enlightenment principles such as reason and liberty. And the imposition of representative democracy was precisely justified on these reasons. The majority of the population is too busy working to know its own interests, but they can eventually be enlightened to see what their interests truly are. In this, the Enlightenment, radical or moderate, has failed. Where the French state in the nineteenth century successfully encompassed all of the French population under a form of common identity and patriotism, notably by turning peasants into Frenchmen, according to the phrase by Eugene Weber (1976), it has not delivered on the promises of material well-being. The promises of emancipation have not materialized, and centuries of representative democracy have not liberated the working classes from the yoke of landlords and bosses. If there was hope in the afterwar period that this Enlightenment promise may be on the agenda again, this hope has been crushed since the 1980s, and was buried after the financial crisis of 2008 and its austerity-driven response by politicians from all sides of the spectrum (Noiriel, 2018).

This has happened, as I noted above, despite the fact that levels of home ownership and education have never been so high. Most working-class people have finished high school and been awarded a *Baccalauréat*, and many are home-owners of one of the millions of bungalows built throughout peripheral France. Yet their ability to secure economic independence, a promise of the Enlightenment, has not materialized and indeed progress may even have been reversed in recent years. Many are worse off than their parents, and those without family assistance are extremely exposed to the ebb-and-flow of macro-economic trends such as global slowdown and recession. A social contract of the future has to address these needs that were posited as the *sine qua non* condition for social advancement more than two centuries ago. The revolt of the gilets jaunes against rent-seeking economic actors, such as landlords, motorway management companies, insurance and mortgage companies, and utilities, is testament to the economic plight that needs redressing. When the proportion of fixed costs – which for many in peripheral France includes the cost of fuel for their car – keeps on rising as a proportion of the household budget to the point where spending on food is being sacrificed to service these fixed costs, the situation is not that dissimilar to the situation France was in back in 1789 after three disastrous harvests. The people are also much better educated, nominally own property, and are better able to defend their interests and organize themselves than in the eighteenth century when the bourgeoisie was the rising social class at the end of the feudal order. Although the gilets jaunes have failed to organize themselves politically in the traditional sense, I have shown that they have provided one of the strongest political challenges to the very existence of the French state as it currently stands. It is this new form of politics, which does not go through political parties but demands social and economic justice directly, that is at the centre of the new social contract they demand.

Conclusion

The office of the president has been at the forefront of the state's response to the gilets jaunes. Unlike presidents of the Fifth Republic before Sarkozy, Macron has opted for an engaged and ever-present role for himself as the leader of the administration. The old style of presidency – a quasi-monarchical office created by De Gaulle in 1958 which combined popular control through seven-year election cycles and a certain distance from the day-to-day politics of running the state, which was typically managed by the prime minister – suited the time and the man that created the office. But the majesty that surrounded the office was exemplified by De Gaulle's infamous saying of 1958, "*je vous ai compris*" [I have understood you], a vague formulation that maintained distance from the nitty-gritty of the political compromise France was going to find for Algeria, combined with a reassuring message that a solution would be found. Placing the presidency above and beyond the dirty business of politics, De Gaulle created a sublime function in the Fifth Republic. This sublime function has now largely disappeared, with three successive presidents (Sarkozy, Hollande and Macron) each playing their part to get rid of the distant character, necessitated by an engaged and participating president. By turning the president into the architect of everything that happens in French politics, these three presidents have managed to take all the credit for France's successes, as well as suffer all the blame for its failures. This shift away from a sublime office had already been theorized by Edmund Burke, considered the founder of modern conservatism, in both his *Reflections on the Revolution in France* written in 1790 (Burke, 1790/2001), and his aesthetic work on the sublime and the beautiful (Burke, 1757/1990). In this conclusion, I show that the whole business of the gilets jaunes has revealed another side of this aesthetic story: it has unearthed the ugliness of day-to-day politics. By juxtaposition, the once-sublime office of the president has itself been made ugly, with far-reaching consequences for the social contract established under the Fifth Republic in France.

The beautiful and the sublime

Burke, though himself critical of social contract theorists in many regards, conceded that 'Society is, indeed, a contract. [...] It is a partnership in all science, a partnership in all art, a partnership in every virtue and in all perfection. As the ends of such a partnership cannot be obtained in many generations, it becomes a partnership not only between those who are living, but between those who are living, those who are dead, and those who are to be born' (Burke, 2001: 261). This contract of the living, the dead and the yet unborn can be placed in Burke's wide political aesthetics, as a form of embodiment of the sublime over the beautiful.

Corey Robin explains Burke's disposition in his book *The Reactionary Mind*. As Robin points out, Burke argued that the problem of the *ancien régime* in France was precisely that its reliance on an ideal of beauty had stratified French society in the eighteenth century. Against the chivalrous ideal of the regime was opposed the brutal violence of the revolutionary struggle, which took the attributes of the sublime over those of the beautiful. The sublime, for Burke, is a sensation we feel when exposed to extreme pain, danger or terror. It emboldens the soul, just as much as it has the capacity to crush its spirit; it inspires action just like it can cause death (Robin, 2017: 46). The tension in the concept of the sublime is never resolved, because the sublime's perfect expression only exists in God, that is, in a divine order unreachable for mere mortals. But we can still experience this feeling of sublimity, and Burke's genius was to show that the sublime has a potent hold on human relations. As Robin puts it: 'In the face of the sublime, the self is annihilated, occupied, crushed, overwhelmed; in the face of the sublime, the self is heightened, aggrandized, magnified' (Robin, 2017: 66).

Such an elevation of the soul requires a sense of mysticism, a distance and lack of understanding that create the conditions for its possibility. The monarch can only be sublime to the people if there is an aura of unknowability around the person that holds sovereign power and the office that perpetrates it. For Burke, the 'power which arises from institution in kings and commanders, has the same connection with terror' (Burke, 1990: 62). Sublime fear of the leader is a necessary attribute, without which the passions of men cannot be held for long. Hobbes had said as much a century and a half before Burke. Too much familiarity with the object of the sublime turns the object into a mere 'beautiful' artefact, to be enjoyed and which causes pleasure, rather than being a source of awe and admiration. Burke understood well that sublimity is easily lost, and that it is most present when violence is a possibility. The possibility of violence is indeed much more effective than its actuality, for too much violence creates familiarity between those who exercise violence, and those on whom violence is exercised. In turn, this familiarity dispels the myth behind violence, and makes it less sublime (Robin, 2017: 87). For violence to remain sublime, it must thus be as occasional as a public appearance of the monarch: rare and brief, carefully orchestrated and symbolic. When violence ceases to inspire dread, it has already lost much of its potency and cannot hope to hold on for long.

The decadence of society can be seen for Burke in an overwhelming presence of the beautiful. Beauty is derived from lust, for Burke, and mixed with social qualities to create love. It is really antithetical to the sublime in that it requires familiarity, proximity and recurrent relations between human beings in order to flourish. But it is also a source of weakness for Burke. Based entirely on our senses, beauty lacks the divine link that the sublime enjoys. Created by sight, touch or smell, beauty has certain natural qualities for Burke, which include smallness, smoothness, delicacy and having clear and bright colours (Burke, 1757/1990: 107). Unlike sublimity, beauty is thus something that we experience through the senses, and at least to an extent can be analysed rationally, measured and understood with a clear analytical analysis. Based on Burke's description, beauty is a virtue of the weak, whereas the sublime is held together by the strong. But the flipside of the beautiful is even more interesting in Burke. Although he only mentions it in passing, the concept of ugliness is an important counterweight to the beautiful.

The ugly

The exact opposite to beauty, ugliness is 'consistent enough with the idea of the sublime' (Burke, 1757/1990: 109). Burke does not elucidate his thought any further, but the consequences of his brief exploration of the ugly remain possible. If beauty lies in a harmonious disposition of forms, ugliness lies in its haphazardness. If beauty leads to love, ugliness leads to hatred. If beauty is a source of elegance and grace, ugliness is a source of irreverence and disrespect. If beauty is linked to smoothness and sweetness, ugliness is blunt and bitter. When beauty is relaxing, ugliness is restless and exhausting. Taking the comparison a step further, we can subvert Burke's message about darkness and brightness. Whereas the sublime thrived on darkness and its dangers, beauty thrives on bright colours. But ugliness is like a fluorescent light in the night: neither totally breaking the darkness nor creating beauty, it reflects the lights that hit it without breaking the sense of dread and fear that darkness instils. It combines some features of the beautiful, though turned on their head, with features of the sublime, though never fully materialized. Ugliness creates no beauty, nor elevates itself to the realm of the sublime. The yellow vest, with its fluorescent bands, is the ultimate ugliness of the (peri-)urban milieu. The light it reflects is neither beautiful nor sublime, it is merely functional and makes one noticeable. Like a particularly ugly building in the middle of an idyllic landscape, one cannot help but stare at the *gilet jaune* and take note of its existence. Its ugliness is its redeeming feature; being ugly is what it was designed for, to be a stain on a canvass we cannot ignore, drawing the gaze and making existence felt. In an advertising campaign in 2008 to justify the new law making yellow vests compulsory in French cars, the government featured the designer Karl Lagerfeld wearing the piece of clothing with a slogan stating: "it's yellow, it's ugly, it doesn't match anything, but it can save your life' (Guerrien, 2018).

The gilets jaunes have been an ugly movement. This is not meant in a pejorative manner, but rather in the conceptual manner derived from the thought of Burke. As such, they are a new challenge to the dichotomy of the beautiful and the sublime that the Irish philosopher had considered, and they open a new avenue of philosophical enquiry into ugliness. In his documentary on the gilets jaunes roundabouts he visited, the French parliamentarian and amateur film-maker François Ruffin argues that the structures that have been erected on the protesters' venues are a sight of beauty. Doubtless there are sporadic expressions of artistic creativity on the sites, but the *cabanes* or huts that the occupiers of roundabouts had erected were sites of resistance and occupation rather than aesthetically pleasing. In many ways, they resembled the hastily constructed structures of the shantytowns of world metropolises, rather than an art gallery or the expression of particular sensitivities. Providing shelter to the protesters from the weather – the protests, after all, started in late autumn, and went on in many places throughout the winter – these *cabanes* served a very utilitarian purpose. Often built in record time with makeshift materials, they became an eyesore for the commuters who passed them on a daily basis, and their presence was a deliberate act of visibility. Just like the high visibility vest itself, the *cabane* was not erected to be beautiful, but to raise awareness of the plight of the protesters, on top of the considerations cited above. It became unavoidable to notice them, precisely because they do not fit in with the vision that France exports to the rest of the world. Known for *haute couture*, designers and perfume, France became synonymous with ugliness and popular expression. The ugly side of France became apparent for all to see, from the wealthy boulevards of Paris to the peri-urban spaces of the roundabouts. By placing ugliness forward, the gilets jaunes made it obvious for all to see that their plight was serious and worthy of attention, that a deep sense of unease and pain was present there. The ugliness of the *cabanes* was also a site of profound reflection on the demands of the movement. As Burke had noted about ugliness, it need not be in contradiction with the sublime. There was something sublime about using ugliness in such a manner, and in subverting the aesthetic of everyday life. The *cabanes*, serving crude functions such as warmth and dryness, were the opposite of the aesthetic dimension sometimes displayed on roundabouts, with sculptures and artwork adorning the most beautiful of these peri-urban structures.

The roundabout, of course, is itself a site of ugliness, where the sight of beauty is an exception rather than the rule. The very first roundabout in France was the Place de l'Étoile, around the Arc de Triomphe in Paris, a sight of considerable beauty. It is there that unidirectional driving in a circle around a monument was first introduced by Eugène Hénard in 1907, with millions of other roundabouts to follow over the next century (Confavreux, 2019: 5). The majestic structure that is the Arc de Triomphe combines the best of the sublime and of beauty. Commissioned by Napoleon after Austerlitz to commemorate his military victories, in the style of Roman arches, it signals to a warrior past and the glories of France. Although it was not finished by the time the Emperor had lost power, it was completed under the Bourbon Restoration in 1836. Contrary to those who lamented the graffiti on the monument following the 1 December 2018 protest by gilets jaunes as an attack on the Republic itself, the Arc is not a republican symbol, but rather an imperial and monarchist monument in the centre of Paris. It is so unrepublican that a plaque needed to be added to the monument, in 1870, to remind Parisians that the republic had been proclaimed and that the Second Empire had fallen. Its one democratic feature, the tomb of the unknown soldier, was a later addition and only came about after the First World War. Unsurprisingly, the tomb itself was not touched by protesters, who focused their degradations on the monument itself and the museum underneath it. With its myriad of statues, list of Napoleon's generals, and commemorations of epic battles fought by imperial armies, it is a monument meant to inspire awe and dread. A sublime feature of Parisian architecture, it even addresses the divine with Roman mythological scenes portrayed on its arches. To make such a symbol of the sublime ugly, by adding graffiti to its walls, was not an attack on the republic, for which the Arc does not stand, but an attack on its beauty. The ugly Arc de Triomphe acted as a victory of the vandals over order, of discontent over obedience, of resisting violence over the violence of the state. Yet such a victory was short-lived. The state quickly re-asserted itself – such symbolic displays of ugliness cannot be tolerated – and the graffiti was gone by the very next day. Far from showing the radical revolutionary potential of the movement, this act reaffirmed the power of the state to impose order. The sublime triumphed, and the tranquil beauty of the monument can still be admired today.

A similar ephemeral fate was shared by the *cabanes* on the roundabouts throughout France. Their ephemeral life was soon replaced by a return to normalcy, with many of the temporary structures being dismantled, bulldozed and destroyed. Yet the ugliness of the roundabout remains, even after the gilets jaunes have left their sites of protests. What has become apparent is how ugly this peri-urban France can be, how grey and empty the entrances to urban spaces are, and how lifeless they seem without a group of people building huts in their midst. The ugliness here stands as a stark absence of beauty, a reminder of the emptiness that revolves around the success of twenty-first-century economic life and its organization. Essential for the fluidity of our commercial exchanges, the roundabouts have filled the outskirts of cities with an ugliness that reminds us of the dread created by these economic activities. To function, a modern economy requires cars and roundabouts, parking lots and supermarkets, industrial estates and the workers that populate them. What is, for some of us, a weekly or monthly trip to these economic powerhouses of cheap consumption is, for many who work there or commute through there, a daily reality. Vermeren notes the extent to which this has affected urban architecture even beyond the site of the roundabouts. The *pavillons* that have been built throughout France in the past decades – small houses, many identical to one another and where boredom reigns – can be seen right across the country on the outskirts of the old villages and the cities (Vermeren, 2019: 161). This has happened while the town centres and historic buildings within them have been abandoned, chased by the movement of businesses to the periphery. The old stones have been abandoned in favour of the concrete blocks of the newbuilds, further out of the sight of tourists and visitors, where the new working classes and lower middle classes (the *small-mean class*) are living. Inhabiting ugliness, with concrete and plastic as their sole companions, the gilets jaunes have often embraced the ugliness and turned it into a site of popular unrest, alternative expression and resistance to the beautiful order. They have politicized the ugly, from the vest they wore to the sites they protested at, and changed social relations along with it. Ultimately, though, the sublime need not be ugly, ugliness can engender feelings of the sublime. Dread of the life of misery to come, hope in common action and democratic discourse, and the solidarity of those who until now suffered in silence have combined to turn the ugly into something greater than itself. The gilets jaunes have not quite turned ugliness into beauty, but they have showed that ugliness can also take part in the sublime, and can live on even after the movement has ended.

One may dream about a renewal of urban architecture, as Vermeren does, with France becoming a leader in combining thoroughly innovative green cities with a wider management of the land, a return of great forests that once populated the land, and a planned urbanization for the rest of us. Or one may see the beauty present in the sites of protests, as Ruffin and Perret (2019) do, and see the gilets jaunes as the embryo of a new social movement that will revive our sense of belonging and bring social beauty. Instead, I conceptualize the future of the movement as a space of healing – a pharmacology of the social movement suggests that much needs to be done for the social contract to be revived. The ugliness the movement has brought forth need not be combatted with the idealized beauty of what could be otherwise, but rather may be embraced as a source of inspiration and sublimity. If the contract, as Burke suggested, is between the dead, the living and the yet unborn, thinking about the future, and acting upon it, are essential parts of any social contract. Ugliness might here do more for a change in social relations than beauty ever could. By embracing the ugly, the gilets jaunes have shown a side of France that it is too easy to turn a blind eye to. By choosing a site that cannot be ignored – the roundabout – for their protests, and by choosing a garment that cannot be unseen, the high visibility jacket, they ensured that ugliness became apparent to all.

The gilets jaunes in comparison

Nor is this phenomenon – of increased inequalities, demands for social justice, and democratic renewal – a uniquely French one. As Adrian Pabst has noted, what unites the three moments of the Brexit vote, the election of Donald Trump, and the gilets jaunes is the failure of liberalism over the past three decades to provide well-being for the majority of citizens. The working and middle classes that have united in these three political moments have all come to a similar conclusion as to the failure of the political system (Pabst, 2019). In Britain and France, it would have been difficult to tell the difference between the social and economic policies of Cameron and Hollande, despite their belonging to different sides of the political spectrum. Both continued austerity measures to get out of the financial crisis of 2008, and both passed homosexual marriage into law. The economics and social measures of these two leaders characterize the liberal consensus that is under question by gilets jaunes, Brexiters, and Trump supporters.

Laurent Joffrin, editor-in-chief of the left-wing *Libération* newspaper, was quick to dismiss the gilets jaunes as a movement that would favour the extreme right (Joffrin, 2018). Joffrin even blames the gilets jaunes for believing and sharing conspiracy theories found online during the outbreak of the COVID-19 pandemic. The gilets jaunes are blamed for attacking the government's lack of preparedness during the epidemic, and for accusing the powers-that-be of knowingly scaling back the ability of the health services to fight back against a pandemic. Joffrin goes so far as to defend Roselyne Bachelot, minister under Sarkozy, for having tried to save public monies when she got rid of the stocks of masks to fight a pandemic in 2011. The gilets jaunes' scepticism against elites that have left a country unprepared is turned into a fundamental affront to the Republic itself, a hatred of anyone with political influence and a closing of the ranks between the left-wing editor that he is, and the right-wing government that preferred to save a few million euros rather than maintain a capacity for the French state to fight a global pandemic (Joffrin, 2020). The liberal consensus, as much a feature of the political left as it is of the political right, has not only produced growth and prosperity, but also exacerbated inequalities and thrown millions into more precarious conditions. In the four examples I take below – the Brexit vote, the election of Trump, the rise of the Law and Justice party in Poland, and the social movement of 2019–20 in Chile – this liberal consensus has come under attack. Although each case has parallels with and differences from the gilets jaunes, it is important to bring the French context into the light of a global phenomenon, to make visible the myriad of ways the demands for political change have articulated themselves in recent years.

Brexit and Trump

Brexiters in the UK voted for the Kingdom to leave the European Union for many reasons, but focus of the media has largely been on immigration. While there clearly was an anti-immigrant Brexit vote, it is doubtful that this alone explains the outcome, as many commentators have noted. Mary Kaldor (2019) discussed what participants in local fora listed as their priorities for Brexit in Mansfield and Pendle: 'lack of skills training, lack of infrastructure, lack of investment and general neglect'. This general neglect, whether it comes from Brussels or Westminster, was highlighted by participants as a key factor in their desire for Brexit, and the need for politics to be devolved at a more local level (Parsons, 2018). These priorities, of increased local, democratic control against the policies of elites at the national or international level, are similar to many of the priorities highlighted by the gilets jaunes in France. Indeed, one of the commonalities between the Brexit vote and the gilets jaunes has been the lack of trust towards the national elites that are taking decisions in London or Paris, and participating in even more remote decisions in Brussels which seem to ignore the peripheries and heartlands outside of the cosmopolitan cities.

The hollowing-out of democracy, at national and international level, has led to disillusionment regarding the policies of major political parties. Since all major political parties in the UK and France are in favour of European Union membership, despite the perceived costs to these regions, it has been seen there as yet another imposition on those who have no access to political lobbying, those who cannot influence politics beyond their local council or *mairie*. Kaldor explains this gulf between the elites and the local people as a lack of substantive democracy, despite the UK and France being two of the oldest democracies in the world and having important structures in place for structural democracy. And certainly there are local and national elections, meaningful political debates, competing political parties and all of the necessities for the procedures of democracy to be in place in both countries. But overall, the feeling among both Brexiters and gilets jaunes has been that their choices seem to be largely ignored by political elites, irrespective of who wins or loses an election. If procedural democracy does not lead to substantive differences, in other words, democracy does seem to be hollowed out altogether.

The parallels can be extended to the sociology of the two phenomena. Robert Ford and Matthew Goodwin (2017) argue that, in the case of Brexit, it was a social shift in favour of the middle classes that led to the rise of popular resentment in the traditional working class. When the New Labour governments of 1997–2010 shifted their focus from their traditional base to the more liberally minded elites of the metropolises, they altered the balance of British politics with drastic consequences. The shift to the values of the liberal middle classes, attracted by issues of race, gender and sexuality, alienated the more socially conservative, working-class white voters. Abandoned by Labour, and not yet seduced by the Conservatives, this large minority, accounting for around one in five voters, became increasingly open to voting for the Brexit-leaning UK Independence Party. Combined with a growing schism between the liberal middle classes and the older white voters, who value order, stability and tradition over diversity, rapid change and mobility, Ford and Goodwin explain that the shift was large enough to gather a majority in the referendum. Unlike in the French case, where the gilets jaunes found few political allies outside of other fringe protest groups, the British working class found another large dissatisfied group that altered the balance of power in the political landscape of the country. The combination of dissatisfied left-behind voters who had turned their backs on Labour with the socially conservative older voters might go a long way to explain the Brexit vote, but it is entirely absent from the French context.

This leads to a first important difference between the Brexit vote and the gilets jaunes. In the first case, there was a fortuitous (for those advocating Brexit) combination of social forces that led to important and long-lasting political consequences in the United Kingdom, and the withdrawal of the country from the EU. In the French case, the few economic concessions secured by the movement led to no long-lasting changes in the policies of the government. Despite other movements erupting at the same time as the gilets jaunes, such as the pension strikes of 2019–20, and some obvious overlaps in strategy and desired outcome from some of their participants, there has been no convergence of struggles, political alliances, or electoral consequences of the movement. This leads to a second fundamental difference between the two phenomena. In the case of Brexit, there was an organized political party advocating for its outcome. The UK Independence Party, and then the Brexit Party in the 2019 election, were structured political institutions using the existing mechanisms of the political system to affect change. Despite a short-lived attempt by some gilets jaunes to run for the European elections in 2019, there has been a strong desire in the movement to avoid such models of representation. This is perhaps the downfall of the movement in terms of its success, but it also raises important consequences for what it desired to achieve. Unlike in the case of Brexit, the end-goal was not a change in a particular policy – however important – but a change in the structure of French democracy at its very core. Although some Brexiters may have desired a similar outcome (Bickerton and Jones, 2018), most largely accepted that the taking back of control would happen within the existing political framework of the UK.

This relative absence of bottom-up networks of association during the Brexit campaign and subsequent negotiations mean that there have been few local solidarities established over the period in the UK. Even where there have been projects to build up democratic involvement from citizens, such as the Citizens' Assembly project (Flinders et al, 2015), they have largely been led by experts and academics in the field, rather than organized at the local level. According to Craig Parsons (2018), Brexit is more anchored in top-down political processes than in bottom-up ones. While this may be good news for those who feared that Brexit was fuelled by mass nationalism and xenophobia, this is bad news for those who hoped for increased democracy as a result of the Brexit vote. With the demise of UKIP and the Brexit Party following the implementation of the referendum, there seem to be few if any organizational remnants at the grassroots level of the spike in political interest and activity generated by Brexit. This may spell a cautionary tale for the gilets jaunes as well. With no permanent organization, the local networks of activists run the risk of losing faith in their own ability to organize, and may lead to further disenfranchisement of those that had been involved in the movement. Fear of the institutionalization of the movement, even on its own terms, may be the ultimate limiter of its success.

A similar comparison has been drawn between the gilets jaunes and the Trump vote in the United States. American media were quick to highlight the parallels, where the economic insecurity of the hinterlands has been identified as a major source of support for Trump in his 2016 presidential bid (Tharoor, 2018). A similar analysis to the parallels with the UK applies here. White, working-class voters who are disillusioned with the political left have abandoned it in favour of other political avenues. But the similarities end here. Donald Trump is far removed from the gilets jaunes, whose key figures such as Priscillia Ludosky, Ingrid Levavasseur and Jérôme Rodrigues share little with the billionaire from New York. Trump was elected president by winning the Republican nomination, entering the political establishment through the back door, whereas the gilets jaunes refused co-optation by political parties. The bottom-up solidarities generated by the French social movement do not compare with the federal reach of the Trump campaign and support. Emily Ekins (2017) has identified five types of Trump voters, 'American Preservationists (20%), Staunch Conservatives (31%), Anti-Elites (19%), Free Marketeers (25%), and the Disengaged (5%)'. As with the Brexit sociology, it is clear that those who resemble the gilets jaunes in the United States, the anti-elites and the disengaged, account for less than a quarter of Trump voters. In the case of the UK, it was the socially conservative older voters that swayed the Brexit vote, and in the United States, it is the alliance of American preservationists, conservatives and free-market supporters that made the electoral maths possible for Trump's election. This shows that in both the Brexit and the Trump case, a wide political alliance made it possible for the respective votes to have their outcome, whereas in France the gilets jaunes failed to capture political momentum for a larger coalition to emerge. In all three cases, the working-class and lower-middle-class citizens that have been left out of the benefits of globalization – who make up the sociological base of the gilets jaunes – represent only around a fifth to a quarter of the citizens in the country. While they share a common dissatisfaction with the political establishment and elites, there is little resemblance beyond this in the three cases, as their modes of organization are very far apart. The gilets jaunes once again stand out as a *sui generis* movement.

Poland and Chile

International parallels are helpful, if only to point out the differences and similarities between movements. While much attention has been focused on Brexit and Trump with regards to the gilets jaunes, two other movements have had closer parallels but have been largely unnoticed. The rise to power of the Law and Justice party in Poland, and the social unrest in Chile in 2019–20 prove to be two important comparisons that shed more light on the movement than Brexit and Trump do.

In Poland, the Law and Justice (PiS) party that came to power in 2015 capitalized on the similar discontent with the political establishment that has affected France along with most Western democracies. In the Polish case, confidence in the state had reached rock bottom after ruling politicians, state officials and businessmen were secretly recorded while dining together in Warsaw (Easton, 2014). The recordings, which showed collusion between senior politicians and other officials, often speaking with great profanity about their allies in London or Washington, raised many eyebrows in Poland by their extravagance. Sometimes referred to as the 'octopus scandal', after the exotic dishes ordered at the dinners, they exemplified a ruling elite far removed from ordinary citizens, often spending equivalent to the monthly minimum wage on a meal. Building on popular resentment towards ruling elites in 2015, the PiS proposed to build what Jarosław Kaczyński has called the 'Polish version of the welfare state'. The party has gone beyond the traditional left/right dichotomy that had ruled Poland since the 1990s and promoted a programme of social spending with conservative social policies. Outraging the international community with its policies on LGBT equality and abortion rights, the party has nevertheless contributed importantly to the economic lives of ordinary Polish citizens. Galvanizing the citizens living outside the main cities of Warsaw, Wrocław and Gdańsk, the party has managed to provide a platform for those 'who feel alienated by the economic, social and cultural changes since the collapse of communism in 1989', according to Chapman (2019). The widespread feeling of bringing back dignity to a country where it had disappeared under previous governments contributed to the rise of the PiS. Its social policies, started in 2016, have included 'a monthly benefit of 500 złoty (£102) per month per child [...] a one-off bonus payment of 1,100 złoty (£225) to pensioners, the abolition of income tax for workers aged 26 and under, and an increase in the minimum monthly wage from 2,250 złoty (£461) to 4,000 złoty (£815.50) by the end of 2023 – a 78 per cent rise' (Chapman, 2019). The government also lowered the retirement age back to its previous limit – at 65 for men and 60 for women. These social measures, estimated at a cost of 30–40 billion złoty (£6–8bn) per year for the Polish state, answer many of the calls for economic justice asked for by those worst hit by globalization. The PiS, though most often characterized as a right-wing party that played on xenophobia to achieve power, has also managed to gather the vote of many citizens who would otherwise have voted for the left. The United Left party (ZL) failed to reach the 8 per cent national threshold for coalitions to enter parliament in 2015, and thus disappeared from the legislative assembly at the same time as the PiS rose to power. In the run-up to the 2019 elections, which it won, the Law and Justice party also promised a further 40 billion złoty (£8bn) in social spending, particularly on healthcare (Moskwa, 2019). The economic policies address many of the demands of the gilets jaunes, although the PiS goes much beyond these in its socially conservative agenda. There is little indication that the family-focused, Christian agenda of the PiS appeals to the gilets jaunes – although there are other political forces in France that might be interested in this agenda. François Fillon, who was the candidate for the main right-wing party Les Républicains in 2017, ran on a similar platform of social conservatism and family values, thinly veiled behind a veneer of secularism but clearly appealing to the Catholic right (Tresca, 2017). An unholy alliance between the conservative right and the gilets jaunes, although not on the cards, would reveal itself as not too dissimilar to the PiS in Poland. It shows, however, that the new social contract the gilets jaunes are advocating for may not favour the traditional left, with an alliance with more conservative forces always possible to guarantee economic justice. The comparison is itself not perfect, as the PiS is a political party that has achieved power, but it shows the potential of an economically left-leaning agenda with more socially conservative positions.

The social movement that took place in Chile in 2019–20 is perhaps the best international comparison with the gilets jaunes. Starting on 18 October 2019 following a rise in the price of the Santiago metro ticket by 30 pesos (around £0.03), widespread protests spread throughout the country. Ignited by the activism of teenage school pupils, who took to the streets advocating for avoiding paying the metro fare altogether in protest against the rise, it received support from wide sections of the Chilean public. Most commentators agree that the rise in the price of the ticket, though small, was the straw that broke the camel's back. The protests against paying the fare increase soon escalated, as clashes with police became widespread and metro stations were occupied, with up to 20 stations sustaining fire damage (Somma et al, 2020). Since the protests were not limited to the metropolitan area of Santiago, but rather spread throughout the country, mobilizing millions of Chileans at their height, it is clear that the social malaise was much more widespread. Repression by the Carabineros, the police force dependent on the Ministry of Defence, was brutal and deadly. Thirty-six people are thought to have died, 28,000 were arrested in the first few weeks alone, and 427 persons suffered mutilations to their eyes (McSherry, 2020). With numbers of casualties at least ten times higher than in France during the gilets jaunes protests, the level of state repression cannot be underestimated. As was the case with Macron, President Piñera of Chile announced urgent measures, starting with a state of emergency, but also promising a rise in the minimum wage and the state pension, increased provision of healthcare, higher taxes for high income earners, and limitations on the salary and electoral terms of politicians (Sehnbruch and Donoso, 2020). Importantly, and more radically than Macron's *Grand Débat*, the Chilean president announced a national plebiscite to be conducted in April 2020 – since rescheduled for October 2020 – on establishing a new constitution for the country, to replace the Pinochet-era 1980 Constitution still in force.

A group of university students and lecturers at the Universidad Alberto Hurtado in Santiago phrased the terms of the social movement precisely as a challenge to the social contract in Chile (Borges et al, 2020), identifying the sources of the movement in citizens' feelings of discrimination, segregation and humiliation, and generally a feeling among the majority of the population of exclusion from the benefits of economic growth. Identifying inequalities based on territories, with the peripheral regions largely participating in the protests outside of the capital Santiago, inequalities based on race, with the exclusion of the *mestizo* population, and inequalities of gender, the authors note the ultimate decline of trust in public institutions, including the executive, legislative, and judicial power of the state, but also private actors – Chile having many of its core sectors run as *for-profit* corporations, including water, roads and education. The authors point to a series of essential contestation points that surfaced during the social movement, and that need to be addressed. They cite social protection, redistribution, income inequalities, development policies, environment protection, public scrutiny of state institutions, the structure of security services, and the renewal of democratic institutions as being key to addressing the root of the protests. With levels of inequalities far surpassing those in France, and poverty levels unseen in the Hexagon, Chile's situation was much more explosive and led to a much more violent form of protest. The sociology of the movement is quite different from either the French gilets jaunes or the Brexit and Trump votes. It is not the white working classes that are mobilizing, simply because Chile has a largely *mestizo*, mixed-race working-class. But it is, as with the gilets jaunes, a mobilization of ordinary citizens against political elites, turned more towards Washington than reflecting the situation on the ground in Freirina, Punta Arenas, Aysén, Calama, Chiloé or Pascua Lama (Salazar, 2019). With widespread distrust of political elites, at times reaching as high as 95 per cent in surveys in the country, it remains to be seen whether the political solution proposed by Piñera will be sufficient to heal the wounds inflicted on Chilean society in the spring of 2019–20. Although it would require more analysis than I can provide here, it is clear that important parallels, notwithstanding the differences between the two cases, could be found between the French gilets jaunes in 2018–20 and the movement in Chile in 2019–20.

The future of the social contract

A social contract for the future will have to address some of the issues raised above. Fortunately, there are avenues to explore for social healing. Conflict studies have looked at truth and reconciliation commissions, for example, as a mode of moving beyond the conflicts of the past. Although these are not a panacea for the ills of society as a whole, it is difficult to imagine a reconciling of French society with its law enforcement forces and its justice system if the response to a social movement has maimed, crippled and killed citizens without consequences. Not all consequences need to be penal or carceral, but the failure of the police and political order to take responsibility for their actions will leave a bitter taste in the mouths of those who have seen the violence in practice. A rethinking of the militarization of police forces equipped with weapons of war for crowd control seems essential, but this is unlikely to occur if those who have used these weapons do not come forward to testify to their use in practice. There is growing evidence that this is a mode of thinking present within the French police system itself. During Act 45 of the weekly gilets jaunes protest, an off-duty police captain was arrested by his colleagues for rebellion, after he insulted a group of police officers riding their motorcycles past him (*Le Figaro*, 2019). Even official discourse by the director of the IGPN, the authority that polices the police, has shown that the use of force against demonstrators is problematized at the highest levels (Merchet, 2019). Police forces are also largely affected by this escalation of violence. No doubt a few police officers relish it – as do some gilets jaunes and black blocs – but others are left with trauma about what they have witnessed, what they have done, and how they treated their fellow citizens. With record-high suicide rates among police officers (54 recorded for the year up to October 2019, up from 35 in 2018; Leboucq, 2019), it is clear that the demanding job for these officers has psychological consequences, as evidenced by their public demonstration organized on 2 October 2019. A public reconciliation process, with open and transparent accounting of who has done what and when, possibly granting immunity from prosecution for those who come forward, will go a long way in addressing the social ill caused by the protests.

Constitutional revisions can go a long way in addressing systemic inequalities, even if the outcomes of the new constitutional arrangements do not exactly meet the demands of either party. I have already suggested in Chapter 4 on democracy that in addition to the referendum demanded by the gilets jaunes, the institution of the Legislator, as seen in Rousseau, could be revived for the twenty-first century. A once-in-a-generation rethinking of the constitutional order of the state, with an opportunity for input by all citizens and not only those with privileged access to state and political structures, could provide a valuable source of contractual thinking. The time for incremental changes, tweaking of the existing procedure and defence of an obsolete model of representative democracy has passed. Representative democracy is not set to disappear immediately, of course, but the emphasis on political parties rallying electoral support now seems to be only part of the political spectrum of engagement. The gilets jaunes have shown, along with other protests both in France and abroad, that there is a popular enthusiasm for politics – alongside a lack of trust in politicians. Changes in communication technology have created a vast gulf between the speed and interactivity of everyday communication, and the slowness and lack of responsiveness of political life. Enthusiasm for democracy has not vanished, but the old question of whether direct or representative democracy is preferable needs a profound rethink. Social movements, such as that of the gilets jaunes, also have a role to play in raising awareness of social ills. It is unthinkable that a set of constitutional arrangements will fully substitute for citizens raising their voices in public, on the streets and roundabouts, in the town centres and on social media. Popular mobilization has shown itself to be resilient and determined, and has already had a profound impact on French society in the case of the gilets jaunes.

While the gilets jaunes have refused to go through channels of representation to find a solution to the current crisis, it is doubtful that this element of political action will disappear altogether. It will be paramount to find ways to renew with models of representation or delegation to find a political solution to the current predicament that France faces. No doubt the incessant weakening of the power of parliament, the National Assembly, in the Fifth Republic and then again in 2002 when the length of political mandates was changed to essentially guarantee a parliamentary majority for the presidential party, has largely weakened parliamentary scrutiny and the ability of members of this representative body to hold the executive to account. Made in the name of efficiency and expedience, these changes have weakened the role of representation to the point where the role of MPs is unclear to many citizens. Many gilets jaunes have asked: if they are merely rubber-stamping decisions made by the executive, what is the point of paying them their salaries at the public's expense? Instead of further undermining representatives' ability to perform important functions such as holding the executive to account, a rethinking of the powers of representatives may also go a long way in ensuring public support for their function. The details of these changes will be left unexplored here, but there is an alternative way to strengthen the tolerance and fortitude of social forces in society other than weakening representatives' ability to challenge executive power.

In terms of economic justice there are also solutions to the issues raised above. As an alternative to increased inequalities caused by public debt, Graeber (2019: 186) proposes that all new moneys could be issued by citizens, rather than financial institutions, creating wealth for all instead of for specific companies and their shareholders. This new type of economic agency, or some other model resembling it, could do much to address the lack of justice felt by the gilets jaunes in their daily interactions with the state. Piketty, on the other hand, proposes a similarly redistributive alternative, where all citizens are granted access to a small amount of capital – he estimates €120,000 – on their twenty-fifth birthday. This measure, financed through a progressive inheritance tax, would be the equivalent of a universal inheritance. Those who today inherit nothing would thus see their patrimony raised substantially, while those who inherit above €2 billion would see the top rate of tax reach 90 per cent. They would still inherit €120,000 at the age of 25, along with everyone else, but would see their parents' fortune largely taxed and redistributed (Piketty, 2019b: 1130). It is beyond the scope of this book to evaluate these measures, but I only want the reader to remember that they exist, and that the French state's steady decline from citizens' lives is not an inevitable movement of history. There is an alternative.

A Sixth Republic is possible in France, and perhaps the above changes to the country's democratic structures and economic organization would necessitate a change of constitutional order. Or, as some gilets jaunes themselves put it, perhaps the republic has run its natural course and it is time to institute the first French democracy. The possibility of widespread constitutional reform has been on some politicians' lips for some time, and the gilets jaunes have provided an opportunity for widespread rethinking of the political that could prove invigorating for French society as a whole. Either way, it is doubtful that the next Legislator will be a single paternal figure – as was doubtless the case in 1958 – and there is hope that the people as a whole, or at least to a wider degree, will have a say in the changes in constitutional arrangements that are to come. If the current wounds inflicted to the social contract are to heal, it seems inevitable that widespread changes occur, rather than piecemeal band-aids. It is the hope of this conclusion that this will be the case, for the alternatives are not worth contemplating. If the run-off to the next presidential election is once again between Macron and Le Pen in 2022, it is doubtful that the gilets jaunes will vote for the candidate of the centre.

Appendix:
The 42 demands of the gilets jaunes, posted online on 28 November 2018[1]

(1) Zero homeless: URGENT.
(2) Income tax more progressive (more tax brackets).
(3) SMIC [minimum wage] set at €1,300 net.
(4) Promote small businesses in villages and town centres. (Stop the construction of large commercial areas around big cities that kill small business.) More free parking in city centres.
(5) Major Insulation Plan for housing (to make ecological and financial savings for households).
(6) That BIG businesses (McDonald's, Google, Amazon, Carrefour …) pay BIG and that small ones (artisans, small and medium-sized businesses) pay small.
(7) The same system of social security for all (including artisans and the self-employed). End of the RSI [self-employed workers' social security scheme, since abolished].
(8) The pension system must remain in solidarity and therefore socialized (no points-based retirement).
(9) End to the tax increase on fuel.
(10) No pension below €1,200.
(11) Every elected representative to have the right to receive the median salary. Their transport costs to be monitored and reimbursed if they can be justified. Right to restaurant and holiday discounts.
(12) The wages of all French people, as well as pensions and allowances, must be indexed to inflation.
(13) Protect French industry: prohibit relocation. Protecting our industry is protecting our skills and jobs.
(14) End to work postings abroad. It is wrong that a person who works on French territory does not benefit from the salary and the same rights as in France. Anyone authorized to work on French territory

must have equal standing with a French citizen, and their employer must make the same contributions as a French employer.
(15) For job security: further limit the number of fixed-term contracts for large companies. We want more permanent contracts.
(16) End to the CICE [Competitiveness and Employment Tax Credit]. This money to be used to launch a French industry making hydrogen-powered cars (which are truly ecological, unlike the electric car).
(17) End to austerity. That we cease to repay the debt interest that is declared illegitimate and we start to repay the debt itself, without taking the money from the poor and the poorest but by going after the €80 billion lost through tax evasion.
(18) That the causes of forced migration are treated.
(19) That asylum seekers are well treated. We owe them housing, security, food, and education for minors. Work with the UN to open reception centres in many countries around the world, pending the outcome of the asylum application.
(20) That unsuccessful asylum seekers are returned to their country of origin.
(21) That proper integration policies are implemented. Living in France means becoming French (courses in French language, the history of France and civic education, with certification at the end).
(22) Maximum salary fixed at €15,000 a month.
(23) That jobs are created for the unemployed.
(24) Increase in disability benefits.
(25) A cap on rent payments and more low-rent housing (especially for students and precarious workers).
(26) Ban on selling off property belonging to France (dams, airports, etc).
(27) Substantial resources to be granted to justice, the police, the gendarmerie and the army. That overtime payments for the forces of law and order are paid or recovered.
(28) All the money earned from highway tolls to be used for the maintenance of motorways and roads in France and road safety.
(29) Since the price of gas and electricity has increased since privatization, we want them to be renationalized and prices to fall significantly.
(30) Immediate end to the closure of small chains, post offices, schools and maternity homes.
(31) Let's bring well-being to our elderly people. Prohibition on making money out of the elderly. Grey wealth is finished, the era of grey well-being begins.
(32) A maximum of 25 students per class, from kindergarten to the final year of education.

(33) Substantial increase in funding for psychiatry.
(34) The People's Referendum must be incorporated into the Constitution. Creation of an accessible and effective website, supervised by an independent control body where people can make a proposal of law. If a proposal obtains 700,000 signatures then this Bill will have to be discussed, completed and amended by the National Assembly, which will be obliged (one year to the day after obtaining the 700,000 signatures) to submit it to the vote of all the French people.
(35) Return to a term of seven years for the President of the Republic. (The election of MPs two years after the election of the President of the Republic has made it possible to send a positive or negative signal to the President concerning his policies, helping to make the voice of the people heard.)
(36) Retirement at age 60, and for all those who have worked in a trade involving physical labour (a builder or butcher, for example) a right to retirement at age 55.
(37) As a six-year-old child is not able to look after themself, continuation of the PAJEMPLOI public child-minding service until the child is 10 years old.
(38) Promote the transport of goods by railway.
(39) No deduction of tax at source.
(40) End to presidential allowances for life.
(41) Ban on charging retailers a fee when their customers use credit cards.
(42) Tax on marine fuel oil and kerosene.

Notes

Intro
1. The hexagon is a popular term to designate France, based on its shape on map, roughly resembling the geometrical figure.

Chapter 2
1. There are, of course, administrative courts in France to which you could refer your case. But the rules are built in such a way that, unless there was an error of procedure, the actual decision of the préfet would be almost impossible to contest.
2. The arguments summarized here are found mainly in chapters 13 and 14, unless otherwise stated.
3. Although they are beings made of passions, as he points out in chapter 6 of *Leviathan*.

Chapter 5
1. According to Google Scholar, there were over 12,000 citations of John Rawls in academic articles for 2019 alone, with an impressive 204,000 citations overall.
2. A translation of the demands is provided in the Appendix.

Chapter 6
1. BFM-TV, the largest 24-hour news network in France, was created in 2005.
2. This figure is slightly higher than the 8 per cent often used in the literature, as recent studies have suggested that this rate was consistently under-estimated, due to a badly phrased question in the surveys used, and inaccurate extrapolation (Pignoni, 2018).

Appendix
1. 'Avant la rencontre à Matignon: Les Gilets jaunes listent leurs revendications', *La Voix du Nord*, 29 Novembre 2018 [https://www.lavoixdunord.fr/497801/article/2018-11-29/les-gilets-jaunes-listent-leurs-revendications], *my translation*.

References

Adenor, J.-L. (2017) 'Fin de l'état d'urgence. Les 4 mesures qui ne disparaissent pas', *Ouest France*, 31 October. Available from: https://www.ouest-france.fr/terrorisme/fin-de-l-etat-d-urgence-les-4-mesures-qui-ne-disparaitront-pas-5349720

AFP (2019) 'Sur les Champs-Elysées, des ballons jaunes et des sifflets pour Macron', *Le Point*, 14 July. Available from: https://www.lepoint.fr/politique/sur-les-champs-elysees-des-ballons-jaunes-et-des-sifflets-pour-macron-14-07-2019-2324481_20.php

Agamben, G. (2005) *State of Exception*, Chicago: University of Chicago Press.

Alemania, L. (2019) 'Pour l'Insee, les gilets jaunes ne font (presque) pas de mal à l'économie', *Libération*, 19 March. Available from: https://www.liberation.fr/france/2019/03/19/pour-l-insee-les-gilets-jaunes-ne-font-presque-pas-de-mal-a-l-economie_1716123

Askenazy, P. (2018) 'The contradictions of Macronism', *Dissent*, Winter. Available from: https://www.dissentmagazine.org/article/emmanuel-macron-contradictions-neoliberalism

Autotrader (2018) 'Voitures brûlées à Paris: pas que des Porsche ...', 3 December. Available from: https://www.autoplus.fr/actualite/Voitures-brulees-Paris-Porsche-Casseurs-Gilets-jaunes-1533731.html

Balibar, É. (2019) 'Le sens du fâce-à-fâce', in J. Confavreux (ed.) *Le fond de l'air est jaune*, Paris: Seuil.

Barry, B. (1989) *Theories of Justice*, London: Harvester-Wheatsheaf.

BBC News (2019) 'Swiss court orders historic referendum re-run', 10 April. Available from: https://www.bbc.co.uk/news/world-europe-47879777

Bentham, J. (2002) *Rights, Representation, and Reform: Nonsense upon Stilts and Other Writings on the French Revolution*, ed. P. Schofield, C. Pease-Watkin and C. Blamires, Oxford: Oxford University Press (The Collected Works of Jeremy Bentham), pp 317–401. (Original work published 1795.)

Berlin, I. (1969) *Four Essays on Liberty*, Oxford: Oxford Paperbacks.

Bickerton, C. and Jones, L. (2018) 'The EU's Democratic Deficit: Why Brexit is Essential for Restoring Popular Sovereignty', *The Full Brexit*, 11 June. Available from: https://www.thefullbrexit.com/the-eu-s-democratic-deficit

Blairon, K. (2015) 'La suppression d'un territoire: le département français et la province italienne en question', *Civitas Europa*, 35(2).

Bloch, M. (2018) 'A l'Elysée, Emmanuel Macron tente l'explication de texte sur les "premiers de cordée"', *Le Journal du Dimanche*, 18 July. Available from: https://www.lejdd.fr/Politique/a-lelysee-emmanuel-macron-tente-lexplication-de-texte-sur-les-premiers-de-cordee-3713504

Blondiaux, L. (2019) 'The French Experiment', *International Politics and Society*, 23 April. Available from: https://www.ips-journal.eu/regions/europe/article/show/the-french-experiment-3413/

Borges, H., Álvarez, R., González, L., Saavedra, E., Llanos, S., García, C., Otero, C., Piñera, P., Edwards, N., Sanfuentes, A., Cáceres, L., Sanderson, D., Palma, J., Soto, I., Tapia, J.A., Mondaca, D., Espinosa, M. and Álvarez, J. (2020) 'Comisión I. Estado. Pensando un nuevo pacto social', *Observatorio Económico*, 26 February. Available from: https://fen.uahurtado.cl/2020/articulos/comision-i-estado-pensando-un-nuevo-pacto-social-para-chile/

Bouchez, Y., Chemin, A., Mestre, A., Besse Desmoulières, R., Bouanchaud, C. and Kaval, A. (2019) 'A Paris, les syndicats débordés lors d'un défilé du 1er-Mai sous les gaz lacrymogènes', *Le Monde*, 2 May. Available from: https://www.lemonde.fr/politique/article/2019/05/02/a-paris-les-syndicats-debordes-lors-d-un-defile-du-1er-mai-sous-les-gaz-lacrymogenes_5457179_823448.html

Bouanchaud, C. (2019) 'Des militants écologistes évacués violemment par les CRS lors d'un rassemblement pour le climat à Paris', *Le Monde*, 29 June. Available from: https://www.lemonde.fr/planete/article/2019/06/29/des-militants-pour-le-climat-evacues-violemment-par-les-crs-lors-d-un-rassemblement-a-paris_5483227_3244.html

Breines, J. (2011) 'Jacques le fataliste et son maître: finding myself in the work of another', in J. Fowler (ed.) *New Essays on Diderot*, Cambridge: Cambridge University Press.

Bristow, G. (2019) 'Yellow fever: populist pangs in France', *Soundings*, 72: 65–78.

Burke, E. (1990) *A philosophical Enquiry into the Origin of our Ideas of the Sublime and Beautiful*, Adam Phillips (ed.), Oxford: Oxford University Press. (Original work published 1757.)

Burke, E. (2001) *Reflections on the Revolution in France*, Stanford: Stanford University Press. (Original work published 1790.)

Carr, E.H. (2016) *The Twenty Years' Crisis, 1919–1939*, London: Palgrave Macmillan. (Original work published 1939.)

Causit, C. (2020) 'Municipales 2020: comment le Rassemblement national a géré les villes conquises en 2014', *FranceInfo*, 11 February 2020. Available from: https://www.francetvinfo.fr/elections/municipales/municipales-2020-comment-le-rassemblement-national-a-gere-les-villes-conquises-en-2014_3793865.html

Chapman, A. (2019) 'Poland's Law and Justice party has triumphed again by fusing left and right', *New Statesman*, 14 October. Available from: https://www.newstatesman.com/world/europe/2019/10/poland-s-law-and-justice-party-has-triumphed-again-fusing-left-and-right

Chauvel, L. (2019) 'Le ressenti ne ment pas', in J. Confavreux (ed.) *Le fond de l'air est jaune*, Paris: Seuil.

Chevillard, T. (2020) '"Gilets jaunes" à Paris: Le parquet dresse un bilan des enquêtes confiées à l'IGPN', *20 minutes*, 21 January. Available from: https://www.20minutes.fr/faits_divers/2700191-20200121-gilets-jaunes-paris-parquet-dresse-bilan-enquetes-confiees-igpn

Christin, O. (2019) 'Pas de pouvoir sans consentement', in S. Bourmeau (ed.) *"Gilets jaunes": Hypothèses sur un movement*, Paris: Édition La Découverte.

Clavel, G. (2016) 'François Hollande et Manuel Valls au plus bas de leur popularité', *Huffington Post*, 5 October. Available from: https://www.huffingtonpost.fr/2016/06/02/popularite-francois-hollande-manuel-valls-record-baisse-yougov_n_10236942.html

Clavel, G. (2018) 'Popularité: Macron atteint son plus bas en pleine crise des gilets jaunes', *Huffington Post*, 6 December. Available from: https://www.huffingtonpost.fr/2018/12/05/popularite-macron-atteint-son-plus-bas-en-pleine-crise-des-gilets-jaunes-sondage-exclusif_a_23609357/

Colin, N. (2018) '"Un pognon de dingue": Macron a 30 ans de retard', *L'Obs*, 28 June. Available from: https://www.nouvelobs.com/chroniques/20180626.OBS8771/un-pognon-de-dingue-macron-a-30-ans-de-retard.html

Confavreux, J. (2019) 'Avant-propos', in J. Confavreux (ed.) *Le fond de l'air est jaune*, Paris: Seuil.

Constant, B. (2010) *De la liberté des anciens comparée à celle des modernes*, Paris: Editions Mille et une Nuits. (Original work published 1819.)

Coquaz, V. (2019) 'Qui sont les 11 morts du mouvement des gilets jaunes mentionnés par Emmanuel Macron?', *Libération*, 30 January. Available from: https://www.liberation.fr/checknews/2019/01/30/qui-sont-les-11-morts-du-mouvement-des-gilets-jaunes-mentionnes-par-emmanuel-macron_1706158

Corey, J.S.A. (2011) *Leviathan Wakes*, London: Orbit Books.

Coutant, I. (2019) 'Les "petits-moyens" prennent la parole', in J. Confavreux (ed.) *Le fond de l'air est jaune*, Paris: Seuil.

Cunliffe, P. (2018) 'Phoney Cosmopolitanism versus Genuine Internationalism', *The Full Brexit*, 11 June. Available from: https://www.thefullbrexit.com/phoney-cosmopolitanism

D'Holbach, P.H.T. (1972) *Essai sur l'art de ramper, à l'usage des Courtisans*, in F. Grimm and D. Diderot (eds) *Correspondance littéraire*, Paris: Hachette. (Original work published 1790.)

D'Holbach, P.H.T. (2001) *La Politique Naturelle*, in J.-P. Jackson (ed.) *Œuvres Philosophiques. Tome III*, Paris: Alive. (Original work published 1773.).

De Fournas, M. (2018) 'Après un an de mandat, Emmanuel Macron sur Twitter ça donne quoi en chiffres?', *20 minutes*, 4 May. Available from: https://www.20minutes.fr/high-tech/2266315-20180504-apres-an-mandat-emmanuel-macron-twitter-ca-donne-quoi-chiffres

De Jong, J. and Gilbert, N. (2019) 'The mixed success of the Stability and Growth Pact', *Vox*, 15 January. Available from: https://voxeu.org/article/mixed-success-stability-and-growth-pact

Delaporte, L. (2019) 'Fréjus, la vitrine "bétonnée" du Rassemblement national', *Mediapart*, 14 September. Available from: https://www.mediapart.fr/journal/france/140919/frejus-la-vitrine-betonnee-du-rassemblement-national?onglet=full

Devellennes, C. (2013) 'A Fourth Musketeer of social contract theory', *History of Political Thought*, 34: 459–78.

Diderot, D. (1986) *Jacques the Fatalist*, London: Penguin. (Original work published 1796.)

Drillon, J. (2014) 'Ouvrières "illettrées": ce qu'Emmanuel Macron aurait dû dire', *L'Obs*, 18 September. Available from: https://www.nouvelobs.com/politique/20140918.OBS9620/ouvrieres-illettrees-ce-qu-emmanuel-macron-aurait-du-dire.html

Dufresne, D. (2019) 'Allô Place Beauveau?', *Mediapart*, 11 July. Available from: https://alloplacebeauvau.mediapart.fr/

Easton, A. (2014) 'Poland bugging: The table talk that shook Warsaw', *BBC News*, 25 June. Available from: https://www.bbc.co.uk/news/world-europe-28001780

Ekins, E. (2017) *The Five Types of Trump Voters. Who They Are and What They Believe*, Democracy Fund Voter Study Group, June. Available from: https://www.voterstudygroup.org/publication/the-five-types-trump-voters

Ertzscheid, O. (2019) 'De l'algorithme des pauvres gens à l'internet des familles modestes', in J. Confavreux (ed.) *Le fond de l'air est jaune*, Paris: Seuil.

Euronews (2019) 'La statue de la liberté en gilet jaune', 2 March. Available from: https://fr.euronews.com/2019/03/02/la-statue-de-la-liberte-en-gilet-jaune

European Commission (2019) 'Report from the Commission. France. Report prepared in accordance with Article 126(3) of the Treaty on the Functioning of the European Union', COM(2019) 529 final. Available from: https://ec.europa.eu/info/sites/info/files/economy-finance/com2019529_fr_en.pdf

European Court of Human Rights (2019) *Chebab vs. France*, Application no. 542/13.

Flinders, M., Ghose, K., Jennings, W., Molloy, E., Prosser, B., Renwick, A., Smith, G. and Spada, P. (2015) *Lessons from the 2015 Citizens' Assemblies on English Devolution*, London: Democracy Matters.

Ford, R. and Goodwin, M. (2017) 'Britain After Brexit: A Nation Divided', *Journal of Democracy*, 28: 17–30.

Foucault, M. (1991) *Discipline and Punish: The Birth of the Prison*, London: Penguin.

Fourquet, J. and Morin, C. (2020) 'Aides-soignantes, caissiers, camionneurs ... Les gilets jaunes sont devenus les "premiers de tranchée"', *Le Figaro*, 9 April. Available from: https://www.lefigaro.fr/vox/societe/aides-soignants-caissiers-camionneurs-les-gilets-jaunes-sont-devenus-les-premiers-de-tranchee-20200409

Fukuyama, F. (1992) *The End of History and the Last Man*, New York: Free Press.

Garcin-Berson, W. (2018) 'Suppression de l'ISF: peut-on déjà dresser un premier bilan?', *Le Figaro*, 18 December. Available from: www.lefigaro.fr/conjoncture/2018/12/18/20002-20181218ARTFIG00087-suppression-de-l-isf-peut-on-deja-dresser-un-premier-bilan.php

Garner, H. (2016) 'Mise en perspective de l'évolution du système social français: genèse et tendances', *Informations sociales*, 193(2), 12–22.

Gaudin, J.-P. (2003) 'Une canicule politique', *Cybergeo: European Journal of Geography, Politique, Culture, Représentations*. Available from: https://journals.openedition.org/cybergeo/5404

Graeber, D. (2015) *The Utopia of Rules: On Technology, Stupidity, and the Secret Joys of Bureaucracy*, Brooklyn: Melville House.

Graeber, D. (2019) 'Rendre la monnaie', in J. Confavreux (ed.) *Le fond de l'air est jaune*, Paris: Seuil.

Guay, J.-H. (2019) 'Espérance de vie à la naissance (année), France', *Perspective monde*. Available from: http://perspective.usherbrooke.ca/bilan/tend/FRA/fr/SP.DYN.LE00.IN.html

Guerrien, F. (2018) 'Gilet jaune, jaune gilet ("c'est jaune, c'est moche, ça ne va avec rien mais ...")', *Mediapart*, 2 December. Available from: https://blogs.mediapart.fr/fredguerrien/blog/021218/gilet-jaune-jaune-gilet-cest-jaune-cest-moche-ca-ne-va-avec-rien-mais

Guilbaud, D. (2019) '"Égoïstes, imbéciles, illuminés, poujadistes, vulgaires": les "gilets jaunes" vus depuis une certaine haute fonction publique', in S. Bourmeau (ed.) *'Gilets jaunes': Hypothèses sur un movement*, Paris: Édition La Découverte.

Guilluy, C. (2019) *Twilight of the Elites: Prosperity, the Periphery, and the Future of France*, New Haven: Yale University Press. (Original work published in French 2016.)

Hayat, S. (2019a) 'L'économie morale et le pouvoir', in J. Confavreux (ed.) *Le fond de l'air est jaune*, Paris: Seuil.

Hayat, S. (2019b) 'The Gilets Jaunes and the democratic question', *Viewpoint Magazine*, 13 February. Available from: https://www.viewpointmag.com/2019/02/13/the-gilets-jaunes-and-the-democratic-question

Hobbes, T. (1996) *Leviathan*, Cambridge: Cambridge University Press. (Original work published 1651.)

Houeix, R. (2019) 'Élections européennes: où sont les Gilets jaunes?', *France 24*, 27 May. Available from: https://www.france24.com/fr/20190527-elections-europeennes-gilets-jaunes-vote-abstention

Huntington, S.P. (1996) *The Clash of Civilizations and the Remaking of World Order*, New York: Simon & Schuster.

James, A. (2012) *Fairness in Practice: A Social Contract for a Global Economy*, Oxford: Oxford University Press.

Jeanbart, B. (2005) 'Les opinions européennes face au traité constitutionnel', *Politique Étrangère* 2: 273-283.

Joffrin, L. (2018) 'Gilets Jaunes, effet brun', *Libération*, 13 December. Available from: https://www.liberation.fr/politiques/2018/12/13/gilets-jaunes-effet-brun_1697665

Joffrin, L. (2020) 'Ils savaient?', *Libération*, 24 March. Available from: https://www.liberation.fr/politiques/2020/03/24/ils-savaient_1782884

Kaldor, M. (2019) 'Democracy and Brexit', *Soundings* 72.

Kirkman, R. (2010) *The Walking Dead*, Orange, CA: Image Comics.

L'Obs (2018) '"Gilets jaunes": on a décortiqué chacune des 42 revendications du movement', 30 November. Available from: https://www.nouvelobs.com/politique/20181129.OBS6307/gilets-jaunes-on-a-decortique-chacune-des-42-revendications-du-mouvement.html

L'Obs (2019) '"Grand débat": un nouveau marathon pour Macron à Souillac', 18 January. Available from: https://www.nouvelobs.com/politique/20190118.OBS8722/grand-debat-un-nouveau-marathon-pour-macron-a-souillac.html

Larsen, S. (2013) 'Notes on the Thought of Walter Benjamin: Critique of Violence', *Critical Legal Thinking*, 11 October. Available from: http://criticallegalthinking.com/2013/10/11/notes-thought-walter-benjamin-critique-violence/

LCI (2019) 'Gilets jaunes: d'où vient le "Ahou! Ahou! Ahou!" chanté dans les manifestations?', 30 March. Available from: https://www.lci.fr/social/gilets-jaunes-d-ou-vient-le-cri-ahou-ahou-ahou-chante-dans-les-manifestations-300-film-2116987.html

Le Figaro (2014) 'Barrage de Sivens: les dernières heures de Rémi Fraisse', *Le Figaro*, 29 October. Available from: https://www.lefigaro.fr/actualite-france/2014/10/29/01016-20141029ARTFIG00406-barrage-de-sivens-les-dernieres-heures-de-remi-fraisse.php

Le Figaro (2019) '"Gilets Jaunes": un capitaine de police arrêté à Paris', 23 September. Available from: www.lefigaro.fr/gilets-jaunes-un-capitaine-de-police-arrete-a-paris-20190922

Le Gall, M. (2018) 'Smic: comment comprendre la hausse de 100€ annoncée par Emmanuel Macron', *La Nouvelle République*, 11 December. Available from: https://www.lanouvellerepublique.fr/a-la-une/smic-comment-comprendre-la-hausse-de-100-annoncee-par-emmanuel-macron

Le Monde (2018a) 'Le recours à l'état d'urgence, une option face aux débordements des "gilets jaunes"?', 3 December. Available from: https://www.lemonde.fr/les-decodeurs/article/2018/12/03/le-recours-a-l-etat-d-urgence-une-option-face-aux-debordements-des-gilets-jaunes_5392147_4355770.html

Le Monde (2018b) 'A Mantes-la-Jolie, des images choquantes de lycéens interpellés par la police', 6 December. Available from: https://www.lemonde.fr/police-justice/video/2018/12/06/images-choquantes-de-lyceens-interpelles-par-la-police-a-mantes-la-jolie_5393761_1653578.html

Lebaron, F., Gallemand, F. and Waldvogel, C. (2009) 'Le "modèle social français" (est à bout de souffle): genèse d'une *doxa*? 2005–2007', *La revue de l'IRES*, 61(2): 129–64.

Leboucq, F. (2019) 'Combien de policiers et de gendarmes se sont suicidés au cours des dernières années?', *Libération*, 21 October. Available from: https://www.liberation.fr/checknews/2019/10/21/combien-de-policiers-et-de-gendarmes-se-sont-suicides-au-cours-des-dernieres-annees_1757682

Loach, K. (dir) (2019) *Sorry We Missed You*.
Locke, J. (1988) *Two Treatises of Government*, Cambridge: Cambridge University Press. (Original work published 1689.)
Lukes, S. (2004) *Power: A Radical View*, London: Red Globe Press.
Machiavelli, N. (2008) *The Prince*, Indianapolis: Hackett Publishing Company. (Original work published 1532.)
Macpherson, C.B. (1973) *Democratic Theory: Essays in Retrieval*, Oxford: Clarendon Press.
Macron, E. (2019) 'Letter from M. Emmanuel Macron, President of the Republic, to the French people', 13 January. Available from: https://uk.ambafrance.org/Read-President-Macron-s-open-letter-to-the-French-people
Masse-Stamberger, B. (2018) '"Fin du monde" contre "fin du mois", la rhétorique méprisante de nos élites', *Marianne*, 29 November. Available from: https://www.marianne.net/debattons/billets/fin-du-monde-contre-fin-du-mois-la-rhetorique-meprisante-de-nos-elites
McSherry, J.P. (2020) 'Chile's struggle to democratize the state', *nacla*, 24 February. Available from: https://nacla.org/news/2020/02/24/chile-struggle-democratize-state-plebescite
Merchet, J.-D. (2019) 'Comment le ministère de l'Intérieur veut s'adapter à la "subversion violente"', *L'Opinion*, 29 Septembre. Available from: https://www.lopinion.fr/edition/politique/comment-ministere-l-interieur-veut-s-adapter-a-subversion-violente-198969
Mills, C.W. (1997) *The Racial Contract*, Ithaca: Cornell University Press.
Moskwa, W. (2019) 'Polish Ruling Party Announces $10 Billion Election-Year Stimulus', *Bloomberg*, 23 February. Available from: https://www.bloomberg.com/news/articles/2019-02-23/polish-ruling-party-announces-10-billion-election-year-stimulus
Mouffe, C. (2005) *On the Political*, Abingdon: Routledge.
Nagesh, A. (2018) 'Killed by my debt', BBC, 29 May. Available from: https://www.bbc.co.uk/news/resources/idt-sh/How_debt_kills
Noiriel, G. (2018) *Une histoire populaire de la France: De la guerre de Cent Ans à nos jours*, Marseille: Agone.
Noiriel, G. (2019) *Les Gilets jaunes à la lumière de l'histoire*, La Tour d'Aigues: Éditions de l'aube.
Nozick, R. (2001) *Anarchy, State, and Utopia*, Hoboken, NJ: Wiley-Blackwell. (Original work originally published 1974.)
Observatoire des inégalités (2013) 'Les inégalités face aux retraites', 5 September. Available from: https://www.inegalites.fr/Les-inegalites-face-aux-retraites

Observatoire Girondin des Libertés Publiques (2019) 'Rapport d'enquête sur le maintien de l'ordre à Bordeaux du 17 novembre 2018 au 16 février 2019. Une politique d'intimidation', 3 March. Available from: https://france3-regions.francetvinfo.fr/nouvelle-aquitaine/sites/regions_france3/files/assets/documents/2019/04/29/rapport_sur_le_maintien_de_lordre_du_17_novembre_au_16_fvrier_final-4211329.pdf

Pabst, A. (2019) 'Brexit, Trump et les "gilets jaunes": révolte contre le libéralisme et politique du paradoxe', *Revue Politique et Parlementaire*, 121 (1090).

Parikh, S. (2019) 'Immigration: The Elephant in the Room Troubling Gilets Jaunes (Yellow Vests) in France', *Maydon*, 15 April. Available from: https://www.themaydan.com/2019/04/immigration-the-elephant-in-the-room-troubling-gilets-jaunes-yellow-vests-in-france/

Parsons, C. (2018) 'Brexit rooted more in elite politics than mass resentment', *The Conversation*, 13 December. Available from: https://theconversation.com/brexit-rooted-more-in-elite-politics-than-mass-resentment-107133

Pateman, C. (1988) *The Sexual Contract*, Cambridge: Polity Press.

Philippe, B. (2019) 'Gilets jaunes: le pourcentage de radars vandalisés a encore bondi en 2019', *Capital*, 1 March. Available from: https://www.capital.fr/economie-politique/gilets-jaunes-le-pourcentage-de-radars-vandalises-a-encore-bondi-en-2019-1329771

Pignoni, M.T. (2018) 'La syndicalisation en France. Des salariés deux fois plus syndiqués dans la fonction publique', *Dares Analyses*, 25. Available from: https://dares.travail-emploi.gouv.fr/IMG/pdf/2016-025.pdf

Piketty, T. (2013) *Le Capital au XXIe siècle*, Paris: Seuil.

Piketty, T. (2019a) 'La couleur de la justice fiscale', in J. Confavreux (ed.) *Le fond de l'air est jaune*, Paris: Seuil.

Piketty, T. (2019b) *Capital et idéologie*, Paris: Seuil.

Plato (2003) *The Last Days of Socrates*, London: Penguin Classics.

Pluyette, C. (2016) 'Le nombre d'assujettis à l'ISF a encore progressé en 2015', *Le Figaro*, 9 June. Available from: https://www.lefigaro.fr/conjoncture/2016/06/09/20002-20160609ARTFIG00264-le-nombre-d-assujettis-a-l-isf-a-encore-progresse-en-2015.php

Rawls, J. (1971) *A Theory of Justice*, Cambridge, MA: Harvard University Press.

Rawls, J. (1993) 'The Law of Peoples', *Critical Inquiry*, 20(1): 36–68.

Rey, A. and Féron, L. (1896) *Histoire du corps des gardiens de la paix: Tome 1, Du Moyen Age à la Commune de 1871*, Paris.

Rhodes, M. and Mény, Y. (eds) (1998) *The Future of European Welfare: A New Social Contract?*, New York: Palgrave.

Robin, C. (2017) *The Reactionary Mind: Conservatism from Edmund Burke to Donald Trump*, 2nd edn, New York: Oxford University Press.

Rogers, S. (2013) 'How Britain changed under Margaret Thatcher. In 15 charts', *The Guardian*, 8 April. Available from: https://www.theguardian.com/politics/datablog/2013/apr/08/britain-changed-margaret-thatcher-charts

Rosanvallon, P. (2000) *La Démocratie inachevée*, Paris: Gallimard.

Rosanvallon, P. (2019) 'Accroître le "pouvoir de vivre"', in J. Confavreux (ed.) *Le fond de l'air est jaune*, Paris: Seuil.

Rosanvallon, P. (2000) *La Démocratie inachevée*, Paris: Gallimard.

Rousseau, D. (2019) 'Les "gilets jaunes": crise politique ou crise de régime?', in S. Bourmeau (ed.) *"Gilets jaunes": Hypothèses sur un movement*, Paris: Édition La Découverte.

Rousseau, J.-J. (2001) *Du Contrat Social*, Paris: Flammarion (original work published 1762).

Ruffin, F. and Perret, G. (dirs) (2019) *J'veux du soleil*, Jour2fête.

Salazar, G. (2019) 'El "reventón social" en Chile: una mirada histórica', *Ciper*, 27 October. Available from: https://ciperchile.cl/2019/10/27/el-reventon-social-en-chile-una-mirada-historica/

Sehnbruch, K. and Donoso, S. (2020) 'Social protests in Chile: inequalities and other inconvenient truths about Latin America's poster child', *Global Labour*, 11(1).

Service Checknews (2019) 'Référendum ADP: 574 000 signatures, et le compteur continue de stagner', *Libération*, 28 July. Available from: https://www.liberation.fr/checknews/2019/07/28/referendum-adp-574-000-signatures-et-le-compteur-continue-de-stagner_1742552

Service Public (2019) 'Organisation de manifestations, défilés ou rassemblements sur la voie publique', 10 October. Available from: https://www.service-public.fr/associations/vosdroits/F21899

Siegelbaum, L. (nd) 'Stalin Constitution'. Available from: http://soviethistory.msu.edu/1936-2/stalin-constitution/

Somma, N.M., Bargsted, M., Disi Pavlic, R. and Medel, R.M. (2020) 'No water in the oasis: the Chilean Spring of 2019–2020', *Social Movement Studies*. Available from: https://doi.org/10.1080/14742837.2020.1727737

Sowerwine, C. (2009) *France since 1870: Culture, Society and the Making of the Republic*, 2nd edn, London: Palgrave Macmillan.

Spinoza, B. (1996) *Ethics*, London: Penguin Classics. (Original work published 1677.)

Spinoza, B. (2007) *Theological-Political Treatise*, Cambridge: Cambridge University Press. (Original work published 1670.)

Tang, F. (2017) 'China has enough state assets to deal with its debt mountain, official think tank says', *South China Morning Post*, 25 August. Available from: https://www.scmp.com/news/china/economy/article/2108344/china-has-enough-state-assets-deal-its-debt-mountain-official

Tharoor, I. (2018) 'The cultural anxiety fueling France's protests, Brexit and Trump', *The Washington Post*, 10 December. Available from: https://www.washingtonpost.com/world/2018/12/10/cultural-anxiety-fueling-frances-protests-brexit-trump/

Tønder, L. (2013) *Tolerance: A Sensorial Orientation to Politics*, Oxford: Oxford University Press.

Tresca, M. (2017) 'Le vote des catholiques: "François Fillon défend les valeurs familiales que je porte", dit Armelle', *La Croix*, 21 April. Available from: https://www.la-croix.com/Religion/Catholicisme/France/Le-vote-catholiques-Francois-Fillon-defend-valeurs-familiales-porte-Armelle-2017-04-21-1200841339

Ventura, A. (2016) '"En Marche": "Emmanuel Macron n'a plus qu'à se faire broder ses initiales sur ses chemises", dit Alba Ventura', *RTL*, 8 April. Available from: https://www.rtl.fr/actu/politique/en-marche-emmanuel-macron-n-a-plus-qu-a-se-faire-broder-ses-initiales-sur-ses-chemises-dit-alba-ventura-7782733162

Vermeren, P. (2019) *La France qui déclasse: Les Gilets jaunes, une jacquerie au XXIe siècle*, Paris: Éditions Tallandier.

Vignaud, M. (2020) 'Coronavirus: la dette française explose, mais les taux d'intérêt baissent', *Le Point*, 17 April. Available from: https://www.lepoint.fr/economie/coronavirus-la-dette-publique-explose-pas-les-interets-17-04-2020-2371806_28.php

Wahnich, S. (2019) 'Sans-culottes et gilets jaunes', in J. Confavreux (ed.) *Le fond de l'air est jaune*, Paris: Seuil.

Weatherall, T. (2015) *Jus Cogens: International Law and Social Contract*, Cambridge: Cambridge University Press.

Weber, E. (1976) *Peasants into Frenchmen: The Modernization of Rural France, 1870–1914*, Stanford: Stanford University Press.

Weber, M. (2009) 'Politics as a vocation', in *From Max Weber: Essays in Sociology*, London: Routledge. (Original work published 1919.)

Index

A
affect 60–1
Agamben, Giorgio 64
agnostic politics 126
airports, privatization of 32, 33, 78–9
Alliance Royale 40
American Declaration of Independence 28
Anarchy, State, and Utopia (Nozick) 95, 127
Ancien Régime 13–14, 122, 134
Arc de Triomphe 2, 137–8
army 48–9, 64
arrests 23, 86, 121, 147
Askenazy, P. 68, 70
austerity policies 3, 8, 22, 131, 139

B
Bachelot, Roselyne 140
banlieues 3, 8, 88
   police repression 89–90
Barry, Brian 100–101
beautiful
   and sublime 133, 134–5
   and ugly 135
Benjamin, Walter 50–1
Bentham, Jeremy 29, 84–5
Berlin, Isaiah 71
BFMTV 123
black blocs 23, 65, 66
Blair, Tony 68
body
   free 61
   ownership 95, 128
Brexit 19, 80, 139, 140–3
Brigade Anti-Criminalité (BAC) 89
broadcast media 123–4
bureaucracy and moral violence 43–5
Burke, Edmund 133, 134–5, 139

C
cabanes 136–7, 138
Cameron, David 139
canonical texts 127
Castener, Christophe 64

chants 22–3
Charlie Hebdo 49
Chile 145–7
China 32–3, 93
Chirac, Jacques 30, 32
citizens 75, 87–9, 131
citizenship lessons 84
civil liberties, repression of 25, 62–3, 64, 69, 70
   deployment of troops and 48–9
   impact on traditional workers' rights 65–6
Clinton, Bill 68
Cold War 30, 93
collective liberty 57
commentators on gilets jaunes 9–10, 14, 90, 123
common good 17, 77, 131
Confédération Générale du Travail (CGT) 17, 65
Constant, Benjamin 57–8
Constitution for Europe 2004 28, 79
Constitution of France 64, 73, 79, 82
   envisaging a Legislator process 82, 148
   possibility of widespread reform 149–50
Constitution of the Carolinas 92
corporations 35, 37
Coutant, Isabelle 8
COVID-19 7, 21, 32, 140
crawling, art of 120–1
credit ratings 6
Cunliffe, Philip 110

D
De Gaulle, Charles 51, 79, 122, 133
deaths 23–4, 41, 54, 63, 89
debt
   COVID-19 and increase in 7
   Eurozone restrictions on raising of 108
   illegitimate state-incurred 102
   national 6–7, 70

personal 8, 44–5
Declaration of the Rights of Man and of the Citizen 26, 28
déclassement (social downgrading) 2, 4
democracy 75–90
  citizens of 87–9
  direct 15, 20, 131
  gilets jaunes' demand for increased 12, 25–6, 77, 78, 130
  hollowing out of 141
  the Legislator 80–3
  power and 83–6
  regaining initiative 78–80
  representative 130, 131, 148
  social contract 75–7
  weakening of power of parliament 149
demonstrations
  banning of 45, 64, 86
  consensus on management of 2, 88
  freedom to philosophize and 60–3
  high school 121–2
  illegal 62, 63
  July 14 86
  legal requirements 61–2
  May Day 25, 65–6
  repression of 65–6, 69, 86
  right to peaceful 43, 54
  symbolism of kneeling at 121
  see also protests
Depardieu, Gérard 33
départements 72–3
Dettinger, Christophe 23
d'Holbach, P.H.T. 116, 120–1, 131
diagonale du vide (the empty diagonal) 4
dialogue 128–9
Diderot, Denis 114–21
  citations 127
  dialogue 128–9
  Encyclopédie 117
  Jacques the Fatalist 114–16, 116–21
  metaphor of the knee 116–21
difference principle 34, 95, 100
dignity, economic 104–106
direct democracy 15, 20, 131
disillusionment with progress 4–5
'distranecdotes' (*fait-diversions*) 123, 124
divine authority 80, 81
doxa, combating new 127–9
Dufresne, David 24–5

E
economic crisis 4, 5, 6–7
economic independence 131–2
economic justice 91–111
  after Second World War 92–4
  dignity 104–106
  fairness 100–102

  gilets jaunes' demands for 96, 98–103
  liberal-libertarian compromise 96–8
  Nozick and 95–6
  Rawls' revival of social contract 93–5, 96
  solidarity 103–104
  solutions to issues of 149
economic model, 'lead climber' 33–5, 69, 95
economic rights 29
economics in social contract tradition 29–33
Ekins, Emily 143
elites 21–2, 72, 73, 79, 101, 106, 130, 141, 143
emancipation 131
employment contracts 37, 69–70
employment status of gilets jaunes 8, 16
Encyclopédie 117
enforced freedom 77
English Civil War 27
European Court of Human Rights 55
European elections May 2019 40, 67, 72, 142
European flag 22, 71
European Union
  Brexit vote to leave 140–3
  observance of treaties of 107–109
  proceduralism of 109–110
Euroscepticism 72
Eurozone 108
Excessive Deficit Procedure (EDP) 108
The Expanse 5
Extinction Rebellion 17, 62

F
Facebook 9, 14, 124
fairness 100–102
fait-diversions 123, 124
'fifth quarter' of political spectrum 11, 12
Fifth Republic 17, 31, 51, 64, 79, 149
  presidents of 122, 133
Fillon, François 11, 145
financial position of gilets jaunes, personal 4, 8–9, 132
financial regulation 101
fiscal justice, demand of gilets jaunes for 5–6, 34, 96, 98
fiscal policy 5–6, 70
  international restrictions on 108–109
  see also taxes
Five Star Movement party 19
flags 22, 71, 73
Ford, Robert 141

foreign workers in France 110
Foucault, Michel 84–5
Fourth Republic 31, 51, 93
freedom
  enforced 77
  of expression 86, 129
  individual 58–9
  see also liberty
French Communist Party (PCF) 16, 17
French Revolution 14–15, 51, 130–1
French social model 31–2
Front National (rebranded as Rassemblement National) 10–11
fuel tax 3, 5, 6, 34, 72, 84, 114
Fukuyama, Francis 1, 10, 30

G

gabelle (salt tax) 13
Game of Thrones 44
Germany 32
gilets jaunes
  achievements of 114
  apolitical claim 1
  being and becoming of 113–14
  Brexit supporters and comparison with 139, 140–3
  calls for resignation of Macron 15, 22, 25, 78, 105, 130
  challenge to social contract 2, 9–10, 12, 17–18, 19
  Chile and parallels with 145–7
  commentators on 9–10, 14, 90, 123
  comparisons with *Jacques the Fatalist* 115, 116
  early days 20–6
  economic plight 4, 8–9, 132
  employment status 8, 16
  as a form of jacqueire 14, 90, 115, 116
  future of 139
  in history of social movements 13–17
  isolated movement 17
  lack of a permanent organization 143
  media reporting and counter movement of social media 123–4
  national movement 14, 17, 87
  non-revolutionary movement 15
  non-unionized protest 16, 17, 127
  origins 3–7, 19, 78
  Poland and parallels with 144–5
  political affiliations 9, 11, 12
  popular movement 1, 17, 22, 87–8, 90
  popularity 17, 21, 49–50
  rejecting an ideology against material interests of 84
  'small-mean class' of 8, 36, 88, 90, 111, 138
  social movement, 15 13–17
  sociology of 8–10
  state response to 34, 62, 69, 129, 133
  sui generis movement 1, 17, 130, 144
  Trump supporters and comparison with 139, 143–4
  ugliness 136–9
  visibility 22, 23, 85, 139
  working class movement 3, 8, 17, 21, 88
  yellow vest 20–1, 58, 85, 136
  see also gilets jaunes, demands of; protests, gilets jaunes
gilets jaunes, demands of 151–3
  economic dignity 104–106
  economic justice 96, 98–103
  end to lifelong presidential indemnities 104
  fiscal justice 5–6, 34, 96, 98
  for a fully human life 30
  highways 102
  immigration 88–9, 99, 110
  increased democracy 12, 25–6, 77, 78, 130
  international solidarity 87, 110
  pension solidarity 103
  reciprocity from elected officials 103–104
  Référendum d'Initiative Citoyenne (RIC) 25–6, 78, 79
  rent control 102
  rent-seeking capitalism 102–103, 132
Goodwin, Matthew 141
Graeber, David 6, 44, 102, 149
grand débat national 20, 64–5, 67, 81
grenades 24, 63, 65, 89
gross domestic product (GDP) 4, 6, 7, 108
Guilluy, Christophe 3, 72, 106

H

Hayat, Samuel 9, 26, 99
heatwave, 2003 52–3
history of social movements, gilets jaunes in 13–17
Hobbes, Thomas 26, 27, 45–8, 52, 53, 58
Hollande, François 5, 25, 64, 133, 139
housing, new 138
Hundred Years' War 13, 27

I

ideology, power as 83–4
immigration, demands of gilets jaunes on 88–9, 99, 110

Impôt de la Fortune Immobiliere (IFI) 6, 33
Impôt de Solidarité sur la Fortune (ISF) 5–6, 33, 34, 88, 97
independence, economic 131–2
individual freedom 58–9
inequalities 2, 5, 68, 92, 100
   alternatives to 149
   difference principle 95
   Locke's justification for 92
   Rawls' justification for 95, 97, 99, 100
   tax system and 97–8
   will of political elites to promote 101–102, 140
inheritance tax 149
initiative 78–80
injuries 24–5, 50
international
   justice 38, 106–110
   solidarity 87, 110
isolated movement of gilets jaunes 17

J

jacqueries 13–14
   gilets jaunes as a form of 14, 90, 115, 116
Jacques the Fatalist (Diderot) 114–16, 127
   metaphor of the knee 116–21
Joffrin, Laurent 140
justice
   fiscal 5–6, 34
   international 106–110
   Rawls' theory of 29, 94–5, 96, 105, 107, 109
   see also economic justice

K

Kant, Immanuel 127
Kirkman, Robert 46
knee
   bending of the 126
   Diderot's metaphor of 116–21
   symbol of submission 121–2

L

La France Insoumise 106
La Manif pour tous 21
Lallement, Didier 62
Law and Justice (PiS) party 144–5
The Law of Peoples (Rawls) 106–107
laws of nature 47–8
LBD 40 24, 50, 89
Le Figaro 89, 147
Le Fouquet's 23, 54–5
Le Pen, Marine 9, 11, 12, 67, 71, 105, 106, 150

'lead climber' model of economic growth 33–5, 69, 95
left/right political divide 10–13
legislation
   anti-terrorist 63–4
   giving unprecedented powers to *préfets* 25, 45
   state of exception 64
the Legislator 80–3
l'ENA (l'Ecole Nationale d'Administration) 69
les évènements 16–17
Leviathan (Hobbes) 26, 27, 45–8, 52, 53, 58
liberal
   -libertarianism 32, 92, 96–8, 99, 111
   religion of 127–8
   meanings of 29
   utopia 67–71
liberalism, failure of 139
Libération 124, 140
liberty 57–74
   freedom to philosophize 59–60
   limitations on 60–3
   individual 58–9
   positive 71–3
   restrictions on 58, 129
   Spinoza's 59–60
   types of 57–9
life expectancy, lowering of 53
Lisbon Treaty 79
Loach, Ken 45
local government 25, 45, 72–3
Locke, John 28, 76, 91–2, 95, 128
loud protests 22–3
Lukes, Steven 83, 84

M

Machiavelli, N. 49, 124–5
Macpherson, Crawford 30
Macron, Emmanuel 9, 11, 133
   approval ratings 21, 130
   calls for resignation of 15, 22, 25, 78, 105, 130
   deployment of *Opération Sentinelle* 48–9
   as disrespectful 104–105, 116, 122
   grand débat national 20, 64–5, 67, 81
   'lead climber' model of economic growth 33–5, 69, 95
   liberal-libertarianism 32, 92, 97, 99, 111, 128
   liberal utopia 67–71
   rise in minimum wage 34, 97
   scrapping of *Impôt de Solidarité sur la Fortune* (ISF) 5–6, 33
   security detail 64

INDEX

sharing in responsibility of deaths 54
similitudes with royal authority 122
target of protesters' anger 25
Twitter use 122–3
Macronism 68, 69–71, 92, 111
Maillotins 14
Marseillaise 14, 16, 22, 87
Matignon accords 15–16
May 1968 events 16–17
May Day 2019 25, 65–6
MC Solaar 85
media, broadcast 123–4
median wage 103–104
Mills, Charles 36, 39
minimum wage (SMIC) 34, 97, 99–100
  in Poland 145
Mitterrand, François 5, 7, 10, 51, 101
monetary system 102
moral economy 99–100
moral violence 41, 42, 43, 48, 126
  and bureaucracy 43–5
More, Thomas 67
multinational corporations 37
mythic violence 50–2

N
Napoleon I 137
Napoleon III 15, 51
National Assembly 78, 103, 149
national movement of gilets jaune 14, 17, 87
negligence 52–3
neoliberalism 30–1, 33
New Labour 68, 141
Noiriel, Gérald 13, 15, 17, 87, 90, 123, 131
Norway 32, 33
Nozick, Robert 92, 95–6, 97, 99, 106, 127
numbers of protesters 21

O
Opération Sentinelle 48–9
original position 94
origins of gilets jaunes 3–7, 19, 78

P
Pabst, Adrian 139
panopticon 84–5
Paris Commune 15, 16
Pateman, Carole 6, 35
peace 47–8
Peace of Westphalia 1648 26
peasant rebellions 13–14
  gilets jaunes as a form of 14, 90, 115, 116
pensions 103

strike 126–7
peri-urban France 3, 84, 90, 106, 136–7, 138
periphery, living on 5, 73, 105, 132, 138, 141
petits-moyens (small-mean class) 8, 36, 88, 111, 138
philosophize, freedom to 59–60
  limitations on 60–3
Piketty, Thomas 5, 6, 11, 12, 68, 97, 100, 149
Plato 57, 75
Poland 144–5
police
  files on protesters 62
  rethinking militarization of 147–8
  suicides 148
  use of weapons 23, 24, 50, 63, 65–6, 89, 147
  violence
    beyond gilets jaunes' protests 62–3, 65–6
    at gilets jaunes' protests 24–5, 50, 55
    and repression in banlieues 89–90
    and repression of May Day demonstration 25, 65–6
political affiliations of gilets jaunes 9, 11, 12
political divide, left/right 10–13
political rights 29, 93
popular movement of gilets jaunes 1, 17, 22, 87–8, 90
  group absent from 88
popularity of gilets jaunes 17, 21, 49–50
populism 10–11, 19
power
  democracy and 83–6
  dimensions of 83–4
  resistance and 85–6, 116
  resting on threat of violence 44, 45, 48, 86
  rise in state 25, 63–4, 67
  social contract and creation of 76–7
  weakening of parliamentary 149
préfets, powers of 25, 45
president, office of 122, 125–6, 130, 133
  sublime function 133
presidential election 2017 10–11
presidential indemnities 104
proceduralism 109–110
property
  destruction of private 54–5
  distribution 131
  Locke's theory 91–2

Nozick's model 95–6
prices 105, 106
redefinition of notion of 30
proportionality of violence 49, 53–5
prosecutions 55
protests
   deployment of army to 48–9
   fête de la musique 62–3
   gilets jaunes
      blockades 41, 54, 58
      chanting 22–3
      consequences of 25, 62
      economic concessions following 34
      in town and city centres 2, 22–3, 54–5, 88, 137
      social malaise during 121–4
      violence at 1, 21, 23–5, 41–2, 43, 50, 54–5
   illegal 62, 63
   see also demonstrations; roundabouts
public spending 70
public support for gilets jaunes 17, 21, 49–50
public transport 3, 4, 84, 105

R
racial contract 36, 39
radicalization 66
Rassemblement National (previously Front National) 9, 12, 71–2, 106
Rawls, John 22, 29, 30, 97, 99, 100
   citations 127
   difference principle 95
   international justice theory 106–107, 109
   philosophical foundations 127–8
   principles of justice 107
   revival of social contract theory 29, 93–5, 96
   The Law of Peoples 106–107, 108, 110
Reagan, Ronald 30, 32
real estate tax 6, 33
reciprocity 103–104
Redouane, Zineb 89
referendums 79–80
   Référendum d'Initiative Citoyenne (RIC) 25–6, 78, 79
   shared initiative (RIP) 78–9
regional
   identities 72–3
   inequalities 4
religion 127–8
religious practice, act of kneeling in 120
rent-seeking capitalism 102–103, 132
Republican Guard (CRS) 16
republics 77

resistance
   power and 85–6, 116
   right to 52–5
respect vs. toleration 124–7
rights
   mutual transfer of 47–8
   two concepts of 93
Robin, Corey 134, 135
Rogers, Jerome 44–5
Rosanvallon, Pierre 8, 9, 10, 25
roundabouts
   acts of violence on 41–2, 54
   cabanes 136–7, 138
   first French 2
   as sites of protest 3, 14, 54, 58, 115
   ugly spaces of 136–7, 138
Rousseau, Jean Jacques 28
   the Legislator 80–3
   social contract 76–7
Ruffin, François 136, 139

S
Sarkozy, Nicolas 25, 32, 122, 133
secularism 89
sécurité sociale (social security) 31, 92–3, 104
security forces 24–5, 48–9, 121
   see also police
self-preservation 46, 47, 52, 53, 55
Seneca 125
sexual contract 35–6
Shadowrun 37
Sixth Republic 149–50
'the small-mean class' 8, 36, 88, 90, 111, 138
social contract 26–9
   becoming of 36, 39–40
   compromise in 130–1
   critique of 35–6
   democratic 75–7
   dialogue between persons 128–9
   economic 29–33, 100
   empirical method of 100–101
   fear and threat of death 49
   future of 147–50
   gilets jaunes' challenge to 2, 9–10, 12, 17–18, 19
   grand débat national 20, 64–5, 67, 81
   Hobbes' justification for 45–8
   as impossible 36, 38–9
   international 38, 106–110
   Legislator and potential involvement in 82–3
   metaphor of repairing broken 119–20, 122
   as necessary 36–8
   and possibility of resistance 53–5
   Rawls revives theory of 29, 93–5, 96

renewal 129–30
rethinking 35–9
revision under a state of exception 64–5
to maximize freedom 60
and virtue of toleration 126
Social Contract (Rousseau) 76–7
social media 122–3, 124
  Facebook 9, 14, 124
  Twitter 50, 122–3, 124
social movements
  Chile 145–6
  contemporary 100
  gilets jaunes in history of 13–17
social roles, reversing of 119–20
social security 31, 92–3, 104
socialist states 30, 93
sociology of gilets jaunes 8–10
Socrates 57, 75, 119
solidarity 103–104
  international 87, 110
Sorry We Missed You (Loach) 45
sovereignty 26, 27, 28, 77
  knee as a symbol of submission to state 121
Soviet Constitution 27–8
speed cameras 22, 43, 44
speed limit 19, 22, 44
Spinoza
  affect 60–1
  liberty 59–60, 129
  toleration 125
Stability and Growth Pact (SGP) 108
standards of living, fall in 4
Star Trek 40
state
  corporations taking over functions of 37
  fear and death at hands of 48–52
  Hobbes' justification for 48
  increase in power of 25, 63–4, 67
  involvement in market practices 101
  monopoly on violence 27–8, 43, 45, 48
  as most important unit of political organization 37
  negligence 52–3
  power to regulate people's beliefs 59
  response to gilets jaune 34, 62, 69, 129, 133
  retreat of 6, 32, 70, 101–102
  rise of modern 27
  selling of assets 31, 32, 33
  similitudes with royal authority 122
  sovereignty 26, 27, 28, 77
    knee as a symbol of submission to 121

Spinoza's free 60, 61
violence
  legitimacy of 27–8, 49–50
  lethal 48, 49, 52
  moral violence 48, 126
  moral violence and bureaucracy 43–5
  right to resist 52, 53–5
state of emergency 63, 64
state of exception 64–5
state of nature 46–7, 49, 58, 76, 94
strikes of 1936 and 1948–9 15–16
structural violence *see* moral violence
sublime 133, 134–5, 138
suffrage 35
sui generis movement, gilets jaunes as a 1, 17, 130, 144
suicides, police 148

T

taxes 6, 34, 97–8
  on dividends of capital 98
  early ability to raise 27
  evasion of 5–6, 34
  fuel tax 3, 5, 6, 34, 72, 84, 114
  Impôt de la Fortune Immobiliere (IFI) 6, 33
  Impôt de Solidarité sur la Fortune (ISF) 5–6, 33, 34, 88, 97
  inheritance 149
  peasant revolts over 13
  proposals of gilets jaunes 96, 98
  US rates 97
tear gas 23, 24, 50, 65
terrorism
  anti-terrorist legislation 63–4
  attacks 49, 63
  suspects 62, 63
Thatcher, Margaret 30, 70
Thatcherism 32, 68
A Theory of Justice (Rawls) 29, 94, 100, 127
thought, freedom of 59–60
  limitations on 60–3
toleration
  metaphors of 126
  need for a spirit of 129–30
  vs. respect 124–7
  Spinoza's theory of 125
totalitarianism 77
trades unions 16, 30, 31, 126
  consensus with police on management of demonstrations 2, 88
  gilets jaunes not a part of 16, 17, 127
  les évènements 16–17
  low membership 31, 126
  targeted for police brutality 65–6
transport
  necessity of private 3, 21, 105

public 3, 4, 84, 105
treaties
    observance of 107–109
    Peace of Westphalia 1648 26
Treaty of Lisbon 28
Trump, Donald 19, 123, 139, 143
trust in politicians 25, 130, 141, 148
    in Chile 147
truth and reconciliation commissions 147
Twitter 50, 122–3, 124
Two Treatises of Government (Locke) 91

U
the ugly 135–9
UK Independence Party 141, 142
United Kingdom
    Brexit 19, 80, 139, 140–3
    English Civil War 27
    New Labour 68, 141
    university strike, 2018 113
United Left Party (ZL) 145
United Nations 24, 37, 38, 93
United States of America
    American Declaration of
        Independence 28
    Clinton administration 32
    Donald Trump 19, 123, 139, 143
    Reagan administration 30, 32
universal inheritance 149
urban architecture 138, 139

V
vehicles
    necessity of private 3, 21, 105
    set alight 24
Vermeren, Pierre 4, 138, 139
violence 41–55
    as coercive and engendering
        resistance 41–2
    as distinct from exercise of power
        85–6
    at gilets jaunes' protests 1, 2, 23–5,
        41–2, 43, 50, 54–5
    knee as a symbol of repression and
        121–2
    moral 41, 42, 43, 48, 126
        bureaucracy and 43–5
    mythic 50–2
    physical 41, 42–3
    police
        beyond gilets jaunes' protests
            62–3, 65–6
        at gilets jaunes' protests 24–5,
            50, 55
        and repression in banlieues
            89–90

and repression of May Day
    demonstration 25, 65–6
power resting on threat of 44, 45,
    48, 86
proportionality 49, 53–5
right to resist 53–5
state
    legitimacy of 27–8, 49–50
    lethal 48, 49, 52
    moral violence 48, 126
    moral violence and bureaucracy
        43–5
    right to resist 52, 53–5
sublime 134–5
visibility
    of gilets jaunes 22, 23, 85, 139
    as an instrument of power 84–5
voltigeurs 89
vote, right to 35
voter apathy 10

W
wage
    median 103–104
    minimum 34, 97, 99–100, 145
    of National Assembly members 103
    policy of gilets jaunes 95, 103–104
The Walking Dead 46
wealth
    redistribution 95, 97
    tax 5–6, 24, 33, 34, 88, 97
weapons
    army 49
    police 23, 24, 50, 63, 65–6, 89
    reconsideration of use of 147
Weber, Eugene 131
Weber, Max 27, 43
welfare state 10, 30, 37, 68, 92–3
'white poor' 8
William III, King 91
workers' rights, demonstrating for 65–6
working class
    appeasement of 93
    British alienated 141
    failure of representative democracy
        to liberate 131–2
    movement of gilets jaunes 3, 8, 17,
        21, 88, 143
    US alienated 143
    workers' movements 15–16

Y
yellow vests
    of supporters 58
    symbol of 20–1, 85
    ugliness of 136